TIME CAPSULE/1950

EVENTS OF THE YEAR

TIME CAPSULE / 1950

HISTORY OF THE YEAR CONDENSED FROM THE PAGES OF TIME

TIME INCORPORATED, NEW YORK

TIME / **1950**

EDITOR-IN-CHIEF *Henry R. Luce*
EDITOR *T. S. Matthews*
MANAGING EDITOR *Roy Alexander*
ASSISTANT MANAGING EDITOR *Dana Tasker*
SENIOR EDITORS *Robert W. Boyd Jr., Otto Fuerbringer,
Thomas Griffith, Hillis Mills, Duncan Norton-Taylor,
Content Peckham, Joseph Purtell, John Tibby,
John Walker, Max Ways*
ASSOCIATE EDITORS *Douglas Auchincloss, A. T. Baker,
Edward O.Cerf, Max Gissen, Frederick Gruin,
Henry Anatole Grunwald, Louis Kronenberger,
Jonathan Norton Leonard, Paul O'Neil,
Margaret Quimby, Marshall Smith, Walter Stockly,
Samuel G. Welles*

EDITOR *Maitland A. Edey*
EXECUTIVE EDITOR *Jerry Korn*
TEXT DIRECTOR *Martin Mann*
ART DIRECTOR *Sheldon Cotler*
CHIEF OF RESEARCH *Beatrice T. Dobie*

SERIES EDITOR *John Dille*
ASSISTANT EDITOR *Simon Johnson*
RESEARCHERS *Don Nelson, Louise Samuels*
ASSISTANT ART DIRECTOR *Arnold Holeywell*
COPYREADER *Rosemarie Conefrey*

PUBLISHER *Rhett Austell*

COVER ILLUSTRATION *Lou Lomonaco*

Editors' Note

This was the year of Korea. Communist troops from North Korea attacked across the 38th parallel on June 25, and from then until the end of the year TIME devoted much of its space to reporting the war. A detailed account of the fighting starts on page 60. But the war also crops up in other sections of this CAPSULE—just as it did in the magazine— sounding its somber note over and over again as the President, the Congress, defense officials and the nation itself are confronted in turn by the fateful events of that day in June.

■

TIME CAPSULE/1950 is one of a series of volumes, each adapted and condensed from a year's contents of TIME, the Weekly Newsmagazine. The words, except for a few connecting passages, are those of the magazine itself, and therefore reflect the flavor, the attitudes and the state of knowledge of the day —sometimes innocent, sometimes opinionated, sometimes prescient. The book is divided, like the magazine, into departments, and is organized so that each department forms a chronological chapter for the entire year. The dates in the margin are the issue dates of the magazine.

$\boxed{\textbf{NATIONAL AFFAIRS}}$

The Presidency

Harry S. Truman was about to go through the most strenuous year of his career. The Republicans were pressing their claim that his administration was soft on Communism, and the effectiveness of their campaign resulted in substantial Democratic losses in the 1950 Congressional elections—including the defeat of veteran Senator Millard Tydings of Maryland, whose bad luck it was to anger the administration's severest congressional enemy, Senator Joseph R. McCarthy of Wisconsin (p. 44). On top of that, Truman's characteristic petulance got him into hot water with the U.S. Marine Corps and with a music critic who disliked Margaret Truman's singing. Then some Puerto Rican nationalists tried to assassinate him.

But the President's greatest problem was Korea. That event, as reported in TIME's July 3 issue, suddenly made all of Truman's other problems seem minor by comparison. In an act of quick courage, the President committed U.S. troops to defend South Korea. Victory over the North Koreans seemed in sight when suddenly hordes of Chinese Communists entered the war and the U.S. faced disaster all over again. During the year Truman also had a disagreement over policy with General Douglas MacArthur. It was smoothed over, but it was an augury. In 1951 Truman finally fired the General.

JAN. 2 **1950 MODEL:** Behind closed office doors and in conference rooms, the Administration's carpenters sawed and hammered away at the big beams of the Fair Deal platform for 1950. The main lines were already well known: don't rock the boat; propose no bold, new experiments, but insist on putting through the controversial Fair Deal measures (civil rights, health plan, etc.) already proposed.

JAN. 16 **THE ANSWER IS YES:** Harry Truman has told members of his Cabinet not to make any plans to run for congressional offices. He wants to keep his team together, he told them, because he is going to run again for President in 1952.

WITH RANCOR TOWARD NONE: For the annual speech on the State of the Union, Harry Truman spoke as chief of the world's mightiest nation. "The state of the Union," he said, "continues to be good." Abroad, "the greatest danger has receded." Standing at the mid-century mark, he took a long look ahead to the year 2000 and presented a heady vision of sustained U.S. prosperity: "If our productive power continues to increase at the same rate as it has increased for the past 50 years . . . the real income of the average family in the year 2000 A.D. would be about three times what it is today." That would mean an average family income of $12,450 a year. This year Truman spoke confidently of pride in U.S. achievement, and with rancor toward none.

Republicans were plaintively aware that Truman had staked a claim to the concept that Republicans had long considered their special political property: the American dream of expansion and prosperity. Columnist Walter Lippmann diagnosed their bafflement: "Truman's technique is never to deal with problems, but only with the excellent results that would be achieved if the problems had been solved . . . leaving the critic no target to shoot at, no antagonist to get hold of, only the thin air to thrash around in. No wonder so many Republican politicians exhibit the symptoms of being on the verge of a nervous breakdown."

NICE WORK: Harry Truman lay late abed at Blair House JAN. 23 [the White House was being renovated]; on several occasions he did not rise until after 7, and one day the good wives of 15th Street saw him taking his morning stroll at the incredibly late hour of 8:30. It was one of those rare weeks when being President was very nice work, and Harry Truman made the most of a free & easy schedule.

THE DECISION IS YES: The decision as to whether the U.S. FEB. 6 should make a hydrogen bomb, said Harry Truman, is mine and nobody else's. This week the President made his decision. He ordered work on the H-bomb to go ahead. Harry Truman's announcement had in it no sabre-rattling swagger, only the reluctant awareness of a duty that had to be done. He knew that he was authorizing construction of the deadliest weapon ever known to man.

MARCH 20 **NONPOLITICAL POLITICS:** With the hustle of a heavyweight champion's entourage heading for training camp, Harry Truman and his retinue filed aboard the presidential yacht *Williamsburg* this week and glided south toward Key West, Fla. By mixing work with three weeks of lolling under the Key West sun, the President and his advisers hoped to sharpen up for a big tour that will take him across the U.S. and back in May. Officially the trip will be billed as "nonpolitical," an ancient device whereby a President can pay his expenses from his $40,000-a-year travel allowance instead of from the party treasury.

MARCH 27 **STORMING INTO THE SUN:** As soon as she passed the last sheltering headland of Chesapeake Bay, the presidential yacht *Williamsburg* ran into heavy weather. The President, who had chosen a sea route to Key West as a gesture of friendliness to the Navy, surrendered to the unfriendliness of the sea and the built-in crankiness of his personal ship; he took to his berth, stopped eating. When the yacht docked at Key West on the fifth day, the President announced that he had lost four pounds.

APRIL 3 **YELLOW SHIRTS:** Harry Truman brought a variegated collection of sartorial exhibits to Key West and wore them with obvious relish; during a week of beach expeditions, he showed one white pith helmet, one cane, one light yellow sport shirt with orange-and-brown palm trees on its front, one black-and-yellow sport shirt with brown trimmings, and one bright yellow sport shirt with a brown grill design on the front. They were worn with light-colored slacks.

APRIL 24 **THE OPTIMIST:** *Harry Truman*: I don't know whether you fellows ever had a load of hay or a bull fall on you. But last night the moon, the stars and all the planets fell on me. If you fellows ever pray, pray for me.
A Reporter: Good luck, Mr. President.
Harry Truman: I wish you didn't have to call me that.

That, on April 13, 1945, was the humble Harry Truman, ex-soldier, unsuccessful haberdasher, minor Missouri politician, able U.S. Senator, thrust suddenly into the White House by the death of Franklin D. Roosevelt. "I never felt so out of place in my life," he confided to his old colleagues in the U.S. Senate that day. "I don't know if I'll ever get used to it." Last week, five years later to the day, President Truman held his 222nd press conference. He no longer looked like an anonymous face in the crowd. He stood erect as a West Pointer, radiated confidence, and looked amazingly trim for a man of 65. He had sampled authority, and liked it. Not only was Harry Truman used to the job he once had feared—he felt jauntily on top of it.

Critics could say that, even in a time of prosperity, the President should worry more about rising unemployment and deepening deficits; in a time when Russia had bulged nearly halfway across Europe and across the full breadth of Asia, he should spend his days & nights acquiring arms and achieving aims. But there was a lot to be said for a man who could walk away from a collision with the moon, the stars and all the planets, lead his nation through five troublesome years and come out of it all a supreme and unabashed optimist.

GOOD-HUMOR MAN: While his armorers, beaters and gunbearers prepared for the big Western vote hunt, the President took one last look at his problems before leaving Washington, and decided that everything was fine. At his weekly news conference, the President was asked about Senator Millard Tydings' assertion that it would be remarkable if the U.S. and Russia avoided a war. The Senator, said the President, was unduly alarmed. Did the President plan a big increase in the defense budget next year because of the growing international tension? No, Mr. Truman answered. The defense budget next year, he went on, will be smaller than this year's $14.2 billion and the Administration will keep on making economy cuts in the armed services where it can.

It didn't seem to bother the President that his top military men were crying for more money, not less. In fact, the President sounded disturbingly like the man at the carnival, happily willing to gamble the farm on the conviction that the pea was under the middle shell.

MAY 15

The 13-car special train clacked along-side the muddy Potomac and across the Midwestern flatlands into the West. At the end was a bulletproof special car, the *Ferdinand Magellan*, and inside it was pessimism-proof Harry Truman, bound for the hunt. Harrold Stassen last week tried to give the Republicans a simple credo to hurl. "President Truman is the cleverest politician . . . and . . . the worst President ever to occupy the White House." Harry just kept traveling, talking, shaking hands and looking for votes.

MAY 22 **THE HIRED MAN:** In depots and on porches, at crossings and atop boxcars, people gathered in little clots to watch the train roll through. When it stopped in the tank towns of Nebraska and Iowa, in the farming centers of Idaho and Washington, in the mining towns in Montana, the crowds swarmed around the rear platform yelling "Hi, Harry."

"I am talking to you as your hired man," Harry Truman told them. "I have come out here to tell you just exactly what I am trying to do, and I am telling it to you firsthand so it can't be garbled. There is no way for me to get the truth to you but to come out and tell it to you."

Back in Washington, he had left a party uneasy about the effect of Senator Joe McCarthy's assault on the State Department and slow to come to his Administration's defense, a Democratic Congress that had flatly refused to enact most of his Fair Deal program. His legislative leaders were rebellious, disgruntled by his failure to consult them, annoyed by his disregard for their views. Congress spent the week ignoring, disregarding or repudiating several of his proposals.

Truman was trying to do what Woodrow Wilson and Franklin Roosevelt had failed to do—plead for his policies over the head of Congress to the people, fighting the traditional off-year slump for the party in power.

There was no disputing it; Harry Truman did well. He reduces the issues, said the New York *Times* admiringly, "to town-size so any dirt farmer can understand them." Harry Truman liked people, and obviously people liked him in a way that included no awe and not necessarily admiration. A reporter who had also traveled with Franklin Roosevelt noted the difference: Roosevelt had inspired worship, but from a distance. Harry Truman was one of the folks.

CHALLENGE ACCEPTED: This time, when the challenge came, JULY 3 the U.S. accepted it. The bulletins on the invasion of South Korea jerked Washington out of the wilted weariness of a steamy summer weekend. Secretary of State Dean Acheson first heard the news by telephone at his Sandy Spring, Md. farm, promptly put through a call to Harry Truman, who was off in Independence, Mo. for a "back porch" visit.

At first the President determined to go through with his round of visiting, partly to keep from upsetting the world by a dramatic return to Washington. But by Sunday noon, after Acheson's second report, he climbed aboard his plane *The Independence* so fast that he left two of his military aides behind. "Don't make it alarmist," he admonished reporters just before taking off. "It could be a dangerous situation, but I hope it isn't."

Dean Acheson and Defense Secretary Johnson met him at Washington's National Airport, quickly brought him up to date. Before the U.N. Security Council, the U.S. had already drawn up its moral position against the Communist invaders. That decision had been beaten out in Saturday night conferences. The big question left for Harry Truman to decide was not whether to help, but how.

Exactly at noon on Tuesday, Presidential Secretary Charles Ross passed out the text of the gravest, hardest-hitting answer to aggression that the U.S. has ever made in its peacetime history: "In Korea the government forces, which were armed to prevent border raids and to preserve internal security, were attacked by invading forces from North Korea.

"The Security Council of the United Nations called upon the invading troops to cease hostilities and to withdraw to the 38th parallel. This they have not done, but on the contrary have pressed the attack. The Security Council called upon all members of the United Nations to render every assistance to the United Nations in the execution of this resolution.

"In these circumstances I have ordered United States Air and Sea forces to give the Korean government troops cover and support.

"The attack upon Korea makes it plain beyond all doubt that Communism has passed beyond the use of subversion to conquer independent nations and will now use armed invasion and war. . . . Accordingly, I have ordered the Seventh Fleet to prevent any attack on Formosa. . . . I have also directed that United States forces in the Philippines be strengthened. . . .

"I have similarly directed acceleration in the furnishing of military assistance to the forces of France and the Associated States in Indo-China and the dispatch of a military mission to provide close working relations with those forces. . . . The United States will continue to uphold the rule of law."

JULY 10 **THE CONSEQUENCES:** From the moment he proclaimed U.S. air & sea support for the reeling Koreans, Harry Truman had seen the next fateful decision marching toward him in seven-league infantry boots. At midweek he ordered the National Security Council into secret session to size up U.S. troop positions in the Far East. Before the council lay Douglas Mac-Arthur's report that the U.S. doughfoot would have to come and come fast to South Korea if the highsounding words of 24 hours before were to have any meaning.

At a White House conference, Congressional leaders and cabinet members listened as General Bradley recited the bad news from Korea. When Bradley had finished, the President slowly read off the text of his decision to throw U.S. troops into the battle, to allow the Air Force to bomb "specific mili-

Before the Korean war, President Truman is jaunty and relaxed. Page 11.

After the outbreak of war, the President walks with a weary tread.

tary targets" in Communist North Korea, and to order the Navy to blockade the entire Korean coast. Later that day 66-year-old Harry Truman seemed to walk with a weary man's heavy tread.

POLICE ACTION: "We are not at war," said the President of the U.S. last week. Then he went on to explain. The U.S., said Harry Truman, was engaged in a police action. A "bunch of bandits" had attacked the Republic of Korea—a government established by the United Nations—and the Security Council had asked U.N. members to suppress this bandit raid.

WHAT IT TAKES: The President called in the members of Congress' Armed Services Committees and talked frankly. He admitted that the U.S. military high command had seriously underestimated the speed and power of the North Korean ground attack and had gone in too slowly with too little. "Now that is being changed," he said. "We're going in with what it takes." JULY 17

A headline sensation of the summer of 1950 was the sudden trip of General MacArthur to Nationalist Formosa to discuss military matters with Chiang Kai-shek. The Administration, anxious to prevent any further widening of the war, had already announced its policy on Formosa: to discourage all talk of a Nationalist attack against the Communist mainland, and to rely on the U.S. Navy to "neutralize" Formosa and protect it from the Communists. MacArthur had differed with the Administration over its Formosa policy, and his dramatic trip at this moment was therefore open to political interpretation.

THE LAST WORD: What did Douglas MacArthur say to Chiang Kai-shek? Harry Truman certainly wished he knew, and so did the State Department and the Pentagon. They did not even know about the general's flying trip to Formosa until he made it. Since Douglas MacArthur is not the kind of man that Washington lightly orders around, there were anxious meetings at the White House. The President profoundly ad- AUG. 14

mires MacArthur as a general, but believes that political and diplomatic decisions affecting the U.S. should be made in Washington, not Tokyo.

Finally, on short notice, quiet, slender Averell Harriman, the President's new foreign affairs troubleshooter, was hustled off by plane to Tokyo. He was to tell the General to make recommendations on non-military matters, not decisions.

AUG. 21 **ALL IS WELL:** All was now well between Douglas MacArthur, Presidential Assistant Averell Harriman and Harry Truman, and had been all along. So said they all last week. MacArthur had not overstepped his military bounds by his trip to Formosa; he was "a soldier," said Harriman, "and he will carry out any orders that the President gives him." The President, for his part, said he was satisfied with MacArthur in his job.

SEPT. 4 **THE WEEK THINGS WENT WRONG:** The war news from Korea continued to be encouraging, but everywhere else the President looked, things seemed to be going wrong. Congress was bent on compelling him to lend money against his will to Franco of Spain, and was loading his war-powers bill with restrictions he didn't want. This was hardly over before the President got a hatpin-sized jab from a new direction: the deadpan announcement from the railway unions that they proposed to strike, after he had just been assured that they would not. But that wasn't all. Douglas MacArthur, speaking his piece on Formosa, got the President so worked up that he ordered the General to withdraw his remarks. It was the kind of week during which a President might well ask himself why he had ever gotten into politics in the first place.

TWO VOICES: Harry Truman did what not even Franklin Roosevelt had had the temerity to do. He ordered Douglas MacArthur to shut up. But for what Harry Truman intended to accomplish, the order had been given too late. A statement by MacArthur, drawn with the obvious intention of making military sense out of the Administration's strange, vacillating policy on Formosa, had already been sent to press in the U.S.

MacArthur had a single, paramount conviction: no matter what, Formosa had to be denied to the enemy—an end which the Administration was also trying to achieve. But Acheson deplored the timing of the General's statement. The President agreed. Mr. Truman sent MacArthur an order to withdraw his statement. White House Aide Charles Ross tried to explain: "In the field of foreign relations there can be only one voice stating the position of the United States."

"WHEN I MAKE A MISTAKE": One morning at the end of last SEPT. 18 month, Harry Truman sat down and tackled the personal mail that he always handles himself. In one letter, Congressman Gordon McDonough respectfully suggested that the U.S. Marines, like the Army, Navy and Air Force, ought to have their own general on the Joint Chiefs of Staff. Mr. Truman popped a gasket.

"For your information," he dictated, "the Marine Corps is the Navy's police force . . . and that is what it will remain. They have a propaganda machine that is almost equal to Stalin's. . . . Sincerely yours, Harry S. Truman."

Congressman McDonough quietly inserted the correspondence in the *Congressional Record*. A journalist spotted it and passed it on, and soon the President was under a heavy counterattack. Mr. Truman has put his foot in his mouth before, but this time the feat seemed to overshadow all others. Harry Truman soon decided he had better do something and prepared to do what no other President within memory has done: make a public apology for an egregious blunder. The White House speech writers were called in to carve out a statement. And the next day he appeared, hat in hand, at a convention of the Marine Corps League which just happened to be taking place at the Hotel Statler.

The convention's official bugler, 70-year-old Herbert Baldwin, tried to blow *Hail to the Chief*, but his upper dentures slipped out, so he just blew Attention.

"You succeeded in enticing me over here," Harry Truman grinned. "When I make a mistake I try to correct it. I try to make as few as possible." The delegates cheered and Mr. Truman joined them in singing, "From the halls of Montezuma to the shores of Tripoli. . . ."

THE FACE IN THE LAMPLIGHT: Twice before, in deep predica- SEPT. 25 ment, Harry Truman had gone looking for a man of honesty, dignity and prestige. Both times he turned in the same direction. Last week the rays of Mr. Truman's lamp fell once again on the homely, sorrowful, willing face of General George Catlett Marshall. The President had seldom been in a worse political fix. At its center was Louis Johnson, the Democratic Party's chief fund raiser in the 1948 presidential campaign, whom Mr. Truman had rewarded with the job of Secretary of Defense. But by now it was clear that to keep Johnson in the Cabinet was to risk the Democrats' political neck, perhaps even jeopardize the country's security. For months White House conferences had been frequently blue with complaints of Johnson's undercutting, hamhandedness, blooper-blowing. One complaint was that Johnson had leaked confidential statements and afterwards blandly denied making them. Mr. Truman had to do something. General Marshall, whom he venerates, was the answer to his prayers, and was named last week to be the new Secretary of Defense. Louis Johnson was fired.

As the differences mounted between General MacArthur and the Administration, President Truman decided on a dramatic trip of his own: a flight to Wake Island to meet his Pacific commander in person and smooth over the controversy.

OCT. 23 **THE GENERAL ROSE AT DAWN:** The President seemed to be in a carefree and folksy mood when he began his long pilgrimage to shake the hand of General Douglas MacArthur. But once the presidential DC-6, *Independence*, left St. Louis for Wake Island, his jocularity vanished. An odd atmosphere of expectancy and something very like tension settled over the expedition for the last leg of the journey. Truman and MacArthur—who had never set eyes on each other, and who had clashed publicly over U.S. policy in Formosa—seemed, at the moment, like the sovereign rulers of separate states, approaching a neutral field.

The illusion was heightened by the hour of meeting—dawn had just begun to silhouette a great black thundercloud east of Wake Island as the *Independence* circled for a landing. A battered 1948 Chevrolet sedan rolled up. Douglas MacArthur stepped forth and advanced, hands in his pockets, his greasy, battered, gold-encrusted cap well down on his head. As the President stepped down, MacArthur held out his hand.

"I've been a long time meeting you, General," said Truman, grinning.

"I hope," the general answered genially, "it won't be so long next time." (Douglas MacArthur has not been to the U.S. since 1937.)

The two men got carefully into the dusty automotive ruin —climbing over the front seat because the rear doors were stuck—and rattled off to a Quonset hut. The door closed. It stayed closed for one hour. Nobody heard what was said.

At 7:45 the two men emerged into the tropic sunshine and made another rattling journey, this time to Wake's new coral-pink administration building where their advisors were waiting. Said MacArthur, pulling out a pipe: "Do you mind if I smoke, Mr. President?"

"No," said non-smoking Harry Truman, "I suppose I have had more smoke blown at me than any other man alive." The President pulled out an agenda penciled on a scratch pad and the conference began. Truman confined the talk to subjects on which he and MacArthur already agreed—Korea, the Philippines, stabilizing the Far East. There was no mention at this roundtable meeting of Chiang Kai-shek or Indo-China. Truman characterized the general as "one of America's greatest soldier-statesmen."

Faced with such hallelujahs, MacArthur authorized Press Secretary Charlie Ross to state: "No field commander in the history of warfare has had more complete and admirable support than I have during the Korean operation."

MARGARET'S PIANO: During a trip to New York City to NOV. 6 commemorate the fifth anniversary of the United Nations, Harry Truman halted for his first look at his daughter Margaret's apartment on upper Madison Avenue. Margaret was away, keeping a singing date in Hartford, Conn., but the President, after exploring, told her over the telephone that her piano was out of tune.

FANATICS' ERRAND: No dictator in his right mind would live NOV. 13 in Washington's historic Blair-Lee House for a minute. Unless the blinds are drawn, passers-by can peer up into its shutter-framed, white-curtained windows. But if Harry Truman had any misgivings for his safety when he moved into the old residence two years ago while the White House was being made over, he gave no sign of it. Only the Secret Servicemen worried: to them, Blair-Lee House was a perilous place.

Agents with sub-machine guns were posted behind both front doors. Uniformed White House guards (who are under the direction of the Secret Service) were stationed at two sidewalk sentry booths and at posts along the curb. Day after day, month after month, fighting monotony, they doggedly worked their eight-hour shifts, watching the limousines which swept up to the house, the streetcars, trucks and cars which rumbled along out in the street, the pedestrians who sauntered day & night under the windows. Nothing ever happened.

One quiet, unseasonably hot afternoon last week, a burly White House cop named Donald Birdzell was reacting like a bear in a zoo to the rigors of boredom and the demands of duty. He paced. Then he stood before the Blair House steps and stared solemnly toward the street. As he did so a sound —a faint, metallic click—disturbed him. He turned his head.

On the sidewalk, ten feet away from him, stood a neat, dark man in a pinstriped, blue-green suit. The man was silently and carefully aiming a German P-38 automatic pistol at him. It went off—just as Birdzell jumped, clawing for his own revolver. The guard bolted instinctively for the street— partly to draw the gunman's fire away from the President's quarters, partly to leave a clear field for the Tommy gunner behind the door. Then hell's own corn popper began to grind in front of Blair-Lee House.

The gunman pivoted, shooting. Birdzell, out in the streetcar tracks of Pennsylvania Avenue, turned and began firing back. A bullet hit one of his legs and he sank to one knee. Another bullet hit his good leg. He tumbled forward, and went on banging steadily away with his pistol held braced at arm's length on the pavement before him.

As other guards and Secret Service men went into action, a second neat, dark man darted up to the guards at the west sentry booth, yanked out a Luger and began shooting at point-blank range. A uniformed private named Leslie Coffelt went down, dying, with bullets in his chest, stomach and legs; Plainclothesman Joseph H. Downs toppled over, shot in the stomach and chest. There was one last cacophony of shots, shouts and tinkling glass. The first gunman, frantically trying to reload, was hit and sprawled out, hat awry, heels kicking; the second lurched backward over a low boxwood hedge, stone dead with a bullet through his ears.

For a few seconds it was so quiet that the ding-ding of distant streetcars was clearly heard. Then hundreds of people were running toward Blair-Lee House. A hefty Secret Service man named Floyd Boring looked up, saw the President, who had been aroused from a nap, peering out an upstairs window in his underwear. Boring bawled: "Get back! Get back!" until the President stepped out of sight.

Down below, guards rolled the living gunman over, jerked roughly at his coat, fumbled through his pockets, carefully snapped the elastic band of his underwear to be certain it was not hooked to a hidden bomb mechanism. They demanded his name. He whispered: "Oscar Collazo." His companion was Griselio Torresola. They were Puerto Ricans, members of a fanatic band of Nationalists.

In Washington's Gallinger Hospital, the wounded Collazo willingly told the tale of his crazy pilgrimage. He and his fellow plotter had agreed that it was their sacred duty to kill the President. Why? With flowery Latin eloquence, Collazo cried that his countrymen had been "enslaved."

Their mistakes, rather than their deadly accomplishments, made Secret Service men shudder. Collazo, who was charged with murder [guards Birdzell and Downs recovered], admitted that neither man had any idea whether the President was at home. Neither had been moved to read a line in Washington newspapers—if they had done so, they would have known that they could have had a free shot at the President when he left for Arlington that afternoon to dedicate a statue.

The President made the trip. Secret Service men hustled him out a rear entrance and into his gold-trimmed Lincoln limousine. Convoyed by automobile loads of hard-faced agents, the big car rolled out of the drive, and off across the Potomac. Harry Truman seemed unmoved by the assassination attempt. Although extra guards accompanied him, he took his usual walk the next morning. Said he: "A President has to expect those things." To Admiral William Leahy he added: "The only thing you have to worry about is bad luck. I never have bad luck."

DEC. 11 **SHOCK WAVES:** The first hint of tough action against the Chinese [who had just entered the Korean war with a massive surprise attack] came during Harry Truman's jampacked press conference at midweek. The President began by reading a prepared statement. It condemned the Communists and warned that the U.N. forces might suffer reverses, but "have no intention of abandoning their mission in Korea." A reporter picked up a presidential remark that every weapon the U.S. had would be made available to General MacArthur: "Mr. President," he asked, "does that mean that there is active consideration of the use of the atomic bomb?"

There has always been, the President replied.

Did this mean that Douglas MacArthur could drop the atomic bomb whenever he felt like it? No, no, no, said the White House. Under the law, only the President may authorize use of the bomb, and "no such authorization has been given."

The State Department, in a matter of minutes, began quaking at such boldness. When the shock waves hit Western Europe, newspapers blazed with headlines. Britain's Prime Minister Clement Attlee swiftly decided to hustle off to Washington for a personal conference with the President.

DEC. 18 **THE LETTER:** When the Washington *Post's* Music Critic Paul Hume got back to his office from Constitution Hall one night last week, he addressed himself to an uncomfortable chore—criticizing the President's daughter. Hume, a well-grounded student of music, had come to the widely shared conclusion that Margaret just "cannot sing very well." "She is flat a good deal of the time," Hume wrote. "She cannot sing with anything approaching professional finish . . . she communicates almost nothing of the music she presents." The day after the review appeared, 34-year-old Critic Hume got a letter that made his eyes pop. It read in part: "I have just read your lousy review of Margaret's concert. . . . It seems to me that you are a frustrated old man. . . . Some day I hope to meet you. When that happens you'll need a new nose, a lot of beefsteak for black eyes, and perhaps a supporter below."

It was signed: "H.S.T."

Margaret, on concert tour, told reporters: "I am absolutely positive my father wouldn't use language like that."

Critic Hume said: "I can only say that a man . . . carrying the terrible burden of the present world crisis ought to be indulged in an occasional outburst of temper."

Critic Hume calls Margaret's singing "flat," is blasted by HST. Page 23.   *Margaret Truman: ". . . my father wouldn't use language like that."*

"HANDICAPS AND BURDENS": The President was a little DEC. 25 taken aback at the worldwide sensation his mule skinner's phrasing had set off. (Critic Hume began a review of another recital last week: "If I may venture to express an opinion. . . .")

During a conference with a committee from the National Association of Broadcasters, Harry Truman bemoaned the "handicaps and burdens" of his office—particularly the handicap of living the lives of two men, that of a President and that of a human being. "Sometimes the frailties of the human get the better of me."

A MESSAGE AT CHRISTMAS: "I am talking to you tonight about what our country is up against and what we are going to do about it."

With those words, President Truman moved the nation

into a quickened mobilization to prepare the country either for World War III or a highly armed, wary era of uneasy peace that might last for years. Among his moves, the President:

¶ Proclaimed a state of national emergency, unsheathing for the second time in less than a decade the extreme powers granted to a President only in times of crisis.

¶ Created a supreme Office of Defense Mobilization.

¶ Ordered a 1,000,000-man increase in the armed forces, to total 3,500,000 by spring.

"I summon every person of every community to make . . . whatever sacrifices are necessary for the welfare of the nation," the President said.

The Nation

It did not take long for the U.S. public to respond to President Truman's straight talk on the crisis of Korea. But in the months before the war started and the straight talk began, the nation was in a mood for business as usual—strikes, fads, politics and all.

FEB. 13   **STRANGERS KEEP OUT:** With the air of a Borgia guest spurning a poisoned chop, John L. Lewis rejected President Truman's proposal for a 70-day truce and a three-man fact-finding board to end a nationwide strike of the United Mine Workers. Wrote Lewis: "The mineworkers do not wish three strangers, however well-intentioned, but necessarily ill-informed, to fix their wages, decree their working conditions, define their living standards and limit the educational opportunities of their children."

This week, with 372,000 now on strike, and the nation facing midwinter with a perilous two- to three-week supply of coal in its bins, Truman invoked the machinery of the Taft-Hartley Act.

John L. Lewis had dared the President to do his worst: "To use the power of the state to drive men into the mines . . . is involuntary servitude."

POWER OF PERSUASION: Federal Judge Richmond Keech FEB. 20 ordered Lewis to order his miners back to work. Lewis went through the motions. Thus he hoped to save himself from another whopping fine for contempt of court ($1,420,000 for him and the U.M.W. in 1948 in similar circumstances).

Plastered as he was with injunctions, septuagenarian John Lewis was far from licked. To no one's surprise, defiance swept through the coal fields. In Pennsylvania and West Virginia, miners shouted: "To hell with them. . . ." "They can't mine coal with an injunction."

"CEASE FORTHWITH": John Lewis issued a second order to FEB. 27 his miners: "Cease forthwith all stoppages and return to work without delay." But the nation's coal mines were still closed. Whether John Lewis actually meant his miners to go back to work, only Lewis could say, and the cat had his tongue. While the grim farce continued, the emergency had become real. Steel plants prepared to shut down and coal was rationed to city-dwellers. Power was cut, railroad service curtailed. Estimates were that the country as a whole had only eight days' supply of coal; some areas were already down to almost nothing.

This week, as the Administration pondered what to do next, Lewis haughtily sat down again to talk things over with the operators.

WAITING GAME: For John Llewellyn Lewis the week began MARCH in acute suspense. It ended in one of the greatest victories of his thunderous career. For the third time in its history, his United Mine Workers had been brought to trial for contempt of court. A conviction might have bankrupted the U.M.W.'s $15 million treasury; at least it could have brought John Lewis to his knees. But there was no conviction.

"It may be," Judge Keech said, "that the mass strike of union members has been ordered, encouraged . . . or in some wise permitted by means not appearing in the record; but this court may not convict on conjecture."

The decision stunned Government attorneys and operators. The miners had worked out a way to beat the Taft-Hartley Act injunction. And the operators quickly agreed to pay higher wages ($14.75 a day) plus added contributions to the union's welfare fund. The operators also accepted a "good faith" clause in the contract which gave Lewis the right to call out miners on a whim. Rumbled John Lewis proudly, "We have benefited all labor and we have benefited all citizens who live under our flag." Lewis' fight had cost the miners around $400 million in wages—an average of around $1,100 each. The permanent damage to the coal industry, already groggy from constant conflict and losing more & more business to competing fuels, was difficult to assess.

MARCH 20 **FUN FOR ALL:** A white-haired old party named Jack Alonzo Goldie got into a Chinese robe at Rockport, Mass. last week, put a black band around his head and announced that 1) he was The Zoom, and 2) that an H-bomb was going to blow the world up on April 7, 1954. He asked one & all to become Zoomites, and join him in burrowing underground.

The more fearless molders of U.S. opinion—the advertising agency, the department store and the beauty salon—paid no attention. Women's skirts were raised to what is known as "mid-calf" for the new season—a maneuver which would doubtless enable the fiends of fashion to start lowering them again in the fall. Women who had cut off most of their hair in 1949 because they looked so frightful with it long, were urged by Elizabeth Arden to grow it out immediately because they looked so frightful with it short.

Because of New York's water shortage, the Brooklyn baseball club started digging a well near the first-base line at Ebbet's Field, planned to use it in irrigating the infield grass. The Treasury Department announced a resurgence of moonshining in the U.S.

The nation, in a word, was still clinging firmly to the proposition that a man had a right to be a little pixilated if he wanted—even though he might be blown into radioactive scrapple next week.

MAY 1 **"DEAR IKE":** It was not a ground swell, but some waves were forming:

❡ In Dallas, a small circle of aroused ladies formed the "Americans for National Coalition," proposed "the drafting of . . . Dwight D. Eisenhower" for President.

❡ In Fort Collins, Colo., a group of young lawyers and

businessmen (Republicans and Democrats) formed themselves into the "Dear Ike" Club, sent out 2,000 letters which invited others to join. The simple rules: write Eisenhower a letter asking him to accept the Republican nomination; write at least ten other letters to friends telling them about the plan.

¶ Pollster George Gallup asked voters of both parties whom they would pick for President if the race should be between Eisenhower and Truman. The results: 60% for Eisenhower; 31% for Truman; 9% don't know.

DOUBLE TROUBLE: The bag of groceries that cost a city JUNE 5 housewife $5 in 1935-39 now costs her $9.83, the Bureau of Labor Statistics reported last week.

PLAGUE OF PLENTY: Across the fertile countenance of the JUNE 19 nation, the farmer bent his back in the June sun and worked the land. In the flatlands of Kansas, deep-tanned men, with wheat dust pasted to their faces, pushed the clattering combines northward in the annual harvest of winter wheat. The Shorthorns and Herefords lumbered lazily across the Great Plains. Down South, where the cotton stretched like a giant snowdrift from North Carolina through Texas, there were watermelons and peaches to be picked, tobacco to be topped, beef and dairy cattle to be tended.

In this mechanized land of milk and honey, there was abundance Moses never dreamed of. There was, in fact, too much of it. America's blessing of plenty had been transformed, by perverse economics and expedient politics, into a plague of plenty.

The result was a contagion of contradictions. Food prices were too high, yet the Government was spending or lending more than $11 million a day to keep them that way. There was more food than people would eat, yet at least 15 million Americans (plus 600 to 700 million in foreign lands) could not get enough of the right kind. One arm of the massive Department of Agriculture was feverishly shuffling schemes for limiting farm production; another arm was busily showing farmers how to grow more. Already the U.S. had stored up enough wheat and corn to fill a freight train stretching almost halfway around the world, enough cotton to loom 90 million bedsheets, enough powdered milk to irrigate the Wheaties of all New York City's schoolchildren for several years to come.

Here was the glowering, complex malady known as "The Farm Problem." The farmer himself, aware of all the complaints about farm subsidies and wasteful gluts, has begun to be touchily defensive about the whole subject.

Actually the average good farmer was riding the crest of the most prosperous wave in farming history. His farmhouse was fresh-painted and stocked with all the comforts a city-dweller could ask. There were some who talked like Corn & Hog Raiser Carroll Brown of Oskaloosa, Iowa. "When the farmer asks too much," he reasoned, "the rest of the guys may gang up on us some of these days and we'll get nothing."

And there were, above all, farmers who spoke out like B. F. Vinson on his 150 Georgia acres. "I might not like some of the Government control," said he, "but I'd rather have it than be turned wild aloose." As long as there were farmers' votes and politicians to covet them, nobody in the foreseeable future was going to turn the farmer wild aloose.

JULY 3 **FROM THE COUNTRY & THE CITY:** Many a small U.S. farm town—big enough for a post office or a bank branch but too small for a movie house or a department store—is dying, judging by new census figures last week. Shannon City, Iowa, for example, has lost 119 of its 288 inhabitants. Said an oldster: "None of the kids ever comes back here to live after they've gone away to school." Four teen-agers complained: 'Nothing to do here—just a square dance once a month."

Where are the people? In 1950, it seems that the U.S. wants to live, not in a big city, but near it. All over the nation, people fleeing the city's crowds and taxes, people fleeing the country's torpor and low wages, have settled in the suburbs. The growing town of 1950 is the bedroom town.

JULY 10 **THE TIME IN KOREA:** No sooner had the President announced his support of Korea than a Dallas citizen was on the telephone, calling his local newspaper. Where was Korea, anyway? Were the people Indians or Japanese? And what time was it there?

It was a rare U.S. citizen who could pass a detailed quiz on the little piece of Asiatic peninsula he had just guaranteed with troops, planes and ships. But that didn't seem to matter. Across the nation there was solid popular agreement that Harry Truman had acted wisely and swiftly. "I'll tell ya," said Evar Malin, 37, who farms his mother's 140 acres north of Sycamore, Ill., "I think we done the right thing. We had to take some kind of action against the Russians; maybe been a good idea if we'd stepped in a little sooner."

ALL QUIET ON THE POTOMAC: Secretary of Defense Louis JULY 17 Johnson made a voluntary contribution of his own to the Korean war effort. "I told the President," he said, "that the Secretaries of the Army, Navy and Air Force and the Joint Chiefs had talked it over and none of us are making any speeches the rest of the month. The President thought it was an excellent idea."

PLAIN TALK: Of the war in Korea Dwight D. Eisenhower last AUG. 7 week said: "You can't win anywhere if you don't win this one."

ALL OUT: Real-estate promoters in Washington, D.C., were keeping up with the times in their newspaper ads. Samples:
¶ "Small Farms—Out Beyond Atom Bombs."
¶ An estate at Belle Meade, Va., "a safe 58 miles from Washington."
¶ A place "out of the radiation zone."

FAR FROM THE CANNON'S ROAR: For all its savagery and AUG. 28 import, the Korean conflict was working little more hardship on most citizens than the Battle of Wounded Knee. The U.S. had seldom had more sugar, meat, steel, gasoline, whisky and nylon, or more manpower for the mink coat, bubble gum and trout-fly trades. The nation so far seemed to accept this plethora of prosperity and plenty with none of the qualms of conscience which had afflicted it during World War II. If there was anything to be done, the U.S. citizen of 1950 figured it was up to Washington to tell him.

ROADS SEIZED: For 17 months, the bosses of the railroad SEPT. 4 brotherhoods had been demanding that the carriers cut the work week in yards from 48 hours to 40, at the same time grant a 31¢-an-hour wage boost so that yardmen would make as much money as when they worked the full 48 (a similar concession was won by a million non-operating employees in 1949). Last week, they gave the signal for a nationwide railroad strike to begin this week.

Harry Truman, hopping mad, seized the railroads; Assistant Secretary of the Army Karl Bendetsen was put in charge. Management, not the Government, would continue to manage the roads. But the union bosses obviously expected that now they would eventually get what they wanted. [The dispute dragged on for three years; in 1952 the railroad workers won increased wages and shorter hours, and the roads were returned to their owners.]

Dwight D. Eisenhower defeats Truman in a Presidential poll. Page 28.   *Senator Lyndon Johnson. His sharp nose senses "business as usual."*

SEPT. 18 **TEXAS WATCHDOG:** In the week that President Truman announced his program for mobilizing the U.S. economy, the Senate's new watchdog committee on U.S. preparedness uttered its first warning growl. Texas' sharp-nosed Chairman Lyndon Johnson had caught the strong scent of "business as usual" in some corners of the Defense Department's planning. Government-owned reserve defense plants, Johnson reported, had been allowed to deteriorate. Rubber stockpiling had slacked off while the need loomed greater than ever. "If we find the same siesta psychology in other fields," said Johnson, "our work is certainly cut out for us." For his task, Freshman Senator Johnson set himself a commendable set of rules: don't spend time looking for headlines, try to avoid politics, be constructive and impartial.

THE CITY UNDER THE BOMB: Time was when a small OCT. 2 American who got vaccinated and looked both ways before crossing streets had a reasonable chance of outliving his boyhood. But a new complication to survival has been added. One recent treatise on the subject seriously inquired: "Can Junior fall instantly, face down, elbow out, forehead on elbow, eyes shut? Have him try it tonight as he gets into bed."

A little practice and an understanding of the situation might save the life of a small boy born into the Atomic Age. Junior's terrifying new problem of survival was the problem of millions of his countrymen. For the first time many Americans were beginning to realize that the U.S. had become the target of a determined and ruthless enemy. And to save lives, to keep a bomb-shattered community going, would require plans and cooperation such as the U.S. had never been forced to think about before.

In New York City, firemen made plans for moving equipment across county lines. The Department of Public Works counted up some 24,000 pieces of equipment for emergency use—*e.g.*, 5,949 dump trucks, 444 hydraulic jacks, 367,240 lbs. of dynamite. The Welfare Department began canvassing the city's schools for shelters. Police officers began training courses under a nuclear physicist. To supplement the existing police radio net, communications experts were thinking about training pigeons to respond to supersonic whistles and plans were afoot to tie the Muzak canned music circuits into the emergency system.

Meanwhile Junior went on practicing throwing himself flat on the ground to escape the blow which would crush all small Americans unlucky enough to be standing in its path.

REPUBLICAN UPSURGE: In Tuesday's elections Republicans NOV. 13 scored a bigger victory than they themselves expected. They came within two seats (49-47) of capturing the Senate, substantially reduced the Fair Deal majority in the House. Four of the Administration's main senatorial pillars were ripped out while Robert A. ("Mr. Republican") Taft, the man the Administration most wanted to beat, won in Ohio by a spectacular majority of around 400,000. Of the Fair Deal's pillars in the Senate, Majority Leader Scott Lucas fell with the most resounding crash.

Almost as spectacular, even more unexpected, was the defeat of elegant, sarcastic Millard Tydings, chairman of the powerful Armed Services Committee, who had served Democratic Maryland as a Senator for 24 years. The thing that chiefly beat him was the charge that he had whitewashed the McCarthy investigation of Communism in the State Department.

Taft's victory in Ohio, he said, was "an omen for 1952." Other Republican victories included that of Richard Nixon, 37, congressional bloodhound of the Hiss case, who decisively beat Fair Dealer Helen Gahagan Douglas in California by making the Administration's failures in Asia his major issue.

In the House, Republicans gained 30 seats. The Democrats held precariously to their control of Congress, but for the next two years, at least, the Fair Deal was dead. For Harry Truman, who had predicted a Democratic landslide, the election of 1950 was a sharp and pointed rebuke.

NOV. 20 **NOT FOR PUBLICATION:** While the President cruised through Chesapeake Bay on the presidential yacht *Williamsburg*, newsmen bobbed behind in a rented yacht, waiting in vain for some specific comment from the President on the election. Press Secretary Charlie Ross finally sent a radio-telephone message and achieved an effect he probably did not intend: "The President has not commented on the elections in any extensive way—certainly not in a way that could be used for publication."

NOV. 27 **A FACE TO THE WORLD:** This was the official face which the U.S. in various statements from its leaders turned to the world last week:

The U.S. is living in fear of war. It is in a jam in Korea, and unable right now to defend Europe. In one breath it begs its enemies to hold their fire; in another breath it confesses its own weaknesses. It does not want to get in trouble with anybody; it just wants brotherhood and peace.

Secretary of State Acheson led off with statements beamed directly at Peking, assuring Mao Tse-tung that "everything in the world" was being done to make the Communist Chinese "understand that their proper interests will be taken care of."

Harry Truman flagged Peking with a message of mild indignation and reassurance, complaining that U.N. forces were being attacked by planes which fly from the "privileged sanctuary" of China. He said solemnly: "We have never at any time entertained any intention to carry hostilities into China."

DEFEAT: The U.S. and its allies stood at the abyss of disaster. DEC. 11 The Chinese Communists, pouring across the Manchurian border in vast formations, had smashed the U.N. army, this week were clawing forward to pursue and destroy its still-organized fragments. Caught in the desperate retreat were 140,000 American troops, the flower of the U.S. Army—almost the whole effective Army the U.S. had. With them, fighting to establish a defensive position, were 20,000 British, Turkish and other allies, some 100,000 South Korean soldiers.

It was defeat—the worst defeat the U.S. had ever suffered.

The Congress

BACK TO WORK: The 81st Congress came back to Capitol JAN. 9 Hill this week with politics on its mind and blood in its eye. At stake this year was more than the unfinished business on the Fair Deal agenda. With 36 Senators and the entire 435-member House facing the voters again next November, the prize was control of the 82nd Congress and a long head start toward the White House in 1952.

A FORGOTTEN BREED: As the 81st Congress returned to JAN. 16 work, Illinois Senator Paul Douglas slouched through the halls of the Capitol, a rumpled, craggy mountain of a man, smoking incessantly, dropping the ashes often as not on his shabby blue suit—the most promising, most controversial freshman the Senate had seen in years.

The Truman Administration was still not sure whether

Senator Paul Douglas: "All I want is to be a damn good Senator."

Senator Hubert Humphrey is ready after a midnight shower. Page 38.

Freshman Douglas was to be its foremost prophet or its subtlest enemy. He had fought for most of its program with a scholarly mastery of facts and a cool, articulate logic that had hopeful Democrats proclaiming him the Fair Deal's answer to Republican Robert Taft. But he had fought Fair Deal waste and extravagance as hard as any Republican. He is against Harry Truman's compulsory health insurance bill, for example, because it tries to do too much too soon.

On the basis of the record so far, Douglas seemed to be the nearest visible approach to an almost forgotten breed of American maverick—the old freewheeling Republican independent like Idaho's William E. Borah or Nebraska's doughty Liberal, George W. Norris. When he first stood in the empty quiet of his new Senate office a year ago, Douglas confided to his secretary: "All I want is to be a damn good Senator." Since then he has modified that ambition somewhat. "All I want is to be half as good a Senator as old George Norris." At 57, he was off to a good start.

FEB. 6 **"IT IS OBVIOUS"**: All week long, the FEPC (Fair Employment Practices Commission bill—to punish an employer for discrimination in hiring because of race or religion) was an issue, but it came no nearer to a vote. "It is obvious to everybody," said Manhattan's sleek, sharp Representative Vito

Marcantonio, who had long been flying the banner of the Red-line American Labor Party, "that everybody wants civil rights as an issue but not as a law." No one expected FEPC to roll very far through the 81st Congress. It might inch its way through the House, but it was almost sure to be talked to death in the Senate.

DENTAL OPERATION: Though the controversial federal MARCH 6 FEPC bill had been buried in congressional committee for five years, the fumes of its persistent and bomb-like smoldering had never left the nostrils of U.S. politicians. Last week, it became obvious that the FEPC bill was going to be trucked in, like an ashcan of nitroglycerin, for consideration on the floor of the House.

The bill's bitter opponents launched a campaign for adjournment which would have automatically kept the measure off the floor for many more months. When that failed, Pennsylvania's bald, stocky Republican Congressman Samuel K. McConnell attacked from the flank, introduced a substitute FEPC bill which included none of the Administration provisions for enforcement. Harlem's Congressman Adam Clayton Powell, pilot of the Administration bill, quoted Daniel Webster in railing against the McConnell substitute: "A law without a penalty is simply good advice." In the final showdown the bill's opponents triumphed; the House perfunctorily approved the McConnell bill. FEPC had been deprived of its teeth.

UNWILLING TO BE COUNTED: Just as the income tax laws JULY 3 had once been used to jail gangsters, when no other charge could be made to stick, Congress has found an oblique way to get at Communists. By asking witnesses at congressional investigations one question: "Are you a Communist?", Congress could cite them for contempt if they refused to answer. Last week House and Senate committees broke all records by citing a total of 43 for refusing to answer questions on Communism.

"THERE IS A DANGER": "I had pictured myself as defending SEPT. 2? civil liberties," said Illinois' Senator Paul Douglas last week. "And yet," he added, "there is a Communist danger in this country." For more than two weeks of agonized soul searching, the Senate had grappled with a problem which the U.S. had never squarely met. And yet, as Douglas pointed out, the country faced an undeniable danger from U.S. Communists who owed their first allegiance to a foreign enemy.

In the end, the Senate came down to a debate over two specific ways of holding the danger in check. One bill bore the name of Nevada's portly Pat McCarran and would require Communist organizations and fronts to register the names of their members and label their propaganda for what it was. President Truman said that he would veto it as an infringement of civil rights. The other bill, drafted by West Virginia's Harley Kilgore, would have left above-ground Communism strictly alone but provided for the roundup and mass detention of possible spies and saboteurs in times of national emergency.

After much debate over the effectiveness and constitutionality of each, the two bills were finally put together in an omnibus bill bearing McCarran's name and passed by an overwhelming 70 to 7 vote. Among other provisions, the new anti-Communist bill authorizes the Attorney General to intern potential spies and saboteurs in time of war or insurrection, requires Communist organizations to register themselves and their members, and makes it a crime to "conspire . . . to perform any act which would substantially contribute to the establishment within the U.S. of a totalitarian dictatorship."

From the White House, Harry Truman continued to regard the bill with disfavor. But the Congress obviously had the strength to override a presidential veto.

OCT. 2 **DAWN OVER CAPITOL HILL:** All week Congress had been tapping its foot, waiting for the President's veto of the McCarran anti-Communist bill. In the House, when the page boys burst in with mimeographed copies of the message, members grabbed eagerly at the bundles, helped pass them out. With little more than a glance, they began shouting: "Vote! Vote!" And minutes after the clerk had intoned Harry Truman's 5,500 words of warning, they had overridden the veto without a word of debate, by a thumping 286 to 48.

In the Senate, half a dozen Democrats—including Minnesota's civil-righteous young Hubert Humphrey—with the gravity of a band of martyrs had just made another kind of decision. They would try to filibuster while attempts were made to swing the votes necessary to uphold the veto. Their arguments were a direct paraphrase of Harry Truman's message. The law, the President had declared, "is about as practical as requiring thieves to register with the sheriff."

North Dakota's unpredictable lone-wolf Republican Bill Langer stepped up with much-needed relief for the Democratic corporal's guard. Shortly after 2 a.m., one of Langer's roars, punctuated by a crashing thump of his fist, frightened a sleeping page boy and sent him sprawling off his chair onto the floor. By 3:25 a.m. Langer's voice was growing hoarse, his face pale and haggard. By 5 o'clock he was in obvious distress. Humphrey, fresh and trim after a midnight shower and shave, sidled up to him. "I can stay until 6 o'clock," hissed Langer. But minutes later the North Dakotan sagged, reached for Humphrey's arm.

Humphrey shouted for a lateral pass: "Will the Senator yield?" "I yield," gasped Langer as his big, heavy hand pawed across his desk and scattered his papers on the floor. The sergeant-at-arms hustled down the aisle to help Humphrey lay Langer out on the floor. They ripped off his coat and tie, tore open his shirt, and bathed his forehead with a damp towel. Just as the first splotches of dawn paled the eastern windows, a stretcher crew hauled Langer off to the Naval Hospital. (Diagnosis: diabetic Bill Langer was totally exhausted.)

By 3:31 o'clock that afternoon, Humphrey admitted that the filibuster had failed. By 57 to 10, the Senate voted the anti-Communist bill into law. Ten minutes later it endorsed a waiting resolution from the House calling for adjournment. (The resolution was carefully phrased. The word was "adjourn," instead of "recess," which meant that Congressmen could qualify for 20¢-a-mile travel pay both to & from their homes.)

So ended the second session of the 81st Congress. It had ignored more major Fair Deal proposals (repeal of Taft-Hartley, federal aid to education, an anti-lynching bill, national health insurance, FEPC, the Brannan Plan) than it had passed. But it had written a solid record of far-reaching foreign-policy measures: extension of ECA (Economic Co-operation Administration) aid, arms for U.S. allies abroad, enough money to get the Point Four program of aid to underdeveloped nations going.

Trials and Conspiracies

This chapter combines several departments that appeared in TIME *under various headings but dealt with the same general subject: the search for possible traitors who favored the cause of Communism. One trail in the search had led, in 1948, to the indictment of Alger Hiss, a former State Department official. Whittaker Chambers, a confessed former member of the Communist Party and for 10 years an editor of* TIME, *testified that Hiss had passed important government documents to him for transmission to the Russians. The documents never reached the Russians, but microfilmed copies of them were found in a hollowed-out pumpkin on Chambers' farm in Maryland.*

Another trail was blazed by Wisconsin Senator Joseph McCarthy, who claimed he had proof that scores of Communists were active in the U.S. State Department. McCarthy's methods were so erratic and irresponsible that in 1954 he would be condemned and effectively silenced by the U.S. Senate.

JAN. 2 **COUNTERATTACK:** As big, brown-mustached U.S. prosecutor Tom Murphy made his second bid to send Alger Hiss off to prison for perjury, it became steadily more obvious that the Government's case was tighter, more dramatically presented and more damaging than it had been in the first trial which had ended last July in a hung jury. But by last week in Manhattan's federal court it was just as obvious that Hiss's defense had improved as well.

Claude Cross, his businesslike little attorney, had new witnesses and new evidence with which to assault important segments of the story told by Whittaker Chambers, onetime Communist courier and espionage agent. Under direct examination, Hiss once more denied Chambers' story—he had never been a Communist, he had never stolen State Department documents, and neither he nor any member of his family had copied State secrets on his old Woodstock typewriter.

There still remained the fact that Chambers had notes concerning secret documents in Hiss's handwriting, and documents typed on Hiss's Woodstock. These things Hiss had not explained away.

PSYCHOPATHIC PERSONALITY: A large, assertive man wearing thick-lensed spectacles took the witness stand last week in the perjury trial of Alger Hiss. He identified himself as Dr. Carl A. L. Binger, a graduate of Harvard Medical School (1914) and the author of three books on psychiatry. JAN. 16

Fortified with his research (which included listening to Chambers' testimony, and reading some of Chambers' writing) and his psychiatric training but without ever having talked to Chambers (unnecessary, he said), Dr. Binger testified that Chambers suffered from a "psychopathic personality." A victim of the disease, said Dr. Binger, "always plays a role . . . must act as if the situation were true though it is true only in his imagination." Other characteristics revealed to Dr. Binger by Chambers' career: "pathological lying," "insensitivity for the feelings of others," "bizarre behavior," "vagabondism."

WHAT IS BIZARRE?: All of Chambers' accusations against Hiss, Dr. Binger indicated, might very well be a pack of pathological lies. JAN. 23

Psychopathic personality, Dr. Binger agreed under Murphy's grilling, was a "wastepaper-basket classification of a lot of symptoms." It covered a type of human behavior somewhere between mere oddness and out & out insanity. "I think that psychiatric diagnosis has a certain vagueness," said the doctor, who admitted he had no full-time training in a mental institution. Piece by piece, Thomas Murphy went about rescuing Chambers, his star witness, from the wastebasket.

Dr. Binger had said that hiding stolen documents in a pumpkin was bizarre behavior on Chambers' part. Was it bizarre, he was asked, for Benedict Arnold, when he sold out West Point to the British, to hide the plans in Major André's shoe? "No," said the doctor. Was it bizarre for Moses' mother to hide him in the bulrushes? "She could scarcely put him in a safety-deposit box," said the doctor brightly. Wasn't the fact that Chambers had held the same job at TIME for ten years strong evidence against a diagnosis of instability? "No," said Dr. Binger.

For 2½ days a fascinated jury listened before a finally exhausted Dr. Binger was allowed to step down.

JAN. 30 **THE RECKONING:** "I find the defendant guilty on the first count and guilty on the second count," said the foreman of the jury.

Prosecutor Tom Murphy. He grills a psychiatrist at the Alger Hiss trial.   *Alger Hiss. The jury foreman said: "I find the defendant guilty."*

Thus came Alger Hiss, 45, to the bitter day of reckoning. He had been found guilty of perjury. Over the long months since August 1948, the case of Alger Hiss had been an agonizing public ordeal that left its mark on those who lived it. For a weary, tarnished man who had trodden the harsh, thankless road to Communism and back, the verdict was at least a partial expiation. Milking the cows on his Maryland farm, Whittaker Chambers said: "My work is finished."

FEB. 6 **"I DO NOT INTEND TO TURN MY BACK":** Within a span of six hours the case of the U.S. *v.* Alger Hiss became a major political issue. In a quiet Manhattan courtroom, Hiss was sentenced to five years in prison. He scarcely had time to post

$10,000 in bail and file an appeal before Secretary of State Dean Acheson set off the storm.

"Whatever the outcome of any appeal which Mr. Hiss or his lawyer may take," said the Secretary of State, "I do not intend to turn my back on Alger Hiss." Acheson spoke in a voice weighted with emotion. "I think every person who has known Alger Hiss . . . has upon his conscience the very serious task of deciding what his attitude is. . . . That must be done by each person in the light of his own principles. For me . . . these principles . . . were stated for us a very long time ago . . . on the Mount of Olives."

Secretary Acheson: "I do not intend to turn my back on Alger Hiss."

Senator McCarthy claims the State Department has 80 Reds. Page 44.

A roar of indignation rose from Capitol Hill and echoed across many of the nation's editorial pages. Snapped California's Representative Richard Nixon: "Disgusting." Harry Truman curtly refused comment. But Acheson had given further embarrassment to Truman, who had himself called the Hiss case "a red herring."

HARRY'S DAY IN COURT: As his perjury case dragged FEB. 27 through its third month in San Francisco's federal court, Harry Renton Bridges finally had the full blaze of the limelight all to himself. His Australian snarl was as sardonic as ever as he tried to refute the Government's charges—that he had been a Communist and had lied in denying it when he became a citizen in 1945.

Bridges had no apologies to offer. In repeating his life story and describing the evolution of his longshoremen's union, he described himself as an old-fashioned radical who took the help of Communists or anyone else if it meant helping the union. But he denied that the comrades had ever controlled him. He assailed the Government witnesses with venom, as "liars, rats and stool pigeons," continually reminded the jury that the Government had tried unsuccessfully to prove him a Communist twice before. His audience roared with laughter when he happily recounted how he typed a series of mysterious notes in 1940, tore them up, planted them in his hotel room wastebasket, then rented another room in a nearby hotel and nightly watched through binoculars as the G-men tried to put the pieces together.

By week's end it was obvious that Harry Bridges had been his own best witness. He seldom missed a chance to throw in a scornful gibe: "These days, people trying to find out where you stand on the U.S. don't ask you that, but where you stand on Russia or Greece." "This is my country," he said.

Said the prosecutor, wryly, to a group of law students: "Gentlemen, if you study hard . . . you might eventually be given the honor of trying the sixth Bridges case."

SIX DOWN: The C.I.O. was cleaning out one more Red-infested corner of its labor empire. This time it was the militant Mine, Mill and Smelter Workers union. The indictment read: "Only the Communist assumption that what is good for the Soviet Union is good for American labor could justify Mine-Mill's position. Only constant subservience to the Communist Party can explain it." Mine-Mill, said Jacob S. Potofsky, President of the C.I.O.'s Amalgamated Clothing Workers, was dominated and its policies set by a four-member steering committee, which took its orders from Eugene Dennis and the rest of the hierarchy of the Communist Party. The veto power of its 44,000 members was only "theoretical."

The boss of Mine-Mill, 39-year-old Maurice Travis, denied the charges, declared that the hearing was a "kangaroo court." But C.I.O. President Philip Murray gave him short shrift. He threw Mine-Mill out of the C.I.O. and, after similar bills, threw out three more unions, making a total of six. Murray had only a few more corners to clean, including Harry Bridges' Longshoremen's union.

205? 57? 80?: In the Senate, Wisconsin's rash-talking Jo- MARCH 6 seph R. McCarthy rose and swung the tails of not one, but 81 Communists and party-liners (or so he said) in a wild attempt to decapitate both Harry Truman and Dean Acheson in one horrendous swing.

In a $5\frac{1}{2}$ hour speech he read case histories of all his exhibits, cried that 80 of them were employed in the State Department, that one card-carrying comrade was a presidential speechwriter. He refused to name one name. And his story was also weakened by the fact that he had been using all kinds of differing figures for weeks: first he had said there were 205 disloyal employees in State, then 57, before settling on 80.

Two days later the Senate voted unanimously to investigate McCarthy's charges. Republicans hoped they might turn up another Alger Hiss case; Democrats felt that they didn't dare stifle an inquiry—and besides, they said confidently, they weren't worried. Was there any fire at all below Joe McCarthy's smoke signals? Maryland's thorough and careful Democratic Senator Millard E. Tydings, chairman of the investigating committee, promised "neither a witch hunt, nor a whitewash."

ACT OF HUMILIATION: "Before you leave," said Alabama's MARCH long-jawed Democratic Senator Lister Hill to Secretary Acheson at the close of a hearing ostensibly called to discuss the budget, "would you like to make any comment about the Alger Hiss conviction of perjury?"

The Secretary paused a moment on the fateful cue. "If the committee wishes me to explain what I said, I'll do it. I have no desire to do it." He reached into his pocket and pulled out a prepared statement. His hands trembling, Dean Acheson began to read: "I have been so harrassed by misrepresentations as to what I said that . . . I hope this will dispose of this matter for good and all." First, he insisted, as a lawyer he would never presume to discuss the charges against Alger Hiss. But, he read on, "one must be true to the things by which one lives. . . . Mr. Hiss is in the greatest trouble in which a man could be. It is in regard to a man in this situation that I referred to Christ's words setting forth compassion as the highest of Christian duties. . . . For the benefit of those who would create doubt where none existed, I will accept the humiliation of stating what should be obvious, that I did not and do not condone in any way the offenses charged, whether committed by a friend or by a total stranger, and that I would never knowingly tolerate any disloyal person in the Department of State." Nobody pushed him further.

RCH 27 **McCARTHY AT THE BARRICADES:** In the six weeks since he charged the State Department with harboring "57 card-carrying Communists," Wisconsin's Republican Senator Joseph R. McCarthy had reaped whole scrapbooks full of scarehead publicity. But, despite congressional immunity, and the urging of a Senate committee set up especially to investigate his charges, he had not named one Communist, or produced any new evidence. Instead, he had dragged a batch of tired old loyalty cases back into the limelight and hashed over charges which had been hashed and rehashed (and in some cases, refuted) in the past. Loud-mouthed Joe McCarthy had been irresponsible and worse. He had made a wretched burlesque of the serious and necessary business of loyalty checkups. His charges were so completely without evidence to support them that he had probably damaged no reputations permanently except his own.

APRIL 3 **STAND OR FALL:** Like a desperate gambler, Wisconsin's Freshman Senator Joe McCarthy was doubling his bet every time he took a loss. Shaken up by angry rebuttals from his victims, McCarthy reached deep and produced the most tremendous sensation yet. He would name a man "now connected" with the State Department who was the "top Russian espionage agent" in the U.S.

McCarthy sat in his Senate office wearing an air of conspiratorial secrecy. He tapped a pencil on his desk and kept the tap water running in the washbasin, to foil, said he, any hidden microphones. McCarthy confided the name of the "Russian agent" to only a few. Soon, every cab driver and casual Washington visitor knew that McCarthy had named

Owen J. Lattimore, director of Johns Hopkins' School of International Relations.

McCarthy apparently hoped his evidence would be found in the files of the FBI, which Harry Truman had steadfastly refused to open. Snapped Joe McCarthy: "It is up to the President to put up or shut up." This week the President authorized FBI Director J. Edgar Hoover—a man in whom Congress has unbounded confidence—to testify before the subcommittee. Hoover said that opening his dossiers would result in a "complete collapse" of FBI procedures and would dry up sources. But he said flatly that the FBI had no proof to support McCarthy's charges. After that, McCarthy could only say lamely that he knew something the FBI didn't. McCarthy had said he would stand or fall on the case of Lattimore. It looked as if he had fallen.

CHARGE & COUNTERCHARGE: Wisconsin's bull-shouldered APRIL 1 Joe McCarthy, batted down time after time, just wouldn't stay down. He fetched up some affidavits which, he claimed, would prove that Owen Lattimore "is a Soviet agent." As usual, McCarthy refused to identify his sources.

Having filled the air with the kind of charge that made for sensational headlines, he then made the kind of retreat that was most likely to escape headline notice. He had already ducked away from his earlier accusations that there were 57 card-carrying Communists in the State Department and had not named a single one. He had ducked again when he was challenged to produce the 205 "security risks."

NO SIR, HE'S YOUR BABY: After 31 hours of deliberation, the APRIL jury decided that Harry Bridges had been a Communist and had lied when he denied it at his naturalization proceedings in 1945.

The jury's decision, if upheld by higher courts, would cost Harry Bridges his U.S. citizenship. But there was a question whether his native Australia would take him back. Said a high official in Sydney: "He is America's baby, not ours—I don't think we want him."

ZEAL AND CONSPIRACIES: There was a conspiracy designed MAY 1 to influence U.S. policy toward China. "Mr. Lattimore can be placed in that conspiracy." The speaker was Louis Budenz, a rumpled man, ten years a Communist Party functionary and managing editor of the *Daily Worker*, testifying in the marble-walled caucus room in the Senate Office Building. At a 1937 meeting, Budenz went on to say, Mr. Lattimore's "zeal in seeing that Communists were placed as writers in *Pacific Affairs*" was commended.

Budenz' hearsay testimony against Lattimore—undocumented and uncorroborated as it was—might be impossible of proof. Lattimore's task of disproving it seemed equally difficult.

MADLY ON: Wisconsin's Senator McCarthy went rushing madly on. To the American Society of Newspaper Editors he declared that General George Marshall had been "pathetic and completely unfitted" to be Secretary of State, and his appointment "little short of a crime." The editors applauded when he sat down.

Two nights later, before the same audience, Secretary of State Dean Acheson responded to McCarthy's attack for the first time. There was a right way and wrong way of combatting disloyalty, he said. "It is as though you said to yourself that the best way to find a fire is to ring every fire alarm in the city; not that you know of any fire, but if you get all the apparatus out and have it wheeling around through the city, you might find one." Neither he nor his department asked for sympathy or for help, said Acheson, but merely asked understanding. "The department is manned today by able, by honorable, by loyal and by clean-living American men & women." When Acheson finished, the editors stood and cheered. Only one man sat glowering at a side table, his hands jammed in his pockets. He was Senator Joe McCarthy.

JUNE 12 **THE ROUNDUP:** Off to jail last week for contempt of Congress went lean, bushy-haired George Marshall (no kin to Soldier-Statesman George Marshall) who lent his name and gave thousands of dollars from his inherited fortune to Communist-line causes. He was convicted for refusing to name contributors to his party-line National Federation for Constitutional Liberties when asked by the House Un-American Activities Committee back in 1946.

Scheduled for jail next: Novelist Howard Fast and ten other board members of another Communist front. Soon to go, and for the same reason: Screen Playwrights Dalton Trumbo, John Howard Lawson and the rest of the "Hollywood Ten" who refused in 1947 to tell the House committee whether or not they were members of the Communist Party.

CALLING A HALT: After 2,000,000 words of testimony, it was JULY 10 time, said Senator Millard Tydings, to take a breather. Over the protests of its two Republican members, the Tydings subcommittee voted to hear no more from Senator Joe McCarthy or any witnesses until it had produced an "interim report" on charges of Communists in Dean Acheson's State Department.

Without even waiting to see the Tydings report, McCarthy announced that it would be "a disgrace to the Senate."

RETURNED IN KIND: "At a time when American blood is JULY 24 a gain being shed to preserve our dream of freedom, we are constrained fearlessly and frankly to call the charges . . . what they truly are: a fraud and a hoax." The Senate report was talking about Joe McCarthy. It accused McCarthy of "hit & run" tactics, of a "cavalier disregard for facts," of "twisting, coloring, perverting and distorting" the truth.

McCarthy, unchastened, called the report "a green light to the red fifth column in the U.S."

NO. 4: Julius Rosenberg and his wife were listening to the JULY 31 *Lone Ranger* with their two young sons when a stranger rapped on the door of their drab apartment. Twelve men filed in from the small hallway and announced that they were from the FBI. They arrested 32-year-old Julius Rosenberg as a spy.

A puffy, spectacled native New Yorker with a smudge-sized mustache and disappearing black hair, Rosenberg was the fourth U.S. citizen arrested in the atomic spy roundup that began after the arrest of British Physicist Klaus Fuchs. The FBI said Rosenberg had been an important cog in the machinery, working directly under Anatoli Yakovlev, Soviet vice consul in New York. Rosenberg recruited his brother-in-law, David Greenglass, who in turn contacted Harry Gold.

Alone of the four arrested so far, Rosenberg stoutly insisted on his innocence. The FBI's story, said he, was "fantastic —something like kids hear on the *Lone Ranger* program." [Ethel Rosenberg, Julius' wife, was arrested the following month. They were both convicted in 1951 of passing atomic secrets to the Soviet Union and were executed in June 1953.]

BOILING OVER: The nation was good and mad at Communists —home-grown as well as the U.S.S.R. and North Korean varieties—and here & there its temper not only boiled up but boiled over. Items:

¶ In Detroit, the common council forbade sidewalk news vendors to sell "subversive literature."

¶ In Birmingham, Ala., big, blustery Police Commissioner Eugene ("Bull") Connor, who had been arresting Communists on charges of vagrancy, pushed a new ordinance through the city commission, banishing Communists from Birmingham on pain of a maximum $100 fine, 180-day jail sentence and constant rearrest.

¶ In Houston, Texas, a marauding gang laid down a midnight rock barrage on the apartment of James J. Green, state secretary of the Communist Party, accidentally pelting the neighbors as well.

¶ In suburban Los Angeles, a World War II veteran named Frank Zaffina, 32, rounded up a posse for a "crusade against Communism," pounced on a half-dozen astonished workmen as they came out of the gates of the Chrysler assembly plant. After three had been badly mauled, Zaffina was surprised to learn that among his victims were included a fellow Navy veteran and another with a South Pacific Air Force record. "I guess it isn't right," he mused next day, "to take the law into your own hands."

AUG. 14 **MOST PROBABLE DANGER:** Probably no judicial phrase in recent years has caused more confusion than the late Justice Holmes's famed rubric that free speech is dangerous only when it constitutes "a clear and present danger" to U.S. security.

For years, squatting behind the rock of the First Amendment (free speech), and insisting blithely that they were a danger to no one, U.S. Communists had screamed their denunciations and thumbed their noses at U.S. democracy. Last week Judge Learned Hand ruled flatly that Communism is a "clear and present danger. We shall be silly dupes if we forget that again and again in the past, just such preparations in other countries have aided to supplant existing governments when the time was ripe. . . . We know of no country," he concluded, ". . . except Great Britain, where they [the Reds] would have had so fair a hearing."

A MORAL CERTAINTY: Said Harry Bridges, as he folded his lean frame into the familiar San Francisco witness chair last week: "I'm against aggression. . . I will continue to speak out against war and if I haven't got that right, I may as well go to jail right now."

Said the U.S. prosecutor: "Harry Bridges is a dangerous enemy to our society and a threat to our national security. He is a source of comfort to our enemy. He is our enemy." By urging his longshoremen to oppose U.S. action in Korea, Bridges had lost his right to freedom, argued the Government. Bridges was out on $25,000 bail while waiting for an appeals court to rule on his five-year sentence for perjury. The Government asked that his bail be revoked.

Said Federal Judge George B. Harris, who had presided over the perjury trial: "I am satisfied to a moral certainty and beyond reasonable doubt that Harry Bridges was and is a member of the Communist Party. . . . As such his allegiance cannot be to the United States of America. . . . I revoke the bail."

Harry Bridges winked at his dark-haired wife, told her not to cry, walked jauntily down the corridor to jail. [After serving 20 days of a five-year sentence, Bridges was once more released on bail. In 1953, the U.S. Supreme Court overruled the 1950 conviction and dismissed the case.]

EVEN FOR NO-GOODS: The only immediate effects of the nation's new anti-Communist law were the indignant yelps from the Reds themselves. Manhattan's *Daily Worker* trumpeted their defiance: they would simply not comply with the McCarran law's provision that all Communists must register. They had 30 days from Sept. 23 to change their minds. OCT. 9

The leaders of the Communist Party convicted under the 1940 Smith Act (which makes it a felony to teach and advocate the violent overthrow of the Government) were also given at least a few more weeks to thrash around, untrammeled. Last week Supreme Court Justice Jackson turned down a Government request that the ten leaders be jailed immediately as dangerous to the public welfare. Even no-good citizens, said Jackson in effect, are entitled to freedom under bail, which will be continued for the ten Reds.

OCT. 23 **REVENGE AT ELLIS ISLAND:** Under the law some 347 Italian and German opera singers, businessmen, musicians and plain citizens were snatched off ships and planes arriving last week in New York, and packed off behind the wire fences of Ellis Island. They were among the first victims of the new restrictions on immigration in the Communist-control bill passed by the Congress over Harry Truman's veto.

Harry Truman had warned Congress of just such trouble. Now he was gleefully proving his point by enforcing the law to the letter.

The letter of the law did not give much choice. It banned any alien who "at any time" had been "affiliated" with any "section, branch, affiliate, or subdivision" of any "totalitarian party." Officials estimated that the new law would exclude 90% of all Germans, more than half of all Italians. It would bar all repentant Communists, interfere with trade with Yugoslavia, exclude many of the 55,000 German refugees from East Europe, whose admission Congress had just authorized last June.

In Europe, the Communist press happily crowed about "American political racism" and referred to Ellis Island as "that well-known concentration camp."

OCT. 30 **CATCH A COMRADE BY THE TOE:** This week the deadline went by for all Communists to register under the McCarran antisubversive law, and not one U.S. Communist stepped forward to sign up.

DEC. 18 **NO ERRORS:** Alger Hiss was near the end of his road. Last week a U.S. court of appeals decided there was enough believable evidence of his guilt. Nor could the court find any reversible errors in his second trial, which ended last January.

Said Hiss: "I reaffirm my innocence."

The Cold War

Communism was on the march almost everywhere. China had fallen under Communist rule in 1949 when Chiang Kai-shek quit the mainland and fled to Formosa; the Soviet Union was hardening its grip on its European satellites. The U.S. had countered with military and economic aid to the countries in greatest danger. In January Secretary of State Acheson spelled out which countries in the Pacific the U.S. would definitely defend; Korea was not among them. Then, on June 25, Communist troops crossed the 38th parallel in Korea and the Cold War turned hot.

APPOINTMENT IN PEKING: The four Chinese Communist JAN. 23 officials and their police escort were just 50 minutes late in keeping the appointment. Shortly before 10 o'clock one morning last week they took possession of the office of U.S. Consul General O. Edmund Clubb in the spacious U.S. legation compound in Peking, precisely as they had said they would seven days earlier. In Washington, the Department of State signaled for the orderly closing down of consulates in Peking, Tientsin, Shanghai, Nanking. For the first time in 105 years, the U.S. would shortly be without listening posts in China.

THE DEFENSE RESTS: Secretary of State Dean Acheson propped only a few notes on the lectern before him. Then, summoning the brightest of his lawyer's talents, he launched into his case for Asia. He said, in effect:

The U.S. policy for China is: we're sorry to see you go [Communist] but we're not at all to blame. Now you must get out of it as best you can, by yourself.

Acheson then staked out a second Asian area in tougher language. The nation's defense, said he, rests on a North Pacific frontier running along the Aleutian Islands to Japan and down through Okinawa to the Philippines. In case of attack on this line, the U.S. would defend all these positions. (For Korea, hanging perilously close to the most naked of Russian ambitions, the Secretary offered only a vaguer acknowledgment of "responsibility.") In effect, the U.S. policy along the island frontier is: Bear, Keep Out.

For the third sector of Asia—the uneasy non-Communist nations of Southeast Asia, India and Pakistan—Acheson had cold words and measured promises: "The direct responsibility lies with the peoples concerned." To the Communists he said, in effect, the U.S. policy is: We're fond of Southeast Asia, but not prepared to fight for it.

ARCH 27 **PEACE, BUT NOT AT ANY PRICE:** The uncertainty and negation were over. Last week, in the most important speech he has made since he took office, Secretary of State Acheson said firmly that the U.S. was intending no new appeal to Russia—and explained why. The U.S., said Acheson, was willing to "coexist" with the Communists—to use the current Soviet phrase—but only on realistic and hardheaded terms.

What kind of terms? Not on Russian promises, said Dean Acheson coldly, for they would not be kept. Russia must prove its good intentions by its conduct. It should, for example, let the people of the Eastern European satellites vote freely for "truly independent national regimes." It should drop the policy of "walkout and boycott" of the United Nations. It should call off the Soviet-controlled Communist agents who attempt "to overthrow established governments."

Obviously, Acheson did not expect the Russian bear to roll over and play dead. What he was demanding was that Russia abandon its determination to enslave the world, and of course he expected no such miracle. But more plainly than ever before, the U.S.S.R. had been told where the U.S. stood on all fronts of the Cold War.

The reaction in Moscow came as quickly as a bludgeon could be raised. The Russian press paid Acheson the compliment of its ugliest abuse. He was called a "simpleton," a "Fascist-minded diplomat," an "incorrigible and unceremonious liar."

The Secretary of State went to California on the advice of his boss. It was high time, Harry Truman had said, that Acheson answered his critics and took his policy to the people.

ARCH 27 **ATTACKS ON ACHESON:** Few Secretaries of State had been under attack from so many different quarters. Some critics charged that Acheson's policy was too often negative. Some who approved his current policy of firmness toward Russia believed that he was late in adopting it. Some Republicans berated Acheson for refusing military aid to Formosa, blamed him for the loss of China to the Communists.

On these grounds last week Minnesota's Representative Walter Judd, an old China hand, called aloud for Acheson's resignation. After all this hue & cry, Acheson was astonished by the response of his California audiences. At each appearance, he won standing ovations that surprised and flustered him pleasurably. And this week at Key West, Harry Truman finally rose to the defense of his besieged Secretary of State. Rumors that he might be replaced, said Presidential Secretary Charlie Ross, were "completely without foundation."

NONSTOP TO COPENHAGEN: The drop-bellied, high-tailed APRIL 24 Navy Privateer was supposed to be flying some kind of navigation training flight "nonstop to Copenhagen and return." There was no return—only a long silence. On the third day of the search for the missing plane in the Baltic Sea, a clue to its fate came, like a face slap, out of Moscow. The Kremlin charged that a "four-engined military plane" had flown 13 miles across the Soviet coastline and "an advanced Soviet fighter was forced to open fire . . . after which the American plane turned toward the sea and disappeared." By week's end, only one scrap of evidence had been picked up in the Baltic—an empty yellow life raft of the type issued to Navy patrol bombers. This week, the U.S. charged that the Russians shot down the plane over open waters. But it was a sign of U.S. awareness of the incidental perils of cold war, that there were no shouts for any hot fighting to begin.

THE CASE OF THE NAVY PRIVATEER: The U.S. dispatched MAY 1 a carefully weighed charge that the missing patrol bomber, because of the known facts of its flight plans and its slow speed, could not have been over Russia's Baltic territory when the Russians said it was. Hence it must have been shot down or crippled by Soviet fighters over the open sea. The U.S. demanded punishment for the offenders and indemnity for loss of ten U.S. lives and property. Three days later the U.S. received a flat Soviet refusal, which insisted that the plane was not a Privateer but a "B-29 Flying Fortress," and had been caught taking pictures over Latvia.

The temper of U.S. reaction was shown in Congress, where both houses unanimously voted posthumous decorations for the Privateer crew members. And the hollowness of the Russian accusations seemed to be established further by the finding of a second rubber life raft, of the type issued to the Privateer, picked up by a Swedish ship in the Baltic. The raft showed evidences of having been blasted on the water by high-powered airborne projectiles.

MAY 22 **ANOTHER SLICE:** Last week the Administration at last decided to go to the defense of another big slice of the world against the assaults of Communism. That area was Southeast Asia; the prescription for it would be like the military and economic aid program which had saved Greece and Turkey. The State Department had finally reached a key decision: if the Communists were to be kept from Burma, Siam, Malaya and even Indonesia, they must be stopped now in Indo-China. Acheson in Paris agreed to speed a $15 million program of military aid to the 180,000 French and native troops already locked in battle with the Indo-Chinese Communists. This was in addition to $60 million in U.S. economic aid.

MAY 29 **THE GOOD WAR:** Hope could be more than a straw. It was possible last week to catch the sound of confident, reassuring voices in the Western World. One of them said: "The cold war is a good war. It is the only war in history where the question of destruction doesn't enter into it at all. Everything we are doing is building up. We have rebuilt Europe, not destroyed it." The voice was that of Paul Hoffman, head of ECA. He spoke in Washington to a group of businessmen. "If the Marshall Plan had not been in effect you would have had part of Western Europe at least under the domination of the Kremlin and we would have spent much more for increased defense than we have spent for the Marshall Plan." Said Hoffman to the businessmen: "All we have to do is carry on intelligently, and at extremely low cost, the political, economic, military and informational measures already under way. Then, with luck, all of us in this room will live to see freedom on the march again."

PROGRESS REPORT: Six months ago South Korea, bedeviled JUNE 5
by guerrilla raids, galloping inflation and the daily threat of
invasion from the north, looked like a candidate for the same
mortuary as Nationalist China. Now the Republic of Korea
looks more like a country on its way to healthy survival.

Most observers now rate the 100,000-man South Korean
army as the best of its size in Asia. Its fast-moving columns
have mopped up all but a few of the Communist guerrilla
bands. And no one now believes that the Russian-trained
North Korean army could pull off a quick, successful invasion of the South without heavy reinforcements. Said a Korean private manning a foxhole along the 38th parallel last
week: "We expect war to come. But we aren't afraid. For
every round they send over, we'll send two back."

Only lack of air power might tip the scales against the
South.

All over South Korea a newly proud people were anxiously
hoping the Americans would stay. Remembering the Russians north of the 38th parallel, a Korean said, half apologet-
ically: "We know that many American leaders think Korea
should be given up. We have trusted and hoped in you. Will
you fail us?"

National Defense

---

*The keystone of U.S. defenses in 1950 was a stockpile of nu-
clear bombs and a fleet of jet aircraft and highly-trained crews
on alert, ready to drop the bombs on a moment's notice anywhere in the Communist world. This served as an effective
deterrent to a massive military attack against Europe or the
U.S. But it failed to prevent the kind of localized warfare that
the North Koreans (and later the Chinese) launched against
South Korea—a sudden onslaught of conventional ground
troops over extremely rugged terrain where nuclear bombs
would have had only a limited effect.*

MAN OF THE HOUR: By his own admission, gregarious, blus- FEB. 27
tering Defense Secretary Louis Johnson is a man with an ele-

Defense Secretary Louis Johnson is accused of cutting military muscle.

General Omar Bradley warns that forces are spread too thin. Page 58.

phant-thick hide. But the mounting charges that his heavy-footed economy was wrecking U.S. defenses stung him last week into a trumpeting war of defiance: "The defenses of the United States as of today are, in the opinion of the Joint Chiefs of Staff, myself, and the President, sufficient unto the needs of the hour." That was not quite saying, as he had the week before, that U.S. defenses were "in grand shape." But it seemed on the face of it almost as far from the truth. After eleven months in office, Louis Johnson's belligerent optimism was beginning to sound a little tinny. Items:

¶ The Air Force, with a minimum of heavy bombers, is also dangerously short of first-line fighters, one of the nation's prime defenses against airborne atomic-bomb attacks.

¶ Navy carrier air groups have been cut. The Marine Corps' ready combat outfits have been cut. Of the Marines' 23 crack fighter squadrons, eleven have been closed out for economy.

¶ In the U.S. there is only one Army division that approaches top combat efficiency.

¶ The U.S. still has no defensive radar screen, no adequate protection against new-type Russian submarines.

Even his severest critics were willing to admit that Johnson had squeezed some fat and inefficiency out of the armed services. The trouble was that he had also ruthlessly sliced away muscle. If by these methods Louis Johnson actually thought he could muster a force "sufficient unto the needs of the hour," it was obvious that Johnson & Co. didn't know what time it was.

In the midst of the argument over the nation's defenses, the U.S. went to the rescue of South Korea, which had just been attacked by North Korea.

FOR SMALL FIRES: Louis Johnson had said expansively that JULY 10 if the Russians attacked at four in the morning, the U.S. would be ready by five. Now, only half a little country had attacked, and it was well past five.

Part of the problem was that the U.S. armed forces were designed for another kind of war: an all-out war in which a direct attack by Moscow was to be directly answered by atom-bomb-packed B-36's. The effectiveness of that kind of force had not been disproved by Korea. But Louis Johnson's economy program was looking downright absurd.

What if the Kremlin's masterminds chose to set other small fires around Communism's vast periphery? To contain such assaults, the Joint Chiefs of Staff headed by General Omar Bradley told President Harry Truman last week, the present U.S. forces, thinly spread, were not enough. What they needed was an immediate transfusion from reserves—a limited mobilization of those who would volunteer. Harry Truman accepted Bradley's arguments, but insisted that he wanted to wait a few days, to measure the Russian reaction before making a call for volunteers.

PIECE BY PIECE: President Truman sent up to Congress the AUG. 7 itemized bill for the first installment of U.S. mobilization. He asked for $10.5 billion immediately, to add over 600,000 men to the nation's armed forces. Nearly half the total—$4.5 billion—was allotted to the Air Force. Some $3.3 billion would go for new planes, $2.6 billion for tanks, guns and ordnance.

BLACK AND WHITE: The Army duty officer at the Pentagon DEC. 11 routed General Lightnin' Joe Collins out of bed at 5:30 one morning last week to read him the first pink secret dispatch about the Chinese counter-offensive in Korea. All that day the Pentagon's brass-level was gloomy with misgivings. The hard, shocking fact they faced was that the U.S. was out of combat-ready reserve strength to meet the new danger.

The flow of men into the armed forces had been cut to a slow dribble. The cutback, the Army explained, was caused by a shortage of trained instructors. It takes 14 weeks to give a soldier basic training; nowadays he must be taught, says the Army, about 25% more than soldiers of World War II.

Equally as serious, in an effort to keep the $226 billion economy unruffled, U.S. industry had not been ordered into even a creeping mobilization. "We are moving," Mobilization Overseer Stuart Symington testified before the Senate Banking Committee, "from a light grey state of mobilization to dark grey." This sounded like murky talk to a nation whose arms crisis had been clear as black & white since last June.

MILESTONES

MARRIED: King Phumiphon of Siam, 22, Boston-born, saxophone-tootling King of Siam; and Princess Sirikit Kitiyakara, 17, his distant royal cousin; in Bangkok. Honeymooning this week, King Phumiphon finally sold five royal compositions to *Michael Todd's Peep Show*, a Broadway musical now in production. At first fearful that having part in a Broadway show might impair his royal dignity, Phumiphon was won over when Todd pointed out that Margaret Truman is also a professional musician.

DIED: Edgar Lee Masters, 81, whose grim, folksy *Spoon River Anthology* (1915) was printed in 55 editions and at least five languages to become one of the biggest commercial successes in modern poetry, in Melrose Park, Pa. Accusing the U.S. of ingratitude to poets, Masters was found broke, ill and half-starved in Manhattan in 1944, two years later was given a $5,000 fellowship by the Academy of American Poets.

MISCELLANY

OUT OF THIS WORLD: In San Francisco, Milton Gill told police he could not explain why his car rolled 400 feet downhill and crashed into a parked car; at the time, he was kissing his girl goodnight.

SILENT WITNESS: In Detroit, Frank Buss, charged with biting a policeman while drunk, got a suspended sentence when the judge learned that he had no teeth.

ONE FOOT IN HEAVEN: In Las Vegas, Nev., Henry Albert Beebe, arrested for illegal possession of morphine syringes, told police he was trying to sell the stuff to pay his tuition through Bible school.

WAR IN ASIA

Battle of Korea

NOT TOO LATE?: It was 4 a.m. Sunday in Korea, still only JULY 3
3 p.m. Saturday in Washington. Just before a grey dawn
came up over the peninsula, North Korea's Communist army
started to roll south. Past terraced hills, green with newly
transplanted rice, rumbled tanks. In the rain-heavy sky
roared an occasional fighter plane. Then the heavy artillery
started to boom.

All along the 38th parallel—the boundary between North
and South Korea—the invaders met little resistance. The
North Korean radio broadcast war whoops. According to
the Communist version of events, the Southerners had invaded the North and were being "repulsed." Cried a North
Korean communiqué: "The People's Republic will be obliged
to resort to decisive countermeasures."

Nobody should have been particularly surprised by the
"countermeasures." For months the Northern army had
limbered up in small-scale raids across the border. Nevertheless, the slender organization and uneasy morale of the young
Korean Republic suffered badly under the first blow.

In South Korea's bustling capital of Seoul, army jeeps
carrying loudspeakers roared through the streets, urging soldiers: "Go and join your units immediately." Buses and
trucks were commandeered by the army to transport troops
to the front. No one was quite sure where the front was; it
seemed to be moving rapidly toward the capital. All night
long, Seoul was kept awake by convoys rumbling through
the streets. Next morning Northern planes machine-gunned
the city streets.

American military advisers spoke worriedly of the collapse
and utter confusion of Korean troops under artillery fire.
Korean government officials spoke bitterly of inadequate
U.S. aid. A spokesman issued a statement from President
Syngman Rhee: "The President is greatly disappointed with
American aid . . . . It is too little and too late."

For two sickening days, it looked as if Rhee might be right. The Northern radio broadcast a triumphant appeal to the South to surrender. For hours, hope teetered in precarious balance with despair. Then came the electrifying news from Washington: the Yanks were coming.

Moscow was widely believed to have launched the Korea attack as a "reconnaissance in force," as a test of American determination. If that was Moscow's purpose, it had succeeded. The Red attack in Korea had at last shocked the U.S. into action.

"WE ARE DETERMINED": At 3 a.m. Sunday, the telephone rang in the Forest Hills, N.Y. home of U.N. Secretary General Trygve Lie. The caller was Ambassador Ernest Gross, U.S. deputy representative to the United Nations. The U.S., said Gross, wanted Lie to call an emergency meeting of the Security Council to deal with the invasion. When the U.N. Security Council was called to order the next afternoon, Russia's seat at the Council table was conspicuously empty. The Soviet Union was still boycotting the U.N. for its refusal to unseat China's Nationalist delegates in favor of the Chinese Communists.

On behalf of the U.S., Gross urged the Council to adopt a resolution demanding that the North Koreans cease fire and withdraw their troops to the 38th parallel.

After four hours the U.S. draft resolution was passed by a vote of 9-to-0. It called on all member nations to "render every assistance" to the U.N. in carrying out the cease-fire order.

JULY 10   **"MORALE IS FINE":** U.S. B-29s were bombing Pyongyang, the Red capital, and other objectives north of the 38th parallel. Douglas MacArthur ordered the 24th Division, equipped with tanks and artillery, to Korea by sea. The issue would turn on whether the defenders could hold out long enough for MacArthur's men to get into the line.

TIME Correspondent Frank Gibney reported from Korea: "We asked a soldier, a stubbled infantryman with a cluster of grenades dangling from his belt, how morale was. 'Morale is fine. We have the best morale in the world,' he said, 'but what can morale do against planes and tanks?'"

"WE GO": Last week, 70-year-old Douglas MacArthur drove through the rain to Haneda airfield outside Tokyo. Waiting for him there was the old *Bataan*, revved up and ready to fly to South Korea. As the night wore on, Army weathermen, looking up at the rain and overcast which shrouded the Japanese capital, shook their heads. Staff officers urged the general to abandon his trip. At each objection the MacArthur jaw jutted out a little farther. "We go," said Douglas Mac-Arthur.

Soon after the plane was airborne, MacArthur pulled out the corncob pipe which had been one of his World War II trademarks. "I don't smoke this back there in Tokyo," he said. "They'd think I was a farmer."

In Suwon MacArthur was met by Syngman Rhee, President of the Korean Republic. After a short conference, Mac-Arthur gave his staff officers more cause for worry. "Let's go to the front and look at the troops," he said. "The only way to judge a war is to see the troops in action." What the general saw was not good. The party pushed on to a hill barely a mile from the 15th Century walls of Seoul. Clearly visible were towers of smoke from fires set by enemy shelling. Clearly audible was the crump of Communist mortars over the river.

When he took off again from Suwon airstrip, MacArthur, who had planned to spend two days in Korea, had been there only eight hours. Some read this change of plans as a bad sign. It was. Behind MacArthur lay a disintegrating South Korean army. Before him lay a battle which might, at the worst, take a place in U.S. history alongside the battle of Bataan.

MacArthur himself seemed to thrive under the new burden. At one point the Pentagon sent him a message: "Do you desire any instructions?" The reply was terse: "No." Inside the Dai Ichi Building, his headquarters in Tokyo, bleary-eyed staff officers looked up from stacks of paper, whispered proudly, "God, the man is great." General Almond, his chief of staff, said straight out, "He's the greatest man alive." And reverent Air Force General George E. Stratemeyer put it as strongly as it could be put: "He's the greatest man in history."

It was upon the reverent Stratemeyer and his Far East Air Forces that MacArthur placed the first heavy burden of U.S.

operations in Korea. Ordered into the fighting along with the Air Force were the light cruiser *Juneau* and four destroyers. But the general's trip to Korea had given him firsthand evidence that air and naval support alone would not save the situation. As the defenders fell back, President Truman on June 30 gave MacArthur permission to send in U.S. ground forces under the command of Lieut. General Walton Harris Walker [a veteran of General George Patton's tank forces in Europe during World War II].

MacArthur visits Korea with his chief of staff, General Almond. "He's the greatest man alive," says Almond.

JULY 17 **DOWN THE PENINSULA:** "The isolated unit of less than one battalion supported by one battery of field artillery, which was at Osan yesterday, was attacked by the best Red division, supported by 40 tanks . . . . The ratio of troops engaged was more than eight to one against the American forces. For more than six hours the American forces held off the invaders until their ammunition was exhausted, and then withdrew. . . ."–Communiqué from Tokyo.

This was the dismal outcome of the first combat for U.S. ground forces since World War II. One U.S. officer in the field admitted that he had been contemptuous of the North Koreans. He lost his contempt.

After Osan fell, the harried U.S. commanders tried road mines and bridge demolitions to delay the invaders, but their green troops did not handle these operations well. One group of G.I.s, before running to safety through crossfire, propped up a wounded buddy in the middle of the road, where he could raise his hands to surrender. As they tore across a paddy field, they turned back to have a last look at their friend. It was just in time to see him cut in half by Red Tommy guns, his feeble, lifeless hands still waving in the crisp summer air.

REARGUARD & HOLDING: The week began, deceptively JULY 24 enough, with the first solid U.S. counterattack of the war, launched with the first Sherman tanks committed to battle. The Reds, who had not expected U.S. tanks in action against them, were caught off balance. Lieut. Joe Griffith of Charleston, S.C. said: "The Commies took off like a bunch of scared rabbits."

Triumph did not last long. The Reds smashed back with 80 of their big tanks. The U.S. tank crews found out what it means to be outnumbered, outweighed and outgunned (their 75-mm cannon were no match for the Reds' 85s). All but two of the U.S. tanks were put out of action. Red armor and infantry tore up the U.S. infantry. Robert Miller of the U.P. gave appalling details of this action: "There were only 30 soldiers left out of an American company of 148 that left Japan two weeks ago. Fewer than 20% of the wounded were being evacuated."

RETREAT FROM TAEJON: Taejon, a ramshackle, war-crowd- JULY 31 ed city (normal pop. 37,000), lies amid the hills and paddy fields of southwestern Korea. Through it runs a double-tracked trunkline railroad, which twists 125 miles through the mountains to Pusan, the U.S. buildup port in the southeast. U.S. troops of the 24th Division were supposed to hold Taejon two days; they held it for three.

On the morning of the third day, Communist tanks broke through the city's northern defenses. The Communists moved swiftly. Their flank attacks had cut the escape routes. In the streets of Taejon, some of the trapped Americans fought the Reds at close quarters; others battled desperately to reopen the southern escape lines. Overhead, U.S. Mustangs and F-80 jet fighters wheeled and roared down to attack Communist tanks with rockets. A hospital train that tried to re-enter the city to take out the wounded was driven off. The engineer was shot dead at the throttle.

Osan and Taejon were only the first of many strange names that Americans would have to learn during the following weeks as the battle was pushed southward by the North Korean invaders through one town after another. The American strategy was to delay the advance as much as possible, to give time for the buildup of the American force that was beginning to pour into the southern tip of Korea through the port of Pusan. But the rapid disintegration of the South Korean units, and the smallness of the American force, made this difficult. The news that filtered home was of retreat and of the heroic activities of isolated detachments of individual soldiers. By August, all of South Korea except for a small perimeter around Pusan was in Communist hands.

"THIS GALLANT OFFICER": Listing him between two G.I.s of his division who shared his fate, the U.S. Army formally announced last week that Major General William F. Dean was missing in Korea. As Red tanks broke into Taejon last week, Dean was up at the front, worked with his bazooka squads. Said a corporal: "The general took a couple of men downtown and went after two tanks. I saw him passing ammunition to the men and directing fire. He was doing a damn good job, too." An aide reported that Dean had apparently managed to get out of Taejon. He had last seen him in the mountains outside the burning city as the general went to look for more stragglers.

Said General Douglas MacArthur last week: "It is hoped that this gallant officer, if alive, has not fallen into enemy hands." [General Dean was captured and imprisoned by the Communists. He was returned to the Allied side on September 4, 1953.]

AUG. 7 **"WE MUST HOLD"**: The Korean war reached its grimmest and most dangerous stage. The North Koreans were trying to turn a stubbornly fought retreat into a rout, seize the Pusan beachhead area, destroy the U.N. forces. Knowing the threat, and sick & tired of retreat, Lieut. General Walton Walker called his division commanders together, gave them a stern order: their troops must hold their lines or die where they stood.

"ARE YOU WILLING TO DIE?": There were plenty of U.S. heroes. "We were pinned down by enemy fire," said a U.S. corporal. "Our rations were only five feet away, but we couldn't get to them. The attack came at dawn. My rifle was jammed and wouldn't shoot. The first enemy wave was past. I figured I had to die, so I dug out a can of fruit cocktail and ate it. Then the lieutenant asked: 'Are you willing to die? If you are, I will call for mortar fire.' I could see the next wave coming, and I said: 'It looks like we're cooked anyway. Go ahead.' He called for mortar fire. Some of it hit near us, but most of it went over the hill, into our little friends."

THE UGLY WAR: It is midnight and all around the hills are AUG. 21 astir. Here a sharp burst of small-arms fire, there the flashing life & death of an American shell, searching out the enemy who are gathering within 5,000 yards of this command post. One of the field telephones rings, an officer of the staff picks it up, listens a moment and says, "Oh, Christ, there's a column of refugees, three or four hundred of them, coming right down on B company." A major in the command tent says to the regimental commander, "Don't let them through."

And of course the major is right. Time & again, at position after position, this silent approach of whitened figures had covered enemy attack. Finally the colonel says, in a voice racked with wretchedness, "All right, don't let them through. But try to tell them to go back."

"Yeah," says a staff officer, "but what if they don't go back?"

"Well," the colonel says, as though dragging himself toward some pit, "then fire over their heads."

"O.K.," an officer says, "we fire over their heads. Then what?"

The colonel seems to brace himself in the semi-darkness of the blacked-out tent.

"Well, then, fire into them if you have to. *If you have to*, I said."

An officer speaks into the telephone and the order goes across the wire into the dark hills.

AUG. 28 **"DEFINITELY SAVED":** The Communists wanted Taegu. The flat, dirty city was the provisional capital of the South Korean government; it was the main Allied supply base and communications hub for the central front; it had a valuable airfield from which U.S. tactical airplanes were blasting the Reds; it also blocked what the Communists considered the main approach to the port of Pusan. The North Koreans last week made frenzied efforts to take Taegu.

The enemy divisions mounted a massive (30,000 men) and skillful attack and smashed due south. But the courageous South Koreans managed to regroup. They were reinforced by the 27th Regiment of the U.S. 25th Division. After a heavy artillery and air bombardment had rocked the Reds, the 27th and the South Koreans, spearheaded by Pershing tanks, recaptured Kumhwa and drove on toward Kunwi. Thus was exorcised what Eighth Army headquarters called the "gravest threat" to the Allied beachhead in Korea. Said General Walton Walker: "Taegu has been definitely saved."

MASSACRE AT HILL 303: At a medical clearing station in South Korea last week, Pfc. Roy Manring, 18, of Chicago, sat up in his litter and told the colonel about the things that had happened to him and his buddies at Hill 303.

Taken prisoner when his platoon mistook North Koreans for South Korean reinforcements, the men were stripped and searched. "They took my watch and billfold," said Roy. "My girl's picture was in it. They took that out and kept it. They like girls' pictures." The next morning the Reds got scared when U.S. mortar fire started dropping near their positions. "They made us take off our boots, and they tied our wrists with the shoestring," said Roy. "A couple of guys raised a fuss. I think they beat 'em to death."

That night the North Koreans tried to march their prisoners across the Naktong River, but U.S. fire stopped them. "We started calling *'Misu, mizu!'* That's Jap for water. But they said 'No, no, American planes go tatatata.' Boy! Are they afraid of airplanes! When our planes came over they kept real quiet and gave us branches to put over our heads.

"About 3 or 4 in the afternoon, they got us up and moved us again down near a ditch. The Reds walked up & down the line of prisoners, shooting. I was hit in the leg. I reached down to my leg and got some blood and smeared it on my head and I laid down under a dead man. . . ."

Of the 31 men who surrendered in Roy's platoon, 26 had been killed and four wounded. Another estimated 10 to 15 U.S. soldiers who had been captured by the Reds before Roy's platoon surrendered, had also been murdered.

NEXT?: In the lines it was widely taken for granted that a breakout would be made in a matter of weeks. In Tokyo, one of General MacArthur's comfortable spokesmen said that the war might, just possibly, be won by Thanksgiving. No man could soundly predict victory in Korea by Thanksgiving or for that matter by the next Thanksgiving unless he ignored the possibility that Moscow might intensify the force in Korea, *e.g.*, by getting China's Communist troops into the battle.

AT THE BOWLING ALLEY: For four nights running, enemy armor slammed at forward elements of Lieut. Col. John Michaelis' 27th ("Wolfhound") Regiment astride a road junction 15 miles northwest of Taegu. The Red tanks would

General William F. Dean. A "gallant officer" is captured. Page 65.

Colonel Michaelis. Enemy tanks slam at his men four nights running.

drive down the road to within 100 yards of the first U.S. foxhole and open flat trajectory fire with their 85-mm. guns; a good many of the shells went screaming down the road, hit the first small elevation in their path and bounced into a nearby hillside, like bowling balls. The men, who did not budge under the assault, nicknamed the road, "the bowling alley."

Two of the best working soldiers in the 27th last week were young (26), blond Captain Martin Merchant of Ilion, N.Y., and Merchant's lead platoon leader, Lieut. Doyle D. Lummis of Waco, Texas. Each night, Lummis and his platoon sergeant had calmly told the artillery and mortars in the rear to get ready. Each night, as the enemy tanks started "bowling" their fire down the road, artillery and mortars would instantly open fire. Red infantrymen would dash ahead of the tanks. Lummis' guns would tear into them. Then, when the tanks themselves got close enough, Lummis' bazookamen—who had orders to hold fire until the enemy was nearly upon them—began to spit death & destruction.

On the morning of the fifth day, Merchant and Lummis sat wearily by the road. They looked like Bill Mauldin's Willie and Joe. Both wore filthy fatigues and a week's growth of beard. Their shoulders slumped and their buttons were unbuttoned.

About their position were strewn the Communists they had killed. There were also scattered legs, arms and heads. The flies were terrible and the stench was worse. A lean and frightened dog skulked nearby. "I know those bastards are Reds, but I still don't like to see dogs eat dead people," a bearded sergeant said with a shudder as he bounced a rock off the dog's ribs and sent him yowling into the paddy field.

With the failure to take Taegu, the North Korean offensive stalled and the all-important port of Pusan remained in American hands. General MacArthur assayed the forces that he had been building up and decided it was time to go on the offensive. His plan was a daring one: to make an assault by sea on a beachhead far up the coast behind the main North Korean armies and cut them off from their source of supply. His strategy succeeded brilliantly.

OVER THE BEACHES: The enemy knew that a U.N. landing SEPT. 25 was hanging over him. His spies had spotted U.S. and South Korean troops embarking from Pusan. But the enemy did not suspect that the place would be Inchon, the port of Seoul, 150 miles northwest of Taegu.

The enemy's beachhead resistance was negligible. Within the first four days of their assault, the Marines swept through Inchon and seized Seoul's Kimpo airfield. Advancing rapidly, they entered the capital's suburbs. In the U.N. beachhead around Pusan, General Walton Walker's Eighth Army went over to a general offensive. The aim was to break the enemy ring and link up with the U.N. forces fighting their way east from Inchon. U.N. planes dropped 3,000,000 leaflets, breaking the news of the Inchon landing and calling on the enemy to surrender or die. At week's end his choice was still death.

OPERATION CHROMITE: "The history of war," said General Douglas MacArthur, "proves that nine times out of ten an army has been destroyed because its supply lines have been cut off. That's what we are trying to do.

"Everything the enemy shoots, and all the additional replenishment he needs, have to come down through Seoul. We are going to try to seize that distributing area, so that it will be impossible for the North Koreans to get more than a trickle of supplies into the present combat area."

On landing day last week, in the dawn's early light, MacArthur picked his way through a confusion of men in helmets and life jackets, climbed onto the admiral's bridge chair. He wore his old braided, sweat-stained garrison cap.

The ship's speaker announced: "The first wave of the attack force is ashore." Then the speaker called: "All boats are ashore from the first and second waves. The troops are fanning out rapidly. No casualties so far." MacArthur lowered his head a little, and then a broad grin spread across his face. The night before, he had said we would not take more than 100 casualties on the morning objectives. Now all waves were ashore, with only 15 casualties reported. The Inchon landing was in the great American tradition developed in World War II. It swept around the sea anchor of the enemy flank and struck at his most vulnerable spot. The combined use of land, sea and air power was brilliantly successful.

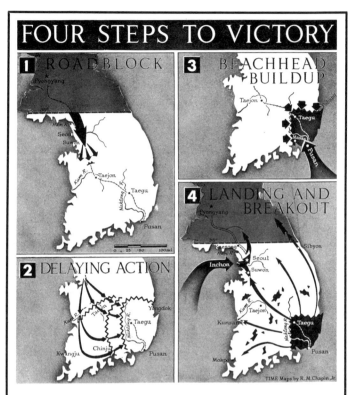

FOUR STEPS TO VICTORY

1 ROADBLOCK

3 BEACHHEAD BUILDUP

4 LANDING AND BREAKOUT

2 DELAYING ACTION

TIME Maps by R.M.Chapin Jr.

As of October 1950, the war in Korea had gone through four phases: 1. North Korean forces cross the 38th Parallel and capture Seoul; 2. United Nations forces are pushed into a perimeter around Pusan; 3. The perimeter holds while U.S. and other allied troops are reinforced; 4. MacArthur outflanks the North Koreans with a landing at Inchon, while other U.N. troops break out of the perimeter to force the enemy back across the parallel. One month later, the Communist Chinese entered the war with a massive assault that sent U.N. forces reeling once more toward the south.

OCT. 2 **SIEGE & RACE:** This week Douglas MacArthur announced that Seoul had fallen. It was the climax of a brilliant week for the United Nations in Korea. As the U.S. Marines moved west from Inchon toward Seoul, the only defense was a brave but hopeless charge by several hundred green Communist security troops. The Marines waited until the screaming Reds were a few yards away, then mowed them down. Said a sweating U.S. staff sergeant: "It was just plain murder."

On Walton Walker's southeastern front, the enemy fought

at first as though they had not heard of the Inchon landings. Finally, however, Walker's men got four bridgeheads across the Naktong River, and all at once someone seemed to have pulled the plug. At some points the North Koreans fought until overrun in their foxholes; at others, they took off so fast that the pursuers found Red laundry still hanging on bushes.

THIS WAS THE WAR: So soon after the battle it was hardly OCT. 9 possible to assess the full extent of what Russia had lost in her ill-starred gamble. But it was clear that she had lost a great deal. She had enabled the U.S. to prove to the whole world that it would shed the blood of its men on foreign soil to defend an ally. Russia had aroused the U.N. to a consciousness of new power and prestige. Russia had showed herself to the troubled peoples of Asia and to all the Red satellites of Europe as a puppetmaster who abandons the puppet when things go wrong.

Stalin's defeat in Korea would not prevent him from trying again—whenever he saw an opportunity to extend the Kremlin's sway. But Korea would almost certainly make Stalin more cautious about further adventures. Korea had looked like a sure thing, and it had blown up in Stalin's face.

ROUT: The enemy's collapse came with avalanche swiftness. By week's end, North Korean organized resistance had ended, U.N. forces were mopping up isolated remnants, the first U.N. Division had crossed the 38th parallel.

LIBERATION: "It's just like old times," said Douglas MacArthur to the assembled big wheels at Kimpo airfield. The Supreme Commander's silvery new Constellation *SCAP* had just flown him in from Tokyo for another historic ceremony of liberation.

The cavalcade pulled up at the Capitol, a fire-blackened, bullet-pocked shell of masonry, its rooms and offices still strewn with the enemy's litter—Russian-made helmets and burp guns, half-consumed bottles of beer and wine. There MacArthur met his friend and ally, South Korea's President Syngman Rhee.

After MacArthur's speech, during which he seemed at times

on the verge of tears, and a prayer, he turned to Syngman Rhee: "Mr. President, my officers and I will now resume our military duties and leave you and your government to the discharge of civil responsibility."

Rhee clasped MacArthur's hand. "We admire you," he exclaimed. "We love you as the savior of our race." Then, in a formal address, Rhee gave Korea's thanks to the U.N. The ceremony over, MacArthur flew back to Tokyo.

STOP SHORT?: Last week thousands of Korean Communist soldiers scampered over the 38th parallel which had divided Korea since 1945. There the Reds hoped to sit in safety while Washington and the United Nations argued over a decision which should have been made weeks before.

In the world's free nations last week there were men who urged that U.N. forces content themselves with shooing North Koreans across the 38th parallel. Leading spokesman for this group was Prime Minister Jawaharlal Nehru of India. Nehru's avowed reasons: fear that invasion of North Korea would bring Communist China, possibly even Russia, into the war; the prospect that by following North Korean aggressors across the parallel the U.N. forces might themselves become guilty of aggression.

The U.S. and its allies in the U.N. offered positive reasons why U.N. troops should cross the parallel:

¶ North Korea's war potential must be destroyed.

¶ The U.N. must demonstrate that international crime does not pay.

¶ The U.N. had repeatedly declared that Korea must be united.

¶ If Russia or China intended to intervene in Korea, they should have done so earlier when they could have pushed U.N. forces into the sea.

OCT. 16 **LAST PHASE:** The stage was set for the final battle in the "police action" in Korea. The U.N. General Assembly last week overwhelmingly approved the British resolution (backed by the U.S.) for a free, united Korea. The resolution recommends "that all appropriate steps be taken to ensure conditions of stability throughout Korea," thereby implicitly instructing U.N. forces to cross the 38th parallel.

This week General Douglas MacArthur broadcast his second ultimatum to the North Koreans: "I, as the United Nations Commander in Chief, for the last time call upon you and the forces under your command. . . forthwith to lay down your arms and cease hostilities."

Only a Chinese Communist or Russian army marching to the aid of the Korean comrades could possibly stave off a swift defeat for the Red aggressors. But more & more such intervention seemed unlikely.

ACROSS THE PARALLEL: An enemy answer to Douglas MacArthur's call for surrender was quickly spotted by a U.N. plane. Winging far up North Korea, a U.S. 5th Air Force fighter-bomber, on a night intruder mission, saw vehicles rolling down from the Manchurian border. They moved in widely spaced clusters, strung over 100 miles of road. Clearly, with supplies from the Chinese and Russian comrades over the border, the enemy was feverishly building up a defense 80 miles north of the 38th parallel. By next dawn a big U.N. aerial hunt was underway. U.N. planes claimed the destruction in one 24-hour period of 85 trucks carrying tanks and artillery.

On the ground, U.N. divisions regrouped for the imminent push across North Korea.

"DAMN GOOD JOB": At 6:30 one morning last week, two OCT. 3 U.N. columns jumped off for the final assault on the North Korean capital, Pyongyang. The cavalrymen, firing from their vehicles, drove swiftly through Pyongyang's outer defenses, left the enemy on their flanks to be mopped up by the men who followed them. About the same time, soldiers of the R.O.K. 1st Division entered Pyongyang's handsome, tree-lined streets from the east. While diehard North Korean snipers blazed away, U.S. and R.O.K. troops met on an avenue flanked with burning buildings. General Paik, commander of the R.O.K.s, slapped the back of every American in sight, repeated exultantly: "Damn good job. Damn good job."

RECONSTRUCTION: Now that the war was ending, the U.N. liberators of Korea faced two big problems—economic reconstruction and political reconstruction. Korea's industry had been shattered. Most of the destruction had been done by U.S. bombing. Now the deadly work would have to be repaired, primarily at the U.S. taxpayers' expense.

FIRST LIBERATED CAPITAL: The people of Pyongyang cheered, waving South Korean flags, British flags, Chinese Nationalist flags and improvised U.N. flags which had been designed from hearsay. The people of Pyongyang, the first Communist capital to be liberated by the forces of the free world, were staging the most spontaneous demonstration seen in any Asiatic city since the liberation of Shanghai from the Japanese.

NOV. 6 **SLIGHT DELAY?:** Early last week nothing but bad roads and poor maps slowed the U.N. advance toward the Korean-Manchurian border. R.O.K. officers whose divisions were racing through northwest Korea jubilantly reported to Eighth Army headquarters: "We will not stop until we bathe our sabers in the Yalu River."

Leading the U.N. pack was the R.O.K. 6th Division's 7th Regiment. Just before dusk one evening the 7th drove to the south bank of the Yalu.

Before the 7th Regiment had a chance to wet a saber, the roof fell in. Throughout northwest Korea the Communists started unexpectedly strong counterattacks supported by tanks, artillery and mortars. R.O.K. commanders in the northwest claimed that the enemy punch had been delivered by Chinese Communist troops brought from Manchuria.

LATE ENTRY: Why the Chinese had sent troops into North Korea so late in the game no one could be sure. Said R.O.K. General Yu: "It may be that the Chinese have come in to save the big [Yalu River] generator at Supung which . . . serves both North Korea and Manchuria."

LATE, BUT WELCOME: On their way to Korea last week were further U.N. reinforcements. Among them:
¶ Nearly 3,000 British troops.
¶ The advance party of a 10,000-man Canadian force.
¶ A volunteer group of 650 Dutch infantrymen.
¶ A South African fighter squadron.

Promised for the future were additional forces including:

¶ A 5,000-man Greek infantry brigade.

¶ About 4,000 Australian infantrymen.

¶ A 1,100-man French battalion.

Landing at Pusan two weeks ago, a Turkish officer said sadly: "We are jealous. We wish we could join the fighting." U.N. forces reaching Korea in the future would have even less chance to see any heavy fighting, but they would be welcome nonetheless. By carrying out mopping-up operations and occupation duties, they could free combat-weary U.S. troops for a return to Japan.

WINTER WAR: With shocking suddenness the U.N. victory NOV. 13 march in Korea was stopped, and hurled back. Generals who two weeks before had promised to have their forces on the Yalu River in a matter of days now discussed a "winter war." Said one U.S. officer grimly: "I think we can hold them."

What happened next depended chiefly on the Chinese Communist government. If Communist troops and aircraft continued to cross the border, sooner or later there would be no choice for the U.N. command except to blow up the Yalu River dams and bridges, to bomb airfields and troop concentrations in Manchuria.

In such a choice, the threat would be a new and greater war, perhaps a World War.

"DO NOT JOSEPHINE!": In northwest Korea last week, an air-ground liaison officer attached to the U.S. 24th Division gave a nervous laugh as he listened to the radio chatter of Mustang pilots overhead. "Do not Josephine," the pilots cautioned one another. In Air Force parlance, "Do not Josephine" means "Don't use up all your ammunition on ground targets; you may need it to fight your way home."

U.N. pilots who had long had the air almost to themselves had their first brushes with enemy jets coming from north of the Yalu—Soviet MIG-15s with swept-back wings and a speed of 600 miles an hour. Ground troops faced enemy units heavily equipped with tanks, automatic weapons, 76-mm. howitzers and multiple rocket launchers. Said one G.I. last week: "Those guys who hit us last night are the best we've run up against."

CRAZY HORSE RIDES AGAIN: On its way to bolster up crumbling R.O.K. forces in northwest Korea, the U.S. 1st Cavalry division's 8th Regiment dug in for the night near Unsan. When morning came, the few troopers who were awake could not believe their ears. Said Pfc. Henry Tapper: "Someone woke me up and asked me if I could hear horses on the gallop. I couldn't hear anything, but then bugles started playing."

Sitting in a battalion command post, Lieut. W. C. Hill thought he was dreaming. "I heard a bugler . . . and the beat of horses' hooves in the distance. Then, as though they came out of a burst of smoke, shadowy figures started shooting and bayoneting everybody they could find."

The infiltrating Red force, probably Chinese, achieved complete surprise. Some cavalrymen thought their attackers were insane. Said a U.S. sergeant: "They would stand right up in front of you laughing to beat hell." Most of the men who escaped the confused, swirling battle swam the icy Kuryong River, fled to a village nine miles south.

Next day a U.S. I Corps spokesman admitted that the Reds had captured 13 U.S. tanks, announced that 500 cavalrymen must be considered dead or captured. A bitter cavalry officer said: "It was a massacre like the one which hit Custer."

Though badly cut up, the 1st Cavalry Division averted a Communist breakthrough—at least for the time being—and dropped its plan to lead an Armistice Day victory parade in Tokyo.

NOV. 20 **"WE HAVE THEM CORNERED":** At 20,000 feet above the burning North Korean border city of Sinuiju last week, fighter planes in history's first jet dogfight streaked across the morning sky. Eight or more Russian-made MIG-15s tangled for a deadly moment with four U.S. Lockheed F-80s. The score: one Communist jet shot down, another damaged; U.S. fighters, untouched.

Major Evans G. Stephens, a Texan, and his wingman Lieut. Russell Brown of Pasadena, Calif., saw two Communist jets pull out of a dive 50 miles south of the Yalu and turn toward the river at the Americans' altitude, closing fast. Said Stephens afterwards, "Brown and I were between the enemy jets and the river. I called to the rest of my flight to come on up—we have two of them cornered."

At week's end the reality of jet combat—the fastest kind of fighting known to man—was becoming routine along the Korean-Manchurian border. Totals for the week: two U.S. planes reported lost or damaged, while the Reds lost 48 in ten days.

DREADFUL WINTER: From Siberia, which harbors the world's NOV. 27 largest cold air mass, bitter winds swept down over Manchuria last week to the mountains and bleak fields of North Korea. In the fighting lines, medical officers treated their first cases of frostbite and trench foot. Units of the 7th Division were fighting last week in 20-below-zero cold. After a U.S. attack near the Manchurian border, medical officers reported as many casualties from cold as from enemy action. Only quick work by litter teams prevented those wounded from freezing to death.

"SOME CRAZY WAR": The Chinese Communist air force had a tactical advantage over the U.S. Far East Air Force last week. U.S. pilots were under strict orders not to cross the Korea-Manchuria border, or even to fire across it. Communist flyers, under no such handicap, were staging hit and run raids across the frontier.

The only way U.S. B-29s could bomb the Yalu River bridges without violating the border was by making long bomb runs just inside and parallel to the line running down the center of the 2,500-ft-wide Yalu. While making such a ten-minute bomb run on Sinuiju, 24 U.S. Superforts at 25,000 ft. were jumped by 16 Russian-made MIG-15s. Attacking in pairs, the Red jets began their dives high on the Manchurian side of the border, swept across the Yalu just long enough to shoot up the slow-moving Superforts, and ended their dives back on the Manchurian side before U.S. jets could catch them.

One frustrated U.S. fighter pilot, watching Communist jets maneuvering north of the border, summed up U.S. resentment thus: "Some crazy war when those bastards can practice stunt flying right in front of you!"

HOME BY CHRISTMAS: To the U.S. 24th Division's Major DEC. 4 General John Church, MacArthur said: "I have already promised wives and mothers that the boys of the 24th Division will be back by Christmas. Don't make me a liar. Get to the Yalu and I will relieve you."

STALLED: On Thanksgiving Day, U.S. troops in the front lines ate turkey with trimmings, some of it delivered by airdrop. Next day, at 8 a.m., the big new push to the Yalu got rolling. The offensive involved about 100,000 Allied troops against about 125,000 of the enemy, mostly Chinese. On the second day, the Reds' resistance stiffened. The next night the Reds staged a furious counterattack, heralded by bugling, whistling, and the brazen clang of cymbals which dismally reminded the G.I.s of the surprise Chinese attack in early November. For the moment, at least, MacArthur's big push was stopped in its tracks. U.S. troops had not been involved in a surprise enemy action of such magnitude since the Battle of the Bulge in World War II.

DEC. 11 **OLD WAYS OF WAR:** Last week the conservative military textbooks, the old ways of war, caught up with the U.S. and with a daring champion of new ways of war, Douglas MacArthur. He had beaten the textbooks again and again; last week they beat him.

In North Korea, he tried what he called a "massive compression envelopment" against greatly superior forces. The enveloped Chinese broke through the envelopment. Their thrust was so wide, deep and strong that his inadequate reserves could not check it. MacArthur's center was gone and the Reds lapped around the two inside flanks of his divided army, pushing both wings back toward the sea.

MacArthur's intelligence failed in not estimating correctly the number of Chinese that had crossed the Yalu, the fighting quality and discipline of the Chinese troops, and the heavy concentration at a point in their line against which MacArthur put his weakest forces, the Korean II Corps. These failures led some observers last week to conclude that a failure of intelligence lost the battle of North Korea.

ON THE GRIDDLE: The crushing Chinese counter-offensive in Korea had put General MacArthur on the griddle at home and in Europe. In Washington, carefully anonymous military officials who love to chuck harpoons at MacArthur leaked reports that he had defied Administration suggestions that he keep his troops well short of the Korean-Manchurian border. MacArthur disputed charges that his "end-the-war" offensive had been ill-advised.

He made the obvious point that intervention on such a scale required elaborate preparation, and consequently must have been decreed by Mao Tse-tung's government long ago. The real reason for the U.N.'s reverses, said MacArthur, was sheer weight of numbers.

AFTER THE BREAKTHROUGH: This week there was no sign of where or how the enemy onrush could be stopped. It was obvious that General Walker would have to keep his whole Eighth Army moving south if it was not to be trapped or rolled up from the flank. A 2nd Division regiment, commanded by Colonel Paul Freeman of Roanoke, Va., fought a rearguard action at Kunu to save as much as possible of an eight-mile vehicle train. Said the colonel: "We will go down the road on trucks, if we can. Otherwise we will destroy the trucks and go over the mountains, shooting backward every step of the way. We've gone through miracle after miracle, and we need one more."

Three marine regiments, which had been in separated positions around the Changjin reservoir, finally fought their way through to the south, after running into bloody ambushes along the roads. The Communists fired on them comfortably at steep grades and hairpin turns, where the Marines' vehicles slowed to a crawl. A dreadful indication of the casualties in this sector was that 1,200 wounded were flown out in the first two days.

WHY WITHDRAW?: Red Chinese soldiers attacking a ridge line last week were shocked to come face to face with swarthy, fiercely mustachioed Turks howling down upon them with bayonets fixed. In this and other Turkish bayonet charges some 200 Chinese were killed, and soon stories of the Turks were spreading like a tonic along the U.N. line.

The brigade of 5,000 smart, tightly disciplined Turks was thrown in to hold the line the R.O.K.s abandoned east of

Kaechon. Estimated Turkish casualties at week's end: 500. A U.S. doctor said it seemed that a Turk waited until he had at least three wounds before he reported to the medics.

After 48 hours of action, the Turks were short of food and ammunition, fighting with knives and fists, hurling stones at endless waves of Chinese attackers. Yet U.S. tanks that went forward to rescue trapped Turkish units found them preparing to attack. Ordered to pull back from positions where they were surrounded by the swarming Chinese, the Turkish commander replied in amazement, "Withdraw? Why withdraw? We are killing lots of them."

In freezing weather, U.S. soldiers escape to the rear by jeep or on foot after the Communist Chinese attack.

DEC. 18 **EXIT?**: The best to be said of Korea was that the worst had not happened. The U.S. forces threatened with annihilation a fortnight ago had not been destroyed, and were not likely to be destroyed.

Despite uncountable acts of individual and group heroism, the morale of the surviving U.S. troops had been severely shaken by the knowledge that all their shiny weapons and equipment, their sensational blitz tactics, their mountain of supplies, their tanks, trucks, artillery and air power could not hold back a horde that moved on foot, without air support, without armor and with hardly any weapon larger than a mortar.

"THIS HURTS": The battered but not broken Eighth Army rolled south, with vehicle columns bumper-to-bumper on the roads and a million refugees alongside. Trucks and jeeps that broke down were not repaired—they were shoved off the road and burned. Said a reconnaissance pilot, looking down on the dreary spectacle of U.S. defeat and retreat: "This hurts. It hurts where I can't scratch."

Because it had wheels, the Eighth outdistanced the pursuing foe. The intelligence estimate was that 18 divisions of Chinese were trying to come to grips with the Eighth Army. The locustlike swarm of the enemy never stopped.

RETREAT OF THE 20,000: "Retreat, hell!" snapped Major General Oliver Prince Smith, commander of the 1st Marine Division. "We're not retreating, we're just advancing in a different direction."

When the order came to start south, the enemy was already closing in on the Marines' makeshift airstrip, whence thousands of wounded and frostbite victims had been flown out. The last plane waited an extra hour for one desperately wounded man. The Marines abandoned none of their disabled men, but bulldozers pushed the dead into mass graves by hundreds.

SHRINKING BEACHHEAD: Early last week, the last units of DEC. 25 the X Corps reached the coast after a skillful fighting retreat from the Changjin reservoir to the Sea of Japan.

LIKE A FIRE DRILL: While the infantrymen in the line drew back slowly before the Chinese assault, the evacuation at the dockside in Hungnam went on apace. A few miles away at the airfield, U.S. troops went grimly about the business of burning or blowing up barracks, buildings and other installations which the Chinese might find useful. Similar demolitions went on at the same time in other parts of the U.S. perimeter. Great orange masses of flame swirled brilliantly up into the skies and then subsided again. The evacuation went on like an orderly, well-rehearsed fire drill.

There was no panic, no disorder. U.S., Norwegian and Japanese ships took on load after load of trucks, tanks, gasoline, rations, jeeps, tents, kitchen stoves and dismantled aircraft. At one warehouse, a steady stream of Korean women threaded their way through huge stacks of flour, rice and millet, emerged with 50 to 100-lb. sacks strapped to their backs or carefully balanced on their heads. There would be some later disappointment. Some of the women had taken their sacks from the wrong part of the warehouse and were heading jubilantly home to the kitchen loaded down with fertilizer.

ABLE TO BAKER TO CHARLIE: The Chinese Communists are noted for sluggishness in victory. More than once, during their civil war with the Nationalists, they needed months after a successful offensive to mount a new one. Last week, having failed to destroy the U.N. forces in Korea, they were moving slowly down the central mountains, with oxcarts and two-humped camels in their supply trains.

During its retreat, the Eighth Army stood first on "Line Able" below Pyongyang, and when that failed to hold, withdrew to "Line Baker" just below the 38th parallel. Since this line would become untenable as soon as the sluggish Chinese were ready to strike, the next move would be to "Position Charlie"—which would consist of only two beachhead perimeters, one around Seoul and Inchon, the other one at Pusan. If they do stop at the 38th parallel, South Korea may be spared the horrors of another Red occupation and some—though not all—of U.S. and U.N. prestige lost in recent weeks may be restored.

MILESTONES

MARRIED: (William) Clark Gable, 48, grand old man of cinema's romantic young men; and British-born Lady Stanley of Alderly, 39, blonde onetime chorus girl and footman's daughter who twice married British titles; both for the fourth time.

DIED: Gustav Krupp von Bohlen und Halbach, 79, owner through both World Wars of the giant Krupp works in Essen, Germany. An early supporter of Hitler, he was indicted as a top war criminal, escaped trial when a medical examination proved him senile.

DIED: Edgar Rice Burroughs, 74, multimillionaire creator of Tarzan; in Encino, Calif.

MISCELLANY

COLD COMFORT: In Rochester, George R. Schiemer of the State Frozen Food Locker Association cheerfully announced that "one of the safest places to be in the event of an atomic explosion" is in a frozen-food locker.

FOREIGN NEWS

Danger Zones

Though the major battle against Communism in 1950 was fought in Korea, there were other areas in the world where the Cold War, then at its height, could also have turned hot. The French were being attacked in their Indo-Chinese empire, where Communist leader Ho Chi Minh was intensifying a military struggle for Vietnam that would later lead to U.S. involvement. In Europe, NATO was little more than a treaty without troops, and the nations of Western Europe were confronted by a mammoth Soviet presence that threatened to engulf the continent. In at least two countries—Austria and Hungary—individual Americans fell victim to the struggle, one as a prisoner, one as a possible victim of murder.

EVEN CORREGIDOR: When Americans grow gloomy about MAY 29 Southeast Asia (as well they may), they tend to look on the Philippine Republic as a bright spot. It is not. In Washington last week the intelligence appraisal was that the four-year-old republic appeared to be coming apart at the seams. Symptoms:

¶ The Communist-led Huks are making ever larger areas unsafe for civilian travel.

¶ Graft and corruption are rampant; the national economy is sagging; the government of ailing, ineffectual President Quirino has lost its grip.

¶ Not even symbolic Corregidor has escaped the rot. With inside help, raiders recently penetrated the island fortress, cut through its armory's steel doors, and with insolent leisure ferried truckloads of arms, ammunition and supplies down to their boats and away.

INDO-CHINA, THE NEW FRONTIER: The U.S. now has a new frontier in the cold war. The place is Indo-China, a Southeast Asian jungle, mountain and delta land that includes the

Republic of Viet Nam and the smaller Kingdoms of Laos and Cambodia, all parts of the French Union.

For more than three years this land has been suffering the ruinous kind of civil war which won China for Communism. The Mao Tse-tung of the Indo-Chinese is a frail, but enduring comrade, who looks like a shriveled wizard; his *nom de guerre* is Ho Chi Minh (or One Who Shines).

In the pre-French past, most of Indo-China had been conquered by the Chinese, who had left their culture indelibly behind. The French converted the area into a tight, profitable colonial monopoly. They invested $2 billion, built up its rice and rubber production. Now the French have bowed grudgingly to the times. They promised limited freedom for Viet Nam within the French Union. But they got up to their necks in a costly campaign to crush Ho Chi Minh and his Communist bid for power.

The French have made more than the usual colonial mistakes. All too often they have been arrogant and brutal toward the Indo-Chinese. They are paying for it now, for the bulk of Communist Ho's support comes from anti-French or anti-colonial Indo-Chinese.

It is Emperor Bao Dai's mission, and the U.S.-French hope, to rally his countrymen in Viet Nam to the anti-Communist camp of the West. In this undertaking he needs time.

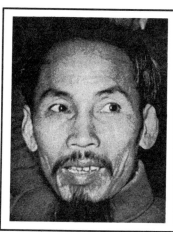

Ho Chi Minh. The Communist leader bids for power in Indo-China.

Emperor Bao Dai has only four battalions to pit against Ho. Page 86.

"Nothing," he says, "can be done overnight." Both Bao Dai and Ho Chi Minh were educated in France. Ho joined the French Communist Party, was sent to Moscow for training, then organized Communist cells in his own country that helped him wage guerrilla warfare against the Japanese. Bao Dai was hunting tigers when the Japanese surprised his party, installed him as puppet emperor.

After the war Bao abdicated and spent most of his time in a château on the French Riviera, dallying in the casinos, conducting jazz bands and treating hangers-on to champagne and caviar. In Indo-China, meanwhile, "Uncle Ho," very much a popular hero, was in the saddle. He spoke a "soft" Communist line, talked more about democracy and reform.

The French eventually broke with Ho Chi Minh and appealed to Bao Dai to come home again and rally his people against the Red menace. Though he has been back for a year, his government has thus far assembled only four battalions of troops, about 4,000 men. All in all, the new U.S. ally in Southeast Asia is a weak reed. Nevertheless, Indo-China had to be defended. The U.S. decision was the result of an idea that it ought to do something, somehow, to stop the Communists in Southeast Asia.

DISASTER ON ROUTE NO. 4: Indo-China adjoins Red China, OCT. 23 but the border has never been pegged out. The real frontier is a string of French forts and outposts connected by a road called Route Coloniale No. 4 which winds between steep hills and dense forests. A month ago, four Viet Minh battalions attacked Dongkhe, a fort at the north end of the frontier, using anti-aircraft guns and 105-mm. artillery, none of which they had had before. The French staff decided to withdraw from Caobang, a fort a few miles to the north.

A column of crack French troops was on its way to protect the withdrawal. The Caobang garrison had already pulled out and was on its way south through the jungle. The two groups, numbering together more than 3,000 men, met and marched southward for two days. Then, in a narrow valley, a force of 20,000 Viet Minh soldiers descended on them. Only about 700 Legionnaires managed to escape the ambuscade. They told of a bloody battle in which over 1,000 were killed & wounded, another 1,000 taken prisoner.

The story of Route Coloniale No. 4 stunned France. Said *Paris-Presse*: "Everybody, from our cabinet ministers down to the man in the street, realizes now that the massacre of Caobang is the outcome of five years of neglect, hesitations, intrigues and balmy optimism."

The French asked the U.S. for $300 million worth of arms for Indo-China. It would take a lot of U.S. supplies to balance Ho's victory, his most important advance in two years.

NOV. 6 **BY FULL MOONLIGHT:** Proclaimed Radio Peking: "People's Army Units have been ordered to advance into Tibet to free 3,000,000 Tibetans from imperialist oppression and to consolidate national defense of the western borders of China."

In New Delhi, India's Prime Minister Nehru could hardly believe the news. For months he had championed China's Communist regime, urged a seat for it in the U.N. He thought he had Mao Tse-tung's promise that the Tibetan issue would be settled amicably. A spokesman announced that India would now give "very careful review" to her sponsorship of Red China. But in New York, Sir Benegal Rau, India's U.N. delegate, indicated that India was still a glutton for diplomatic punishment. Said he: "If the new government of China had been seated in the U.N., it might have deterred any invasion."

When Indian newsmen in New Delhi converged on the Chinese Communist Embassy, they were told that Ambassador Yuan was off on a holiday to see the Taj Mahal by full moonlight.

NOV. 27 **DIKES AGAINST A FLOOD:** The French forces in Indo-China are outnumbered 2 to 1 in the crucial northern theater. The danger of a French defeat is serious. The terrain held by the French is complex—a network of dikes, soggy paddy fields and islandlike villages fringed with bamboo and banana trees.

In Hanoi (pop. 177,000), civilians are jittery. While planes into Hanoi are only half full these days, every seat on outgoing planes is taken and people of means are quietly making their arrangements to pull out. It is known that members of Ho's army come in dressed as civilians. Said a Frenchman: "I wouldn't be surprised if Ho Chi Minh himself were in Hanoi." In the thinking of many natives, Ho's forces are not regarded as Communists, but as the most active fighters for independence.

CROWN IN PERIL: From the gilded rooftop of Lhasa's Potala Palace, heralds blew 14-foot-long copper trumpets. Below, in the building's ornate Assembly Hall, a bright-eyed, 16-year-old boy sat on a high throne, about which clustered Tibet's most powerful lamas, abbots and monks. They had come in the country's hour of peril, with Chinese Communist invaders lodged deep in the Himalayan upland, to witness the coronation of the 14th Dalai Lama, the reincarnated Budda of Mercy.

It was an emergency investiture. Traditionally, the Dalai Lama waits for his 18th birthday before formally assuming power. By staging the ceremony two years ahead of schedule, Lhasa's theocrats seemed to be preparing for the worst. They bolstered the spiritual position of the Dalai Lama should he be forced to leave Lhasa for exile abroad and should the Communists try to install a rival on his throne.

TOO LATE FOR MIRACLES: Last week French authorities or- DEC. 11 dered the evacuation of all French women & children from gravely threatened Hanoi and the Red River delta. It would take something of a miracle to save Indo-China now.

But neither the French nor their chosen native instrument, Bao Dai, showed any signs last week of being able to work miracles. Bao Dai recently flew to Hanoi, supposedly to bolster the people's morale in the face of an expected Communist offensive. He arrived in his C-45 along with a Scotty named Bubi, two bottles of King George Scotch, two guitars, three tennis rackets and a cute, red-headed airline hostess named Esther.

AT LAKE FLAMINGO: *Alice thought she had never seen such a* JAN. 23 *curious croquet-ground in her life; it was all ridges and furrows; the croquetballs were live hedgehogs, and the mallets live flamingoes. . . . The players all played at once without waiting for turns, quarreling all the while, and fighting for the hedgehogs.*
　　　　　　　　　　　　　　　　　—*Alice in Wonderland*

Nationalist China's delegate, Dr. T. F. Tsiang, was in the

Security Council chair because it was his month, by rotation, to preside. He recognized the Soviet delegate, Jacob A. Malik. Delegate Malik did not return the compliment: he said he did not recognize Dr. Tsiang's right even to sit at the Council table. Dr. Tsiang was just a "person who represents nobody," said Malik. Then Malik (having less difficulty than Alice had had with her flamingo) tucked his papers under his arm and stalked out.

Two days later, although Tsiang was still present but not presiding, Malik came back. Saying that he would not "participate" in a meeting at which Tsiang was present, he went right on participating vociferously.

Britain's Sir Alexander Cadogan was well entangled with his flamingo. His government has withdrawn recognition from Dr. Tsiang's government, and recognized that of Malik's Communist friends. Yet Sir Alexander voted for Tsiang and against Malik.

To figure out the next step, everybody at the meeting fluttered yellow booklets called *Provisional Rules of Procedure of the Security Council*. If a majority of the Council nations follow the fashion of recognizing Red China, can the Council oust Tsiang? Or can Tsiang use China's Big Power veto to block this? India's Sir Benegal Rau said the U.N. had better straighten out some rules, otherwise "a government of party 'A' might be recognized by the General Assembly while that of party 'B' would be recognized by the Security Council." Clearly, that would never do.

Hardly had the excitement abated and U.N.'s normal boredom been restored, when the Russians this week announced a general walkout from all U.N. agencies and committees. The strike was to continue until the Chinese Nationalists were turned out of the U.N. Everybody fluttered the rule books again. Not in months had the Lake Success croquet-ground seen such a scurrying of hedgehogs, such a squirming of flamingoes.

RCH 13 HOW THEY DO IT: The U.S. State Department last week published a remarkable document. It was one answer to a question which has become increasingly urgent with such postwar trials as that of Hungary's Cardinal Mindszenty and the U.S.'s Robert Vogeler in Hungary [a U.S. businessman sentenced by Hungary on charges of espionage]: How do Communist secret police extort "confessions?"

The Communists' first victim to tell his first-hand story is Michael Shipkov, a Bulgarian, now in the hands of the Bulgarian State Security Militia (secret police) for the second time. The first time, he was tortured into a false confession that he had been an espionage agent for the U.S. and Britain. Then the secret police sent him back to spy on the U.S. Legation. Instead, he wrote an account of his 32-hour interrogation:

"I was ordered to stand facing the wall upright at a distance which allowed me to touch the wall with two fingers of my outstretched arms. Then to step back some twelve inches, keep my heels touching the floor, and maintain balance only with the contact of one finger on each hand. While standing so, the interrogation continued. I recall that the muscles on my legs and shoulders began to get cramped and to tremble, that my two fingers began to bend down under the pressure, to get red all over and to ache, I remember that I was drenched with sweat and that I began to faint, although I had not exerted myself in any way. If I would try to substitute [fingers], I would be instantly called to order. . . . And when the trembling increased up to the point when I collapsed, they made me sit and speak . . . but when I had uttered again that I was innocent, it was the wall again.

"After a time of this, I broke down."

BREAKTHROUGH?: Around the blue baize table in London's MAY 22 gloomy Lancaster House, the Western Big Three Foreign Ministers conferred for three days. Dean Acheson, crisp, clear and didactic, drove home his sharp points with a wagging forefinger. Britain's ailing Ernest Bevin, chomping away at his dentures, was his usual solid and grumpy self. France's Robert Schuman punctuated his speeches with faint smiles and exquisite little gestures of courtesy; he sat modestly hunched over the table, as if he were the least important man in the room.

In fact, last week, Schuman was the most important. The conference was dominated by his dramatic proposal to merge the French and German coal and steel industries. The proposal was far more than an imaginative economic project;

it was the offer of full partnership to Germany by its thrice-invaded, long-suffering and long-hating enemy.

Dean Acheson had gone to London haunted by the feeling that the West had to do something—but he did not know just what. The Schuman plan was a totally unexpected assertion that France could and would assume the leadership. It gave genuine promise that the idea of Western European integration would finally emerge from the realm of dreamers and talkers into regions as real as coal and steel.

Said the Schuman plan: "A united Europe will not be achieved all at once. . . . It will be formed by concrete measures which first of all create a solidarity in fact . . . [It will] introduce a broader and deeper community of interest between countries which have long been divided by bloody conflict."

Reported TIME's Washington Bureau: "Washington estimated tentatively that the Western Allies may be on the edge of their most important strategic breakthrough in the cold war since the Kremlin was forced, a year ago, to abandon the siege of Berlin."

MAY 29 **TO HANG TOGETHER:** "Great events are happening," said Winston Churchill, who knows a great event when he sees one. A communiqué from the North Atlantic Council in London spoke of "the creation of balanced collective forces in the progressive buildup of the defense of the North Atlantic area."

In simple English, that meant a military division of labor, with the U.S. providing the bulk of strategic bombers and heavy naval forces, the British concentrating on light tactical bombers and fighters, the French supplying the bulk of the land forces. It was an unprecedented step toward military interdependence among the allies which asserted beyond all solemn assurances that they would hang together.

Said Churchill: "I still hope that the unity now being established among all the Western democracies and Atlantic powers will ward off from us the terror and unspeakable miseries of a third world war."

JUNE 12 **NO HANDS ACROSS THE CHANNEL:** That politely muffled scraping sound on the international stage last week was the

British dragging their feet again. France, Italy, West Germany and the Benelux countries had announced that they were ready to start talks to implement the Schuman Plan to pool French and German coal and steel industries under an international authority. The British had grudgingly agreed to send delegates. But when the French suggested that the participating nations issue a joint communiqué stating the purposes of the talks, the British refused; they argued that this would mean an advance commitment to the plan.

As in most other recent instances when Britain was urged to participate in measures toward Western European integration, the Labor government was afraid that the Schuman Plan would interfere with its planned economy.

THE RETURN: For most of the six months and 18 days while AUG. 14 the Russians boycotted it, the U.N. Council had been an effective body. When the North Koreans attacked, the Council took the most important action of its life, became the world's voice in denouncing the Communist aggressors.

The Russians decided that staying out of the U.N. was doing them more harm than good. Last week, Russian Delegate Jacob Malik, a Russian career diplomat with a clean-cut, almost American-looking face, was back.

His terms for "peaceful settlement" were immediate cease-fire and withdrawal of U.N. troops—*i.e.*, the surrender of all Korea to its Communist aggressors. The Council was not intimidated. Four times it voted, and four times Malik was defeated.

FRIGHTENING TRUTH: All the shooting was in Asia, and Asia AUG. 14 was a long way from Europe. But Western Europe still embodied a frightening truth: if the Russians choose to risk all-out war with the U.S., they can roll through Western Europe like a color guard crossing a parade ground. With Mao's Chinese armies to protect their rear, the Russians could throw the better part of their 175 divisions, 25,000 tanks and 19,000 warplanes into a sweep to the Atlantic.

To oppose the Russians, the West has on hand a pathetic collection of 12 to 15 divisions. Some of these are next to worthless, almost all are under-equipped. Some French units are armed with aged machine guns saved from World War I.

Italian soldiers have 1891 Mannlicher-Carcano rifles which as long ago as 1915 they called "humanitarian rifles" because they usually missed the enemy.

The reasons why Western Europe is not prepared to do more are political, not military. An all-out military effort would require drastic cuts in Western Europe's standards of living. But the Russians have forced the free world, in any choice between guns and butter, to choose guns. If Western Europe ignores that lesson, it will one day have neither guns, butter, nor the freedom to choose.

AUG. 21 **BATTLE OF LAKE SUCCESS:** For the past fortnight that Russian face on the nation's television screens blocked not only *Howdy Doody,* but such other favorites as *Lucky Pup,* and *Life with Snarky Parker.* But the show that replaced them— a curious mixture of boredom and excitement, alternating long-winded oratory with sharp, electrifying statements of historic rights and wrongs—was definitely worth America's while. To millions of Americans it brought the unique experience of seeing the enemy right in their living room.

The name that went with the face was Jacob Malik. Hour after hour, in a dry voice that rarely rose in audible anger, meticulously using the same phrases and arguments, meticulously carrying out his orders, he lied.

As the second week of Security Council meetings opened, under Malik's presidency, the first business should have been a discussion of North Korean aggression, with South Korean representatives taking part. But not with Malik presiding. That was why the Kremlin had sent him back to the U.N.— to hamstring, delay, obstruct, make sure that nothing was done.

Americans who watched the show at Lake Success tended to boo when Malik threw a dirty punch, to cheer when U.S. representative Warren Austin put a hard glove on his opponent. But what was the point of the whole prizefight? U.N., which has been around these five years, is regarded by most people, at worst, as an irritating check on U.S. policy, at best as a windy forum for East and West. Is it worth all the fuss and bother—and the TV time?

U.N. is certainly worth more now than at any time since the first round at San Francisco. Said one experienced reporter last week: "The differences between the U.N. of 1946 and 1950 are striking: then, it had just begun to function; now it has begun to act."

U.S. Delegate Warren Austin at the United Nations. The gun, made by the Russians, was captured in Korea by U.N. troops.

EXHIBIT A: The Russians insist that they sent no arms to OCT. 2 their North Korean friends after the Red Army pulled out of Korea in 1948. Last week, General Douglas MacArthur formally reported to the U.N. Security Council that ten different types of Soviet war materiel, plainly stamped 1949 or 1950, have been seized by U.N. troops in Korea.

The report, read to the Security Council by U.S. Delegate Warren Austin, specified among other items, "a 7.62-mm. PPSH-41 submachine gun. . . ." As he came to this passage in the report, Austin reached behind his chair and dramatically produced a Russian-made gun, labeled 1950. Russian Delegate Jacob Malik got up and walked out of the Council Chamber. Later he furiously denounced MacArthur as a "fascist" and Warren Austin's gesture as a provocation designed for simpletons. Lawyer Austin had scored a telling point with Exhibit A.

PEACEMAKER: For his success in ending the war between Israel and her Arab neighbors in 1948, broad-shouldered Dr. Ralph Johnson Bunche had been showered with 40 awards and 20 honorary degrees. Last week as Bunche was eating lunch in the U.N. delegates' dining room at Lake Success, his secretary dashed up with news of another honor. "I have a surprise for you," she said. "You've won the Nobel Peace Prize."

The first Negro to win the Peace Prize, he had been chosen from a list of 28 nominees that included Harry Truman, George Marshall, Winston Churchill and India's Prime Minister Nehru. The road to greatness has been a steep one for the greying, 46-year-old man whose grandmother was born in slavery. In Oslo this December he will get a gold medal and a cash award of about $31,700. To celebrate the news, the usually abstemious Bunche had bought a champagne cocktail—"which was more than I could afford."

DEC. 4 **COAL-STEEL POOL:** This week the Schuman Plan will be embodied in a draft treaty. Europe's most important postwar act of statesmanship—after the Marshall Plan and the North Atlantic Treaty—will be ready for initialing by technical experts of France, West Germany, Italy, Belgium, Luxembourg and The Netherlands.

It had taken Europe seven months to reach this notable stage in its quest for unity. Argument and counterargument had been sifted down into 94 pages of agreement. Highlights: ¶ The six nations will pool their coal & steel resources. ¶ Within this vast single market of 155 million customers, customs duties for coal and steel will be abolished, inefficient mines and mills will be closed. Last year the six produced 214 million tons of coal, 28 million tons of steel. By 1953, after modernizations have been made, they hope to have raised coal output to 220 million tons, steel to 38 million tons. [The actual figures of 1953 were even better: nearly 329 million tons of coal, 44 million tons of steel.]

JAN 2 **WHAT, NO SHERRY COW?:**

> *If I had a cow that gave such milk*
> *I'd dress her in the finest silk,*
> *Feed her on the choicest hay,*
> *And milk her 40 times a day!*

Ever since the 17th Century, Britons have drunk a sherry called "Bristol Milk." Samuel Pepys wrote in its praise. The entry in his diary of June 13, 1668 reads: ". . . and did give us good entertainment of strawberries, a whole venison-pasty, cold, and plenty of brave wine, and above all, Bristol milk."

But John Harvey & Sons, makers of Bristol Milk and a better sherry called Bristol Cream, never got around to registering the trademark of their mellow product. Recently, intending to enter the U.S. market on a larger scale, Harvey's finally applied to the British Food Ministry for a registration certificate protecting the Bristol Milk label.

"You are doubtless aware," replied the Ministry gravely, "the Regulation No. 1 of the Defense Regulations [covering sales of food] makes it an offense to mislead as to the nature, substance and quality of a food. . . . In the Ministry's opinion, the use of the word 'milk' might be held to contravene the said regulation on the grounds that this indicates the presence of milk, and as such suggests that the wine has certain special nutritive qualities. We advise you to omit the word 'milk' from the trademark and replace it by a word not open to objection."

Harvey's retorted, dead pan, that the change in the well-known name might cut down sales in dollar countries. Someone in the Food Ministry recognized the boner, and last week the advice was withdrawn. Said a contrite Ministry spokesman: "Nobody but an imbecile would connect sherry with the product of a cow."

SLOW STARTER: One day last week, Prime Minister Clement JAN. 23 Attlee summoned his ministers to the white-pillared cabinet room at No. 10 Downing Street to announce that Britain's next general election would be held Feb. 23.

Winston Churchill, on vacation on the island of Madeira, received the news of the election date by telephone from London, promptly flew home. The old Tory praised Attlee for giving six weeks' notice of the election. Said Churchill: "It's just what I did the last time. I hope it will be an equally good result—the other way around."

OSMOSIS IN QUEUETOPIA: To mark an event which will put FEB. 6 his name in the history books for generations, Clement Attlee slipped one afternoon last week into a crowded room of London's India House. When flashbulbs flared, he grimaced and ducked behind his wife. Politely, the photographers went away, and the Prime Minister who had given India its freedom stood quietly sipping his tea in the midst of an austere celebration.

Despite his self-effacement (immediately after his smashing Labor victory of 1945, uncomplimentary legends began to cluster about Attlee's retiring and "colorless" personality; such cracks as "An empty limousine drew up at the gate and Attlee stepped out" became standard cocktail-party fodder), Clement Attlee's mark was all over the Indian Independence Day tea party. The tea came in thick cups because Britain's fine china must be exported. The cream on the cakes was synthetic because Britain must keep her imports down. Under their gossamer saris, many of the Indian women present wore homely sweaters because Britain's coal must not be wasted.

Prime Minister Attlee. He has given Britain a new way of life.

Sir Winston Churchill has a word for Attlee's program: "Queuetopia."

In four years and five months as Prime Minister, Clement Attlee had not only given freedom to India, Burma, Ceylon (combined pop. 411 million); he had also given to Britain a new way of life. Some of Attlee's followers called it Socialism; some called it "fair shares for all"; some called it the welfare state. Winston Churchill last week scornfully snarled out another name for it: "Queuetopia."

Whatever it was, the regime of queues and 40% taxes and womb-to-tomb security had come to judgment. If the pollsters are right, only an all-out crusade can put the Tories in office. Last week there was no sign of a crusade.

SHOCK: For several years Britons have been looking down FEB. 13 their noses at what they called "American spy hysteria." Last week, when one of their top atomic scientists was arrested as a Russian spy, the superior British stare turned slightly glassy. Dr. Klaus Fuchs, once a trusted top-level worker at the U.S. Atomic Laboratory at Los Alamos, N. Mex., had been detected, not by famed British Intelligence or Scotland Yard, but by the FBI, whom the British called into the case. Fuchs, said the FBI, had made a partial confession. He had been a secret member of the Communist Party for at least eight years, probably longer. Since 1943 he had had access to the tenderest U.S. and British atomic secrets.

COMEDY IN CARDIFF: Britain's election campaign had been FEB. 20 a dull fight so far, even by sedate British standards. Last week, Winston Churchill provided a touch of comic relief. During a speech at Cardiff, Churchill was expounding his views on the Socialists' housing program. "In official Socialist jargon," Churchill said, "houses are called accommodation units. . . . I don't know how we are going to sing our old song, *Home, Sweet Home*." Then he paused, put his left hand on his breast, stretched out his right hand appealingly and hoarsely burst into song:

> *Accommodation unit, sweet accommodation unit,*
> *There's no place like our accommodation unit.*

When his audience stopped laughing, Churchill got grim again. Said he: "I hope to live to see the British democracy spit all this rubbish from their lips."

"WE CAN'T RUN AWAY": On election day, Tory Anthony MARCH Eden put on a brown tweed suit and set out hatless to tour the polling stations in his Warwickshire constituency. After making the rounds, Eden sipped a gin & French at Warwick Castle. Said he: "I'm convinced we've got out every middle-class Tory vote today, but I see no sign of a trend." While Eden was sipping his cocktail, Aneurin Bevan, Labor's handsome dynamo, was completing a tour of 40 polling places in his Welsh mining constituency Ebbw Vale. In contrast to Eden's cautious doubts, Bevan was in a mood of exuberant confidence. But his tune changed when his secretary brought him the news that Labor's lead was slipping fast.

Bevan sucked in his breath, grunted: "We don't seem to have much success wooing the middle classes, do we? You can't woo them; they want a strong man to lead them."

At the Savoy Hotel, champagne, opened for toasts, stood on the tables going flat. Winston Churchill had promised to show up if the early returns were good. He did not show.

But though Clement Attlee won, the election was a very sharp setback for the Labor Party, a powerful comeback for the Conservatives. With 313 seats needed for an absolute majority, Labor had 315, the Conservatives 296, the Liberals 9, independents 3.

Prime Minister Attlee announced that despite his narrow majority, he would carry on the "King's government." His Party Secretary agreed. Said he: "We can't run away."

MARCH 13 **CHILL IN COURT**: Preceded by the bearers of mace and sword, England's Lord Chief Justice, Lord Goddard, robed in icy dignity and a scarlet gown, entered the oak-paneled courtroom of the Old Bailey. "My Lord," began the Prosecutor, his grey wig clamped firmly forward over his forehead, "this is a case of the utmost gravity." He went over the story that Klaus Fuchs had told in his confession—the course of a brilliant, morally blind man from confusion to total, irretrievable corruption.

Fuchs stood up in the dock, read a statement from notes in a high tinny voice, barely intelligible underneath his heavy German accent. "I have had a fair trial," he said, "and I wish to thank you, My Lord." Then Lord Goddard leaned forward on his bench; a chill passed through the courtroom.

"You have betrayed the hospitality and protection given to you with the grossest treachery. . . ." said Lord Goddard, hard-voiced. "It is not so much for punishment that I impose [the penalty], for punishment to a man of your mentality means nothing. My duty is to safeguard this country."

Then Lord Goddard imposed the maximum sentence under British law—14 years.

OFFICIAL: "Her Royal Highness, Princess Elizabeth," ran a APRIL 24 Buckingham Palace announcement this week, "will undertake no further public engagements." Translation: the Princess, mother of Prince Charlie, 17 months, was expecting again.

POINT COMFORT: "This is one of the happiest days of my MAY 29 life," trilled Grocer Billy Brown of Whitby, Yorkshire, as he hung the Union Jack outside his shop. "I'm sick of points. With me, it's been nothing but scissors, scissors, scissors for years."

During 8½ years, to be exact, Grocer Brown and his fellow food merchants in Britain had snipped their scissors at some 68 billion pesky, elusive food coupons in the ration books of Britain's housewives, stored them in little tins to send to the Food Ministry at the end of each month. Each year they had filled out 20 million official forms. At 5:02 p.m. one day last week the Ministry called a halt to the point system. "Thank heaven," gasped one housewife. "What a relief!"

GREAT EXPECTATIONS: Britain's Margaret, the world's most AUG. 14 eligible princess, was giving her suitors—and the breathless watchers of royal romance—a breathless time. Just when London was momentarily expecting an announcement of her engagement to Walter Francis John ("Johnny") Montagu-Douglas-Scott, Earl of Dalkeith and heir to the Duke of Buccleuch, Margaret began to be squired about by young-man-about-town William ("Billy") Wallace, son of the late Captain Euan Wallace, M.P. and Minister of Transport in Neville Chamberlain's government. Gossips felt that Billy might appeal more to Margaret's volatile character than "quiet and friendly" Dalkeith, who is bored by nightclubs.

Said one observer: "My dear, you can *never* rely on Margaret. . . . Oh, heavens, won't it be a relief when she makes up her mind!"

TO REMEMBER YOU BY: "When one is very old, as I am," SEPT. 2 George Bernard Shaw wrote in 1946, "one of the unpleasant things seems to be that your legs give in before your head does, and you are always stumbling about. I tumble down about three times a week quite regularly. . . ." Fortnight ago, while walking in the garden of his home at Ayot St. Lawrence in Hertfordshire, the 94-year-old playwright fell and broke his left thigh bone. Carted off to Luton and Dunstable Hospital, he soon got into an argument about his 74-year-old once-red beard, which the anesthetists wanted snipped. Shaw won by having the offending whiskers plastered to his face. Next day, in his cream-and-green private room, with his fractured femur fastened together by steel pins, Vegetarian Shaw sat up to munch on nuts and fruit, listened with gusto over a portable radio to BBC reports on his progress. When a nurse finished washing him, Shaw grumbled that he wanted a bath certificate: "Otherwise someone will come along tomorrow and want to do the same thing again. Too much washing is not good for antiques."

On the third day the amazing old man stood up on his good leg for a few seconds and lightheartedly wiggled the injured one. Next day he presented his doctor with a dilemma: "It will do you no good if I get over this," said Shaw. "A doctor's reputation is made by the number of eminent men who die under his care."

OCT. 2 **CLASH OF STEEL:** Winston Churchill had a question to ask the Prime Minister: Would the government promise that no steps would be taken to nationalize steel—at least until there had been a further appeal to the country? Supply Minister George R. Strauss rose to give the cabinet's answer: the government's Iron & Steel Corp. would be set up on Oct. 2.

For a few minutes the House of Commons was in an uproar.

Churchill said: "To disturb and damage the steel industry . . . is to disturb and damage the whole [rearmament] effort." He accused Prime Minister Attlee of acting at the dictates of a "fanatical intelligentsia obsessed by economic fallacies."

Canny Herbert Morrison, no fanatic intellectual, carried the brunt of the government's defense. His main argument: the government was merely implementing an act already passed.

Conservative Party whips, foreseeing a close vote, had pulled M.P. Sir George Harvie-Watt off a New Zealand-bound liner, were flying him back from Gibraltar. Outside

Princess Margaret. A guessing game:
whom will she marry? Page 100.

Sir Stafford Cripps says he does not
consider meat "an edible substance."

the House of Commons, hundreds watched the arrival of the invalids. Labor's Sir Stafford Cripps and Hugh Dalton were brought back from rest cures, R.W.G. Mackay from a hospital. Thomas Hubbard, awaiting an operation, turned up, pale and haggard, with two attending doctors. J.P.W. Mallalieu, who had been suffering from shingles, afterwards wrote: "Medical science is wonderful. First it was deep X rays. Then it was penicillin. Now it's divisions in the House of Commons." The sound of the division bells, he said, had done wonders for his shingles.

For other Socialists the result was tonic: when the division bells had stopped ringing the count was 300 for, 306 against Churchill's motion opposing nationalization.

Thus the nation which, more than any other, had pioneered the great age of steel and the great age of free enterprise had finally socialized its basic industry. But the chapter was not quite ended. Said Conservative Party Leader Churchill: "We shall if we should obtain the responsibility and the power, in any future which is possible to foresee, repeal the existing Iron and Steel Act." [The Conservatives did so in 1953.]

CARROT CHANCELLOR: "My trouble is a tired heart," said OCT. 30 61-year-old Sir Stafford Cripps last week as he resigned the Chancellorship of the Exchequer. The twelve years had been strenuous ones. Cripps was the walking symbol as well as the architect of Britain's postwar austerity program. It was not Cripps's fault that meat was scarce but many Britons blamed him for that when he looked coldly through his half-moon glasses and announced that he did not consider meat "an edible substance." His very name suggested the sound of a crunching cold raw carrot, which was, in fact, one of Vegetarian Cripps's favorite staples.

Nevertheless, Old Austerity had served his country well. Tory Winston Churchill, gazing at Cripps, had once said: "There, but for the grace of God, goes God." Yet Churchill respected Cripps, made him Ambassador to Russia in 1940, special emissary to India in 1942 and later Minister of Aircraft Production. Cripps was, said Churchill in 1947, "the greatest brain in the [Labor] administration."

The man who would replace Sir Stafford Cripps was Hugh Gaitskell, 44. He is 17 years younger than Cripps and in many respects different. He is neither vegetarian nor teetotaler. Gaitskell is a cautious politician who makes few mistakes. He is best known, however, for an incautious remark made in 1947 when as Fuel Minister he was trying to persuade Britons to burn less coal for heating bath water. Said he: "I have never had a great many baths myself. It does not make a great difference to health." Since then he has been one of the quietest of Laborite leaders and Attlee likes his orderly mind. Gaitskell has made enemies because of his rapid rise in the party hierarchy. They think that as Chancellor of the Exchequer moderate bather Gaitskell may soon find himself in hot water.

NOV. 6 **MISSING FISSIONIST:** Scholarly Dr. Bruno Pontecorvo, 37, was well-liked by his fellow nuclear physicists at Britain's Harwell atomic research plant. The Italian-born Briton was jolly and fun-loving, a good dancer, an enthusiastic tennis player. His pretty Swedish wife Helena Marianne was just as gay, had a flair for flamboyant clothes, including red slacks.

A pupil of famed Enrico Fermi, Pontecorvo fled Italy in the 1930s to escape Mussolini's Hitler-inspired anti-Semitism. He spent some time in France, the U.S. and Canada—where he became a British subject. Eventually he made his way to Harwell, where he rose to the post of chief scientific officer.

Like many a colleague, he was an associate in Canada of Dr. Allan Nunn May, later convicted of passing atomic information to Russian agents; and in Britain of Dr. Klaus Fuchs, also convicted of atomic spying for Russia.

But Pontecorvo stayed above suspicion. Last July he resigned from Harwell to take a post at the University of Liverpool, which has one of Britain's finest atomic research departments. He was doing work on tritium, key element for the hydrogen bomb. Before going to Liverpool, Pontecorvo planned a holiday.

With his wife and three children, the physicist went to visit his parents in Milan. Without telling his parents, he and his family went to Rome. He put up his grey Vanguard at a garage, said he'd be back next day to start a long trip. But he never came back. Instead the Pontecorvos bought airline tickets to Stockholm. From Stockholm, without calling Mrs. Pontecorvo's mother, who lives in a suburb of the Swedish capital, they quickly flew on to Helsinki. During the trip, one of their little sons prattled to a fellow passenger: "We're going to Russia."

As the airline bus drove them into Helsinki, the boy asked, "Are we now in Russia?" Just outside the Finnish Airways office, the bus stopped. The Pontecorvos picked up a taxicab and sped off. After that, no trace. They did not register at any hotel or private home. No border station had any record of their crossing. But if Pontecorvo had entered Russia, the Kremlin had one of the world's top physicists in its domain. [In 1955 the Russians displayed Pontecorvo at a Moscow press conference. He became a research director at the Dubna Institute, a leading Soviet nuclear research center.]

"I'M DONE": "Sister," the old man told Nurse Gwendoline NOV. 13 Howell, "you're trying to keep me alive as an old curiosity, but I'm done, I'm finished, I'm going to die." Before the next dawn, George Bernard Shaw had lapsed into final unconsciousness. A little over 24 hours later, the 94-year-old philosopher, playwright, professional pixie and self-styled "Bishop of Everywhere" was dead.

The end that came so peacefully and quietly was not unwelcome. When Shaw guessed that he might live only to become a bedridden invalid, he lost interest in the business.

Last week Lady Astor drove down from London to pay him a visit. "Oh, Nancy," Shaw murmured to his longtime friend as she sat gently stroking the parchment skin on his still defiantly bearded white head, "I want to sleep, to sleep." These quiet words were among the last that voluble Bernard Shaw was heard to speak.

In the tiny (pop. 110) village of Ayot St. Lawrence where Shaw had spent the last 44 years of his life, the parting amenities were those due an old man and a kindly neighbor. A few neighbors, family servants and the daughter of a local publican gathered in Shaw's parlor for a brief service read by the local Anglican pastor, the Reverend R.J. Davies. "Mr. Shaw was not really an atheist," Pastor Davies said later, "I would call him rather an Irishman."

DEC. 25 **SUSPENDED, BUT NOT ENDED:** Thirty months after Marshall aid began, Chancellor of the Exchequer Hugh Gaitskell last week had an announcement for the House of Commons: Britain could go it alone; Marshall Plan aid would be suspended Jan. 1, 18 months ahead of schedule. "Now we can begin to walk proudly again," said an M.P.

The skies had not cleared completely. Britain's present gold and dollar surplus could be wiped out by British rearmament costs or by a fall in exports. For this reason, Hugh Gaitskell stressed that Marshall Plan aid was suspended, not ended.

But last week, once more able to pay its way, Britain was hopeful and grateful. "Ordinary words of thanks are inadequate," cried the *Manchester Guardian*. "Here is one of the most brilliant successes in the history of international relations." Gaitskell said: "We are not an emotional people . . . and not very articulate, but these characteristics should not . . . hide the real and profound sense of gratitude we feel toward the American people."

France

RCH 13 **THE PAUSE THAT AROUSES:** France's Communist press bristled with warnings against U.S. "Cola-Colonization." Coke salesmen were described as agents of the OSS and the U.S. State Department.

Last November the Reds introduced a bill into the French Assembly to "prohibit the import, manufacture and sale of Coca-Cola in France, Algeria and the French colonial empire." A Communist deputy shouted at France's Health Minister: "Are you going to permit the poisoning of French men and women by this toxic American drink. . . ?" Health Minister Pierre Schneiter answered calmly: "Let the French drink what they like and trust their good taste." That good sense carried the day and the Communist bill was defeated.

Meanwhile, the Communists had found unexpected allies: France's wine growers and the complacently chauvinistic members of Premier Bidault's own M.R.P. Paris' *Le Monde* spoke for the conservatives: "What the French criticize in Coca-Cola is less the drink itself than the civilization, the style of life of which it is a sign and . . . a symbol."

Last week, the Communists tried again. The bill passed by 366 to 202.

In New York, James Aloysius Farley, generalissimo of Coca-Cola's overseas expeditionary forces, sizzled like a shaken Coke bottle on a hot stove. "Coca-Cola wasn't injurious to the health of American soldiers who liberated France from the Nazi," he exploded.

If Coca-Cola is barred from France, U.S. Congressmen might be tempted to raise tariffs on French wines. One Congressman expressed his views on the matter. "Coca-Cola," said Representative Prince H. Preston Jr., from Coke's home state of Georgia, "would give the French something they have needed since the war ended, and that is a good belch."

ANOTHER: France last week got its 13th cabinet since the JULY 24 liberation. At week's end it was still in office. New Premier:: René Pleven.

THE BIG IF: France's Robert Schuman will arrive in the U.S. SEPT. 1 next week to attend the Foreign Ministers' conference in New York. He will bring with him a special problem requiring special U.S. attention. Schuman is a sincere anti-Communist who would like to strengthen France's defenses against Communist attack; but he is also a member of a shaky French cabinet which is afraid to take vigorous anti-Communist action. It is reliably reported that Schuman hopes the U.S. will twist his arm a bit and force his government to get cracking on rearmament. Without such a display of U.S. pressure, the present French government would not dare to ask for essential defense measures.

OCT. 30 **ASSEMBLY AGAIN:** The French Constitution of 1946 gave almost all executive as well as legislative powers to the National Assembly. Since then it has been almost impossible for a French government to do anything without the Assembly. On the other hand, the failure of French parties to unite against Communism has made it almost impossible to do anything important with the Assembly. For four years France has found no way out of the dilemma.

Premier René Pleven proposed a *"système majoritaire,"* which would build up a few strong parties at the expense of the weakest. Pleven was determined to fight for this program, even if it meant his downfall.

One of the beneficiaries of a *système majoritaire* would be Charles de Gaulle's RPF (Rally of the People of France). Last week at a fervent national council of his party in Paris, complete with the Cross of Lorraine, the V-for-victory sign of World War II, and chants of "De Gaulle to power!" the general proclaimed: "Once again, we shall be called in at *moins cinq*"—(meaning "five minutes of," the French equivalent of "the eleventh hour"). The Gaullists still believed themselves to be the wave of the future.

NOV. 20 **THE PLANE TO MOSCOW:** The green C-47 from Moscow circled above Paris' Orly Field, showing the bright red stars on its fuselage as it came in for a landing. Half an hour later, an ambulance drove up, opened its doors. From the ambulance Maurice Thorez, France's Communist boss, was carried to the aircraft to start what may be his final pilgrimage to Moscow.

Hard-driving, 50-year-old Maurice Thorez was a very sick man. In the month since he was struck down by a cerebral hemorrhage he had lain partially paralyzed in his party-owned villa near Paris. He had frequent spells during which he blacked out. Five French specialists had agreed that Thorez seemed incurable. Moscow had sent Professor Sergei Davidenkov to attend Stalin's "very dear Comrade Thorez."

Davidenkov disagreed with the French doctors, said that he would personally guarantee a cure in a Moscow clinic.

The Kremlin could congratulate itself on a delicate job, well—if brusquely—handled. It would not be safe to leave a bedridden Thorez in France. He could not easily be hidden underground if the French government decided to arrest the Red leaders. A sick man whose brain or nervous system was affected might talk. He had to be whisked out of the country. [Thorez returned to France in 1953, continued to lead France's Communist Party until his death in 1964.]

Germany

"FROM OVER THERE": On a drizzly afternoon last week, a JAN. 30 train from Oranienburg rolled into Gesundbrunnen Station in Berlin's French sector. Haggard men in tattered clothes and bony, hollow-eyed women straggled onto the platform. Last to get out was a white-faced, white-haired old man with a frayed velvet-collared overcoat. He leaned gasping against a wall. "Yes, yes, from over there," he muttered. "I must be dreaming. Please don't ask me any questions."

The gaunt men & women were survivors of Eastern Germany's concentration camps. Released by the Russians as a propaganda gesture, they were the last of some 200,000 political prisoners whom the Russians had interned since the end of the war in the infamous Nazi camps at Sachsenhausen, Buchenwald and elsewhere. About half of the prisoners died of cold, hunger, disease or beatings. Another 70,000 were shipped off to Russia as slave laborers.

One wreck of a man slowly unfolded a story of seven years' suffering under two dictatorships. The Nazis had thrown him into Sachsenhausen in 1943 for listening to foreign broadcasts. Released in 1945, he headed for home in Schleswig-Holstein. Somewhere along the road, the Russians seized him again, sent him back to Sachsenhausen. In nine years of marriage, he had lived with his wife for only eight months. "God only knows if I'll find her," he said, "or what I'll find if I do."

"OUR MAIN PURPOSE": This week in Stuttgart, U.S. High FEB. 13 Commissioner John J. McCloy spoke before an audience of

1,400 at the opening of a new *Amerika-Haus*. His speech was a milestone in the development of the U.S. attitude toward Germany. Said McCloy: "No one ... is charging the Germans with the responsibility for Hitler's crimes. . . . But what I do expect is an end to the arguments of those Germans who would not only deny their own guilt, but also seek to place the responsibility for the consequences of that guilt exclusively upon the shortcomings of other peoples. . . .

"We Americans are not here exclusively to feed the German people. . . . Our main purpose is to help Germany achieve political recovery."

VERONICA TOWN: Wherever G.I.s were stationed the story was the same. They had money, the Germans needed it; prices soared and the black market and prostitutes flourished. But in 1948-49 when the Berlin airlift brought 8,000 U.S. pilots and enlisted airmen to former *Luftwaffe* airfields in the neighborhood of the quiet old town of Celle (pop. 33,000), the city council was deeply shocked by changes in Celle's way of life.

By train, by bus, by bicycle and by thumb, more than 2,000 trollops came to Celle. The girls increased the shortage of space until the staid people of Celle, swept along on the tide of vice and opportunism, began renting rooms for the night only. Some mothers even sent their children into the streets to lure the G.I.s home: "Nice warm *Stube* with big bed, Joe." Celle was beginning to be known elsewhere in Germany as "Veronica Town" (from a *Stars and Stripes* cartoon character parodying the initials VD).

When the airlift ended and the Americans left, the council cracked down, summoned to court some 200 of the people who had rented rooms to fräuleins. Only 50 were actually sentenced. At last the Bonn government set all offenders free by amnesty, explaining that it was impossible to single out "individual crimes for something of which a whole town is guilty."

CHILL FROM THE EAST: Last week, from Moscow, came news that chilled the hearts of thousands. All German prisoners of war in Russia, said the Soviet radio, had now been returned to Germany.

The Germans were almost too stunned to speak. By the most conservative estimate, the Russians still had not accounted for more than 200,000 prisoners of war. Socialist Leader Kurt Schumacher expressed in one word the feelings of millions: "Monstrous."

LAST CALL FOR EUROPE: The key to Europe is Germany. SEPT. 18 The key to Germany is Berlin, and not since the Russian blockade of 1948-49 has the outpost city seemed more menaced by the Red domain that surrounded it. Berliners and West Germans know that only token defenses stand between them and the threat from the East. Under the circumstances, it is not surprising that many Germans (and other Europeans) are profoundly discouraged and defeatist.

Few men understood this danger so clearly as Berlin's indomitable Mayor, Ernst Reuter. For the past four years he had made it his business to rouse in his countrymen the love of freedom that all men have and to urge the free world to let the Germans have the means of defending themselves.

In last week's decision to send more U.S. troops to Germany, Reuter's long campaign was beginning finally to bear fruit. But the Allied sense of urgency was still muffled by distrust of the Germans. Twice within a generation they had goose-stepped Europe, and the world, into war. Fellow Europeans had a saying: "The Hun is always either at your throat or at your feet."

But the Western world was slowly coming to the realization that its choice was not between an armed and a disarmed Germany. Its choice was between a Germany armed by the West and willing to fight and a Germany armed by and made to fight for the Kremlin.

Time, as Reuter well knew, was all-important. Last week in Washington, John J. McCloy, U.S. High Commissioner for Germany, was anxiously discussing European morale with a friend.

"You speak," said the friend, "as if you are sounding the last call for Europe."

Said McCloy, "That's exactly what it is."

END & BEGINNING: On orders from Washington, Lieut. DEC. General Manton S. Eddy, U.S. Army commander in Europe, last week reactivated the Seventh Army with himself as commanding general and headquarters in Stuttgart. This marked the end of the U.S. troops' role in Germany as an occupation force and the beginning of a fighting force to stand against Communist aggression.

DEC. 25 **"VERY SPECIAL PRESENT":** "I am guilty! I am a sinner!" screamed fat-faced Ilse Koch to her jailers. In her frenzy— whether genuine or faked—she smashed the furniture in her cell and babbled about heaven, hell and sin.

U.S. Commissioner McCloy: "We are not here to feed Germany." Page 109.   *Ilse Koch, the "Bitch of Buchenwald": "I am guilty! I am a sinner!"*

Later last week the "Bitch of Buchenwald" collapsed in a hysterical heap in an Augsburg courtroom, was carried off to a hospital for mental observation. The 43-year-old widow of Karl Koch, commander of the Nazi extermination camp, was on trial for the second time for crimes committed at Buchenwald where 50,000 died.

This time Ilse was being tried by her own countrymen, who grabbed her when the U.S. set her free from Landsberg prison last year. Ilse had served four years for crimes against allied inmates, got out when an Army review board concluded that although she "encouraged, aided and participated" in Buchenwald's operation, "there was no convincing evidence that she had selected inmates for extermination in order to secure tattooed skins, or that she possessed any articles made of human skin."

Last week Witness Peter Planiseck testified that he once saw Ilse order a prisoner to strip so she could see his tattoos; then she wrote down the prisoner's number. That night he was executed.

Another former laboratory worker, Joseph Ackermann, said the director ordered a "very special present" for Koch's birthday, a lamp of human skin and bone. "The light was switched on by pressure against the little toe of one of the three human feet which formed the stand."

Ilse's hysterics and absence from the courtroom did not delay her trial. The procession of witnesses went on. Since West Germany has abolished the death penalty, the prosecution hopes to put Ilse behind bars for life. [She was sentenced to prison for life.]

Russia

THE MAO WHO CAME TO DINNER: It was more than a month JAN. 23 since Mao Tse-tung, boss of Red China, had arrived in Moscow. His talks with Stalin and top Soviet officials were taking longer than the three or four days usually needed for a Stalin puppet to reach agreement with Stalin. Mao and Stalin well knew that the Western world was hoping that they had fallen out. The hope was probably illusory; nevertheless, Mao's prolonged visit might be a sign that all was not well between Soviet Russia and her new Communist neighbor.

MR. QUID PRO QUO: After 60 days of secret dickering, the FEB. 2 time had come for the masters of 700 million people to seal their alliance with open panoply. Soviet dignitaries repaired to a Kremlin Hall. In their center stood Comrades Joseph Stalin of Russia and Mao Tse-tung of China. The documents their foreign ministers signed proclaimed that:

¶ For 30 years, Russia and China would aid each other "with all means . . . in the event of . . . attack by Japan or any state allied with her. . . ." (*i.e.*, the U.S.).

¶ Russia would extend to China a $300 million credit over five years to buy Soviet industrial and railway equipment.

It was hard for the Western world to believe that Mao had spent 60 days in the Kremlin merely to negotiate a variation of the customary treaty between the Soviet Union and its satellites elsewhere. "We know something about Mr. Mao Tse-tung and Mr. Chou En-lai," observed a British Foreign Office spokesman, "but, frankly, the gentleman we are most interested in is Mr. *Quid Pro Quo*."

Most likely *quid pro quos*:

¶ In return for an extension of Russia's stay in Manchuria, support for Chinese Communist infiltration in Southeast Asia.

¶ In return for Soviet military advice and equipment, the installation of Russian watchdogs in the Chinese army and government.

The Sino-Soviet pact gave world Communism another notable diplomatic and propaganda triumph in Asia. Mao made a not unreasonable prediction: "This treaty will inevitably influence not only the flourishing of the great powers, China and the Soviet Union, but also the future of all mankind." [From 1960 on there were signs of a widening rift between the two countries and Soviet technicians were called home from China. By 1964, when Premier Khrushchev publicly attacked Mao Tse-tung, the break seemed complete.]

RCH 13 DELUSION ON SUNDAY: "Comrades, these are not merely elections—this is also a holiday." —J. Stalin

In a holiday spirit, Russia was preparing for its quadrennial national elections next Sunday. Thousands of agitators swarmed out from thousands of *agit* points to address rallies as if there were actually issues that could be decided by the voters. The Russian people, never having known anything better, believe that the show that they will enact next Sunday is really an election as well as a holiday.

ALL THAT GLITTERS . . . : Moscow wrote a financial fairy tale. The Soviet Council of Ministers announced last week that the ruble, which had previously been fixed as worth about 19¢, would henceforth be worth 25¢. The new "exchange rate" was purely imaginary. Nobody ever gets a chance to exchange any rubles into foreign currency; if one did, on a free market, a ruble would be worth more nearly a nickel than a quarter. Ignoring the phony exchange rate, U.S. economists estimate that an American works 30 minutes for a pound of butter, a Russian five hours.

THE MASTERS: The results of the Russian election last week MARCH were—after the figures had been adjusted—better than ever. Voting for the Stalin "bloc" of deputies (there were no other candidates) were 110,788,377 patriots (99.73%), while 300,146 others (0.27%) were listed as having voted against the Stalin bloc by drawing a line through the names. Crowed *Pravda*: "What stirring and decisive figures they are! . . . Only under Socialism are the people the masters of their fate."

THE CAT IN THE KREMLIN: Where is the Korean war leading JULY 17 the world? Will it spread around the globe, to sear the capitals of the world with atomic fire? Or is 1950 the beginning of a series of slow, limited wars that will keep the U.S. and its allies committed in battle for generations?

The answer was buried in the mind of a grey, catlike old man behind the walls of the Kremlin. Would the cat in the Kremlin jump again? Anthony Eden put the question very clearly last week. "I recall a conversation which I had with Marshal Stalin," said Eden, "at a very grim period of the war in December, 1941. 'We should not underrate Hitler,' Stalin said. 'But he made one mistake. He did not know when to stop.' Then Stalin turned to me and said: 'You think that if we are victorious, I shall not know when to stop. You are wrong. I shall know.'"

Stalin is the No. 1 Communist not merely because he has the top job but because he himself is in a notably advanced stage of Communism. It is not true, as the Trotskyists say, that he sneaked into power. He got it because he deserved it— by the standards deeply imbedded in Communist philosophy. To stay in power, Stalin has killed millions—literally millions—including most of his oldest and closest colleagues.

A lot of people in Russia who should know believe that he also killed his second wife. The story goes that on Nov. 7, 1932, the Stalins gave a party at the Kremlin. Alliluyeva,

Stalin's bright, attractive wife, was all keyed up because she was about to take her final law-school examinations. During the evening she got a bit tight and started needling Stalin about a political decision he had been postponing. Stalin tried to shut her up and she threw an inkstand at him.

Even in Moscow, few parties ever ended so quickly. Next night Stalin called Molotov's wife. When Mrs. Molotov got to the Stalin apartment, Mrs. Stalin was dead on the floor—shot. A pistol was on Stalin's desk. He said that she had killed herself: worry over the examination, no doubt.

The story is told not to hang another murder on Stalin; one more would hardly affect the balance. The point is that Stalin's country is the kind of place where a lot of people can believe that the ruler killed his own wife, yet nobody can do anything about it. The present Mrs. Stalin keeps very quiet—and presumably minds her manners. [The dead Mrs. Stalin's daughter, Svetlana Alliluyeva, left Russia for asylum in the West, came to the U.S. in 1967.]

Italy

FEB. 27 **BRAWL:** "Democracy," warned Premier Alcide de Gasperi before the packed Chamber of Deputies, "will be defended at all costs to compel respect for free institutions and prevent violence." De Gasperi reviewed recent violent events, dwelling particularly on Communist-led riots.

Communist Boss Palmiro Togliatti shot to his feet, raced for the government bench. Christian Democratic deputies rushed up to form a barricade between the government and the Left. Within seconds, rival partymen were hard at it. The Reds' thick-nosed Milanese Labor Leader Gaetano Invernizzi made a flying leap from the top of the Communist benches into the heart of enemy territory. He was promptly kicked in the skull.

A swarthy young (30) Communist from Sicily, Luigi di Mauro, slipped through the melee, cocked his fist, was set to throw a haymaker against Italy's motionless Premier when another huge fist, belonging to Labor Minister Achille Marazza, appeared from nowhere and knocked him flat. In frustrated rage, Comrade Di Mauro bit Marazza's thumb to the bone.

Postwar Italy's worst parliamentary brawl ended a few minutes later, quelled by chamber ushers acting as a riot squad. "Fortunately," said Milan's moderate *Corriere della Sera*, "what might have been catastrophe turned into grotesquerie. But the nation is tired of grotesquerie in parliament." That evening the deputies gave a firm vote of confidence to De Gasperi's government.

Communist boss Togliatti starts a brawl in the Chamber. Page 115.

Bandit Giuliano of Sicily. He suffered from a fatal vanity.

BANDIT'S END: Few Sicilians could believe at first that Salvatore Giuliano was really dead. He had been as handsome as a schoolgirl's dream, as vain and indestructible as a god on Olympus. For seven years in the mountain fastnesses of Sicily, he had been the king of bandits in a land where every bandit is looked upon as a king and had gathered around him an army of 600 or more followers.

Like Robin Hood's men, his army would strike swiftly in small groups—kidnaping some purse-proud landlord here, killing a sheriff's man there—and fade elusively into mountain caves, vineyards and wheatfields. In seven years Giuliano's men had killed 79 national *carabinieri*, 25 local policemen, 40 civilians. They had collected more than $1,000,000 in ransoms from 30 kidnapings. They were said to rob only

JULY 1

the rich & powerful. Half in hero worship and half in fear, the local peasants clamped their lips tight when police asked questions about Giuliano.

Last year Rome sent to Sicily hard-eyed Colonel Ugo Luca with a task force of 2,000 picked men, mostly bachelors. Probing the hills and villages, Luca painstakingly weaned peasants away from their hero worship of Giuliano. Some of the bandits surrendered. When word got around that Luca treated them well, others followed. But the bandit king himself remained in the hills.

Two months ago, Luca ordered his men out of uniform and baited a trap for Giuliano's vanity. He sent a troop of *carabinieri* into the wine district camouflaged as a moving picture unit. They were ordered to spread the word that they were making a picture about bandits and to drop strong hints that a leading role might be available for Giuliano. A series of return hints from Giuliano soon led the "moviemakers" into the town of Castelvetrano.

There one night last week they found their man. The *carabinieri* opened fire. Giuliano fled, firing over his shoulder as he went. For 15 minutes the chase led through twisted alleys and courtyards 'Captain Antonio Perenze, leader of the *carabinieri*, hid in a doorway. A stalking figure crept up, machine gun set. Perenze blasted point-blank. The figure whirled, tottered and fell face down, a dark red splotch welling up under his white shirt. In Salvatore Giuliano's pocket was a package of mentholated cigarettes, a small flashlight and a photograph of himself.

NOV. 6 **SKEPTICS & REFORMERS:** Land reform in Italy is a desperate human need and an almost insuperable problem. The Communists propose their usual Draconian solution: confiscate and redistribute large estates, eventually collectivize. The middle-way Christian Democratic government of Premier Alcide de Gasperi rejects revolution for evolution.

For the past year De Gasperi has been pushing a comprehensive land reform act through Parliament. Its core: buy out large land-holdings, cut them into small plots (about 15 acres), help the peasantry to buy and cultivate them. Called the "Sila Project," it is now under way in Calabria, on the heel of the Italian peninsula. Last week TIME Correspondent William Rospigliosi saw the reform. His report:

Though it had been shouted from hilltops, none in Santa Severina believed it would really come about. A system that for generations had kept Santa Severinians hungry, thirsty, dirty, diseased and in despair could never end. Amerigo Marescalchi, a gaunt, soft-eyed Communist, was one of the skeptical ones. When I asked about the following morning's distribution, Amerigo shrugged. "Tonight there will be bread at home," he said. "That's enough for me. Let tomorrow take care of itself."

Distribution day dawned brightly. A beribboned six-year-old girl dipped her hand into a box and drew out the first name: Vincenzo Nocella. But Nocella had not come to the meeting because he did not believe the land would ever be distributed. Then the child drew a plot for Nocella.

Santa Severina land is divided into good and less good zones. Nocella drew a poor plot. A long sigh went through the crowd. The next name drew a middling plot. The crowd lost some of its tenseness. It was past noon before Amerigo Marescalchi drew middling lands. Still uncertain, he rushed home. When he caught sight of his wife Concetta in the doorway of the small, smoke-darkened room they share with eleven relatives, he cried, "It may be not much good as farming land but we can build a house there. It will save us our rent, 2,000 lire a month." Concetta had tears in her eyes. "If only I can get out of this filth," she said.

When we came to Amerigo's plot, a bright-eyed official led the way through a hedge. "This is where your land begins," he explained. Amerigo's jaw dropped. "But this garden?" The official answered: "It's included. Your land goes to the ditch down there. Takes in half that oak tree." Amerigo exclaimed: "The acorns from that tree will be enough to keep a pig. We will have sausage."

The inspection over, Amerigo stood momentarily silent, then said: "I am glad I have got this land. Now it's up to the Communists to show us if they can get us more than this." Slowly he removed his cap. He said: "But tonight I can pray to a resurrected Christ." [The benefits of land reform varied with the locality but on the whole the program was moderately successful. By 1959 nearly two million acres had been distributed.]

Argentina

In 1950 Argentina was still in the grip of Dictator Juan Perón, a career army officer who began his rise to power in the early '40s. In 1945, after a brief period in prison, he was freed as the result of a mass demonstration of workers which had been organized with the help of a beautiful radio actress named Evita Duarte. Four days later Perón and Evita were married—he was 50, she was 26. Her popularity with the masses helped to elect Perón President in 1946, and until her death in 1952 the Peróns were virtually co-dictators of Argentina. Perón was forced to flee the country after a military coup in 1955.

FEB. 6   **NEWS BUTCHER:** *"The President of the Argentine nation proclaims his respect for the Constitution and promises that freedom of the press will always be maintained."*
              —Juan Domingo Perón Nov. 13, 1946

The President did say "always." But then, that was more than three years ago. For the past two months Perón has authorized, if he has not actively directed, the most widespread and relentless attack on press freedom that modern Argentina has ever seen. In that time his favorite congressional hatchet man, José Emilio Visca, onetime butcher, has closed 58 newspapers and magazines outright. By taking control of the country's chief newsprint stocks he has gained the power of life or death over virtually all the rest of the press.

Only 100% *Peronista* newspapers are safe from zealous Deputy Visca and the congressional committee of investigation that he directs. At first Visca took the trouble to find some legalistic excuse for suspending publication of anti-Perón papers. The last six he shut down without explanation; ten more papers, deprived of newsprint, quietly ceased to appear. As long as President Perón continued to support Congressman Visca, Argentines would be entitled to only such press freedom as Visca cared to give them.

MAY 15   **HAPPY TALK:** "One of these days," President Perón declared last week, "mankind in order to find its guiding star will set its eyes on Argentina. . . . I tell you that Argentina has not one single economic problem of any gravity. Economically we could be the greatest nation in the world!"

CALCULATED RISK: Argentina's energetic little Finance Minis- MAY 22
ter, Ramón Cereijo, bounced aboard his plane at New York's Idlewild Airport one morning last week, and flew homeward with gladsome news. Argentina had been promised $200 million in U.S. Government and private bank credits. If U.S. bankers and Government officials had ever felt reluctant about extending Argentina credit, that feeling had evaporated. The State Department hoped that this economic assistance might also help to make Argentina a better political risk. But that remained to be seen.

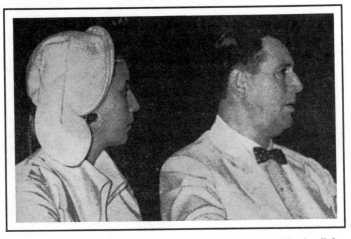

President Juan Perón and wife Evita. Their supporters are "shirtless," but they give her a $42,000 diamond and emerald necklace.

EXIT THE BUTCHER BOY: An old friend of President Juan JUNE 1
Perón's recently returned from a visit to the U.S. and paid a call at government house. Perón asked what the people in North America thought of his regime. "Well, Mr. President," replied the visitor, "they are worried about the lack of freedom in the Argentine press." "What do you mean?" said Perón. "We have freedom of the press. Just look at *La Nación* and *La Prensa*. They attack me all the time. I read them every morning myself." The visitor answered: "This man Vis-

ca you have here has brought lots of bad publicity to Argentina. They say he goes around closing newspapers." Whereupon Perón pressed a button, barked an order through an inter-office microphone: "Get rid of Visca!"

JUNE 26 **FROM THE CRADLE:** Evita Perón told an Argentine governors' conference last week that the country's children are now learning to say "Perón" before they say "Papá."

OCT. 30 **THANKS:** Last week Argentines celebrated the fifth anniversary of Loyalty Day, commemorating Juan Perón's final accession to power. As the high point of a full week of exhibitions, dedications and oratory, 100,000 *descamisados* ("shirtless ones") gathered in Buenos Aires' historic Plaza de Mayo to see Evita Perón accept a glittering necklace of diamonds and emeralds as "a gift from the workers." The bauble was valued at 600,000 pesos ($42,254) and presented on the workers' behalf by the secretary of the General Confederation of Labor, which is bossed by Evita Perón.

DEC. 4 **A MATTER OF RESPECT:** Eight months ago, Radical Party Leader Ricardo Balbín was arrested by *Peronista* police on charges of being "disrespectful" to the President of the Republic. In *Peronista* eyes, the 46-year-old lawyer had added injury to insult when he dared run for governor of Buenos Aires Province against a Perón-backed candidate. Last week he was sentenced to five years in jail.

At no point in the 46-page decision did the judge specify Balbín's offending words or deeds. Balbín recalled speeches in which he had called Perón a "real enemy of the country." But this was no different from what some other Argentine politicians were saying.

In various speeches, Balbín had mentioned another subject —Evita Perón. "The public charities of the President's wife," Balbín once said, "seem to redound to her private good." Observers believed that it was disrespect not so much to the President as to the President's wife that had earned Balbín his harsh sentence.

Prisoner Balbín was not cowed. Said he: "I have no regrets. I would say what I said again. I am less a prisoner than those on the outside."

Austria

Austria was still being occupied in 1950 by troops from the U.S., the Soviet Union, Great Britain and France (they did not leave until 1955). Because of the Cold War, the situation was ripe for intrigue, and Vienna was a hotbed of cloak-and-dagger activity.

MURDER ON THE EXPRESS?: After three years as U.S. naval MARCH (attaché in Rumania, genial Captain Eugene ("Fish") Karpe, 45, was on his way home for reassignment. At Vienna he boarded the blue-and-gold *Arlberg-Orient Express* for Paris. A touch of gout caused him to limp a bit as he climbed aboard the train, but otherwise, Fish Karpe seemed his usual relaxed and cheerful self.

The *Arlberg-Orient* is one of the Continent's glamour trains, a storied track for international diplomats and intrigue. Karpe had Compartment 11 of the Bucharest sleeper. There were six other passengers in the car, including Secretary John Oliver Wright II, of the British legation in Bucharest, Mrs. Wright, a king's messenger (diplomatic courier) and his military guard.

At Salzburg, Karpe chatted on the platform with friends who had come to say goodbye. A small, shifty-eyed stranger lolled in the background, staring at Karpe and listening to the talk. Shortly after 12:30 p.m. the *Arlberg* pulled out of Salzburg.

Fifteen minutes later the Wrights saw Captain Karpe walking forward to the diner. He drank only a bottle of seltzer water, then left the table. Neither the Wrights, the king's messenger nor the messenger's guard saw Karpe return to Compartment 11. "I would have seen him," said the guard. "I kept the door of my compartment open to watch the girls pass by—it's an old habit."

At ten minutes past 2 p.m., a railway repairman found Karpe's mangled, dismembered body scattered along the track in Lueg Pass tunnel, not far out of Salzburg. Had he fallen or been thrown from the train? U.S. Army occupation police said that they found no specific evidence of "foul play." On the other hand, U.S. Intelligence officers thought that it was murder. On the dead man's body were his diplomatic passport, personal papers, $180, and a silver cigarette lighter that had belonged to his friend Robert Vogeler, the American businessman who was jailed as a spy by Communist Hungary. In his compartment, luggage and attaché case were intact. No signs of struggle were evident.

Austrians sensed something more than accident in Karpe's death. "POLITICAL MURDER IN LUEG TUNNEL," cried a Salzburg headline. Dr. Wilhelm Gugl noticed almost no blood on the spot where Karpe was supposedly dashed to death. Had the American been killed before his body fell into the tunnel? His remains were so mangled that an autopsy was useless.

Vienna's diplomatic circles looked on Karpe as no ordinary attaché. He had unusual intelligence contacts. Possibly he had information regarding Russia's spring plans for dealing with Tito. One American, with long experience in central Europe, speculated:

"Karpe's death could be an integral part of the cold war. An international train passing through the wild mountain country of U.S.-occupied Austria could be the perfect place to murder a diplomat who had probed too deeply behind the Iron Curtain." [The mystery was never solved.]

Belgium

Ever since the end of the war the Belgians had been without a king. Leopold III, who was on the throne when the Germans overran Belgium, had surrendered his troops to the Germans and had been imprisoned by the Nazis. His countrymen were furious that he had not fled Belgium and joined its government in exile. Nevertheless, Leopold was anxious to resume the throne after the war. Belgians were sharply divided. The Dutch-speaking Flemings were for him; the French-speaking Walloons were against him, as was the powerful Belgian Socialist party. Many Belgians hoped to solve the problem—and unite the country—by turning the throne over to Leopold's 19-year-old son Baudouin. But the King was adamant and preferred to risk a national referendum on whether he or his son would sit on the throne.

A KING RETURNS: The Socialists insisted that the return of JULY 31 King Leopold III to Belgium would mean revolution. When the Social Christians, with their absolute majority won in the recent election, called for a vote in Parliament, 139 Socialists, 38 Liberals and ten Communists walked out. The vote was 198 to 0 for the recall of Leopold.

Last Saturday Leopold flew back to Belgium in a military transport plane. Few of his subjects were on hand to greet him. The airfield and the roads nearby were guarded by 10,000 soldiers, blackhelmeted gendarmes armed with carbines, and squads of special police in riot cars. In a broadcast to the nation Leopold said: "I address a solemn appeal to you for concord. . . . Whatever additional tests the future can impose on me, this role will be mine."

Moderates who had hoped that the King would clear the air by abdicating in favor of Prince Baudouin were disappointed. The broadcast had the tone of a king who wanted to be king.

TEMPORARY RETREAT: Half of Belgium last week rose against AUG. 7 King Leopold III, who had returned to the throne the week before. More than half a million workers walked out in a general strike called by Paul-Henri Spaak's Socialist Party. In a Liège suburb, gendarmes tried to break up a strikers' meeting. When the strikers resisted, the gendarmes opened fire, killing three and wounding two, including the burgomaster.

Leopold agreed verbally to delegate his powers to his son, Prince Baudouin, and to abdicate in September 1951, when Baudouin will become 21. When this agreement was handed to Leopold for his signature, he at first balked, but later consented.

PRINCE ROYAL: *So you are the King. Dull work at your age,* AUG. *eh?*—Bernard Shaw, *Caesar and Cleopatra.*

At 19, Belgium's Prince Baudouin last week assumed the dull duties (though not yet the full pomps) of kingship. In Brussels, the Parliament voted to accept King Leopold III's offer to stand down from the throne; Baudouin would become "Prince Royal" and act as regent until his 21st birthday, then become king.

Later that day, lanky, bespectacled Baudouin drove to Parliament. Entering the Chamber, he had difficulty managing his sword and fumbled the salutes. That evening, the new regent got down to work and began consultations with political leaders to select a Premier. His father, meanwhile, who had so desperately wanted to be King of the Belgians, stayed at gloomy Laeken palace, a virtual prisoner.

The Cameroons

FEB. 20 **SOCIAL SECURITY:** Was it fitting & proper for the Fon (King) of Bikom to have as many wives as he liked? The U.N. has been burdened with this question since July 1948 when St. Joan's Social and Political Alliance of London (a Roman Catholic lay organization dedicated to women's rights) presented a complaint concerning plural marriage in the British Cameroons. One missionary, said the complaint, had reported that the Fon had 600 wives, charged that he had taken one girl to his harem by force. Last year the U.N. Trusteeship Council sent a visiting mission off to West Africa to investigate. Last week the mission sent in its report of the Fon:

"Probably more than 80 years of age [he himself claims to be more than 100], he is now in a stage when he can take a lenient view of this interference in what he might regard as his private affairs." But the Fon pointed out that he did not deliver opinions upon the peculiar habits of Christian society; why, then, had the outside world taken exception to his own tribe's age-old customs? In his capacity as King of all Kom Villages, Rainmaker, Custodian of the Tribal Lands and Link between the Dead, the Living and the Unborn, it was his job to see that tradition was preserved.

Furthermore, by latest census, the Fon has only 110 wives, not 600. Forty-four of them are very old ladies whom he inherited from his predecessor. The U.N. investigators found no case where a girl had been forced into marriage. The wives of the aged Fon had only one regret: he was too old to sire any more children.

"Plural marriage in Bikom," the U.N. mission report concluded, ". . . is a type of social security which will have to remain until Western civilization through education convinces the Africans that other ways are better."

Canada

SOME PEOPLE ARE SENSITIVE: In a high-school classroom APRIL 3 one night last week a group of Ottawa's retail store clerks listened attentively to the first in a series of lectures, sponsored by the Ottawa Board of Trade, on a delicate subject: how to captivate tourists. Above all, Ottawans ought to take care when driving through puddles not to splash pedestrians. "The people you splash might be tourists," the lecturer warned, "and tourists are highly insulted when splashed."

THE SUMMER'S TALES: Summer waxed strong across Canada AUG. 7 last week and garrulous anglers were telling new fictions to prove an old fact about fishing. Samples:

¶ William Bauer of Kingston, Ont. caught a 32-inch pike, but that was not all. Inside the pike was a large-mouthed bass, inside the bass a perch and inside the perch a minnow.

¶ A fisherman in Port Arthur, Ont. claimed a double strike on his two-hook line. A fish grabbed one hook, a bat gobbled the other. The intrepid angler landed both fish & foul.

¶ While eating lunch on Manitoba's Brereton Lake, Jim Turner of Winnipeg let an orange slip overboard. Before he could recover it the fruit disappeared. A few minutes later, Turner heard a violent threshing in the reeds near shore, rowed over and gaffed a northern pike that was slowly choking to death with an orange stuck in its throat.

PROGRESS REPORT: On a speaking trip to the U.S. last week, OCT. 30 Canada's Finance Minister Douglas Abbott had a confession to make: "Our public men have failed to tell our story in your country. Today I intend to cast aside any restraining influence of modesty and talk to you unblushingly of the virtual transformation which has been wrought in the Canadian economy within the past ten years."

The story Abbott had to tell was a tale of rapid expansion and booming prosperity. A few of the transformations:

¶ Population rose from some 11 million in 1939 to nearly 14 million, a gain of almost 25%.

¶ Gross national production climbed from $5½ billion in 1939 to nearly $17 billion.

¶ Exports were up 200%.

China

Within a year after Mao Tse-tung had set up his Communist regime on the mainland, the Nationalists under Chiang Kai-shek were holed up on the two large islands they had retreated to—Formosa and Hainan.

JAN. 30 **IF THEY HAVE THE HEART:** Tiny, thin-faced General Hsueh Yueh is known as Nationalist China's Little Tiger. Thrice he clawed the Japanese at Changsha in 1941. Now, on tropical Hainan, the Little Tiger watches the weather with a prayerful eye. It is the season for fogs. This season they could cover a Communist invasion armada.

So far the fog has held off. Every day the small Nationalist air force roars from the black-topped airstrip at Haikow across Hainan Strait to drop bombs and leaflets on the mainland. The Communists are smarting. "Landing operations," admitted a recently captured Red field order, "may be delayed."

One old Hainan hand, a foreigner who has lived on the island for 25 years, gives the Little Tiger and his men credit:: "If they have the heart to fight, these troops could make it tough for the Communists."

Tough or not, it is only a matter of time before the Reds strike.

MAY 1 **HAINAN FALLS:** Six months after he had conquered the South China mainland, Red General Lin Piao was ready for the over-water jump to Hainan. Unlike Nationalist China's other island, Formosa, which lies 100 deep-water miles from the Red-held coast, Hainan has only a narrow channel (15 miles) separating it from the continental shore. Behind a thin shield of gunboats and planes, Nationalist General Hsueh Yueh had tried to pull together Hainan's army of 160,000, mostly remnants of the south China retreat.

Early last week, under cover of night, a fleet of Red junks crossed the channel southwest of Hoihow. The Nationalist press claimed a victory after the first four days—6,000 Reds captured, up to 4,000 killed, the invasion assault blocked. In

Hoihow, firecrackers popped jubilantly. Next day the celebration fizzled. The Communists had won again. On the sixth day after making their beachhead, the men of Lin Piao's army marched triumphantly into Hoihow.

It was more than just another chunk of territory (about twice the size of New Jersey, 3,000,000 population) for the vast Red Asiatic domain. It furnished further proof that Nationalist troops still could not or would not fight effectively. More than 400 miles to the northeast, in Formosa, invasion day for Nationalist China's last citadel seemed closer.

INVASION SEASON: May, June, July and August are the best MAY 22 months for an invasion of Formosa. During the rest of the year weather conditions, including typhoons, protect the island. This summer, then, may bring an event to which the U.S. has already officially resigned itself—the Communist conquest of Formosa.

Chiang Kai-shek. His troops face the season of Communist invasion.

Communist General Lin Piao captures one of Chiang's islands. Page 127.

Formosa represents the greatest irony in Asia today. Here, in its last refuge, Chiang Kai-shek's government has shed the chaos and despair of the mainland, and, at least temporarily, appears to be leading an almost serene and even well-managed existence. This rich, green, formerly Japanese-ruled island is a spot of unaccustomed order. The Nationalist government has pulled itself into presentable shape.

The exact strength of Nationalist troops on Formosa is a military secret, but including some 60,000 to 80,000 troops who arrived last week after the abandonment of Hainan Island, the island's defensive force probably numbers around 400,000. There is some indication that it is a better force than the dispirited Nationalist armies that lost the mainland.

What do the Nationalists now ask of the U.S.? First of all, further economic aid and also military aid. Chiang Kai-shek's formula: "The U.S. should match the forms of aid given to the Communists by Soviet Russia. We do not expect more than what the Soviet is giving." This would imply everything up to jet planes manned by American pilots.

What about this durable and much-debated personality, the Generalissimo, now that he has taken back the presidency? Chiang, now 64, has done nothing to revive himself as a hero; if he is a reviving force, it is because the Communists have made him so. Most impressive are the younger men far beneath the stature of Chiang—earnest Chinese who still seem to want to save their people from Communism. They are the men who cannot escape; they have no place else to go. Somewhere along the ragged route of failure, the U.S. rightly or wrongly assumed a moral obligation to these younger Chinese. The look of a hungry friend is in their eyes now.

Egypt

AN. 9 **"THY BROTHER'S BETROTHED":** Egypt's King Farouk, 29, who recently divorced Farida ("Peerless"), was getting ready to marry again. The most reliable account of how this came to pass:

Narriman Sadek, 16, daughter of a civil servant, has been betrothed for the past five years to Zaki Hachem, 27, a Harvard-trained economic aide to the United Nations Secretariat. Narriman and Zaki had set their wedding day for Dec. 8, and went shopping for a ring at the Cairo store of Ahmed Nagib Pasha. Ahmed, who in his spare time helps out Farouk with new telephone numbers, told the young couple to come back next day. His Majesty hustled down to size up Ahmed's

King Farouk. He sized up Narriman from a hidden balcony.

Narriman Sadek cancels her wedding to please the king.

find from a concealed balcony. Narriman, beautiful to look upon, Farouk decided, was for him.

Since that moment she has not been allowed to leave her home, where she is being tutored in court etiquette as she waits for Farouk to name the day. Her wedding to Zaki, which had been hailed by Cairo society editors as "the wedding of the year," has, of course, been called off. Zaki charges that his apartment has been entered by Farouk's agents and that all letters and pictures of Narriman have been stolen.

Farouk's advisers are worried over the King's public flouting of the ancient command: "Thou shalt not usurp thy brother's betrothed." By censoring the Egyptian press, the government for years has tried to conceal Farouk's way of life and other noxious matter lying beneath Cairo's glitter. The King, however, will not cooperate in concealment; his private life is about as private as the Pyramids.

Zaki, at first stunned, is now furious, and prudently dosing himself with sedatives to keep himself quiet. "I will marry no one else," he says. "I still love Narriman, and I know she still loves me. I did not think such things could happen in the 20th Century. Now I know better." [Farouk married Narriman in May 1951, was deposed by a military coup in 1952. They had one son, were divorced in 1954. Farouk died in exile in 1965.]

Greece

Occupied by Italian and German troops in World War II and almost taken over by Communist guerrillas after the war, Greece finally won its battle against the Reds in 1949 with the help of economic and military aid from the United States under the Truman Doctrine. During the war thousands of Greek children between the ages of three and 14 had been taken away from their parents and sent to neighboring Communist countries for political indoctrination. Many of them never returned.

JAN. 9 **INNOCENTS' DAY:** Peace had come to battered, impoverished Greece; the Communist guerrillas had been driven out, perhaps for good. But last week, on Innocents' Day (the Church calendar's anniversary of Herod's Slaughter of the Innocents in Judea), Greece had a day of mourning—for 28,000 children abducted by the bandits and now living on foreign Communist soil.

Earnest young Queen Frederika, mother of three, broadcast a poignant message from the royal palace. She begged for the return of the 28,000—"as a mother, because queens are not supposed to beg." Added Frederika: "The civilized world has remained silent too long."

In the palace with Frederika was a group of black-clad peasant women huddled at her side. Kaliroe Gouloumi, from Gorgopotamos, in Epirus, remembered how the Communists took her children: "They were in our village for a year. First they took our animals, then our food, then our children. I had three." Kaliroe wiped her eyes with her black shawl. "They did not even let me say goodbye. They said they were no longer my children but their children."

In Fourka Konitsa, the villagers learned in advance of the guerrillas' abduction plans. They hid the children in ditches. The guerrillas, frustrated, took Sofia Makri and 20 other mothers to the mountains and tortured them. Said Sofia last week: "They hung us from pine trees. They burned our feet with coals. They beat us. When we fainted they revived us with cold water from the spring. Fourteen of us died up there but we did not tell. When the Greek army entered our village they found the dead living, for out of the earth came our children."

There is no evidence that the Greek children living in Communist countries are physically abused. International Red Cross investigators have seen some of the children and reported that they are well fed. They are being schooled as young Communists and they are expected to feel and show enthusiasm. Said a U.N. delegate in despair: "In ten years there will be no abducted Greek children; they will have been absorbed."

WAR & WORK: For years, when they were hungry, Greeks had JAN. 16 been told by their government: "It is the war. The fighting has destroyed the crops. Things will be better when we have peace." This year, the Greeks had peace. Peasants plowed their fields, and new houses went up amid the rubble. Of Greece's 700,000 refugees, 500,000 have returned to their old homes, with a $35 government bonus in their pockets, free bread rations, and (if they were lucky) a "Baby Truman"— as the peasants call the large frisky mules which ECA [Economic Cooperation Administration] has brought from the U.S.

But Greece's long-deferred hopes were still far from fulfillment. The country's administration is flabby and corrupt; despite ECAid, its economy is semi-paralyzed by public distrust. Recently, when a Greek businessman sought ECA backing for a gold-mining project in Macedonia, an ECA official snapped: "The best place to dig for gold in Greece is in people's mattresses." The imprint of war still remains heavy on the land—and even on the language. A Greek washerwoman, bent over her heaped sink, will say: "I am making war on the laundry." A driver sprawling underneath his truck will say: "I am at war with the engine." After nine years of invasion, occupation and civil war, *polemen* (to make war) in colloquial Greek has replaced *ergazer* (to work).

Hungary

FRIGHTENED FACE: For the first time Budapest's Red regime FEB. was trying its tactics on Anglo-American businessmen and their alleged Hungarian associates [by trying them as spies]. Among them stood an American, handsome Robert Vogeler, 38, a graduate of Annapolis and M.I.T. He had come to Hungary in 1948 as U.S. representative of the International Telephone & Telegraph Corp. Friends knew him as a skilled sportsman (fencer, marksman, skier, golfer) and a gay companion.

One day last November, Bob Vogeler stepped from Budapest's Hotel Astoria and into his black Buick sedan, intending to drive to Vienna to see his pretty, blond wife Lucile and their two children. He never made it. Secret police hauled him off as a spy. For three months, Vogeler lay in a Budapest jail, denied counsel or bail, while the U.S. ineffectually protested.

Beside the American stood his British assistant, once debonair Edgar Sanders; a Hungarian barmaid, Edina Dory, who had worked as an I.T. & T. switchboard operator; a Hungarian official of I.T. & T., Imre Geiger; and three more Hungarians accused of complicity in the "spy ring."

Dressed in neat black with a clean white handkerchief in his pocket, Vogeler took the stand. He stood for almost three hours facing the judges. "Bob is a nervous, quick-moving, high-strung guy," said one of his close friends later. "He could no more stand calmly and confess than he could fly to the moon." Nevertheless, Vogeler stood almost motionless before the court and, in a voice as monotonous as the drone of a litany, confessed to having plotted against the Red regime. His answers were so ready that he interrupted the judge in mid-question. He even used the penitential kind of phrase coined by Red inquisitors: "I am sorry for the detrimental deeds that I have committed."

Judge Olti nodded, at last directed the prisoner to sit down. As Vogeler turned to find his chair, the spectators saw for the first time the face of the American who had been confined, friendless and isolated, under nameless dread and threat, for three months in a Red Hungarian jail.

"It looked," said one American correspondent, "like the face of a frightened rabbit. He was scanning the courtroom as if trying in vain to catch the eye of another American."

This week Hangman Olti pronounced sentence: for Bob Vogeler, whose country was not even powerful enough to get him a lawyer, 15 years; for Sanders, 13 years; for Geiger and another Hungarian, death. [Vogeler was later released and returned to the U.S. in 1951. He recanted his confession.]

RUM: Hungary's socialized candy industry last week polled APRIL 10 "elite schoolchildren" to find out just how to flavor the new "Elite Pupil" candy bar (target for the first year of the Five-Year Plan: 1,000,000). The children sampled bars of orange, vanilla and rum flavors. The country kids liked vanilla; those in Budapest, rum. So there will be two kinds. Said a Communist official of the candy trust: "Candies are no longer the monopoly of the wealthy capitalist children."

SURRENDER: One year and a half after Joseph Cardinal SEPT. 11 Mindszenty went to prison, for refusing to come to terms with the Communists, Hungary's Roman Catholic bishops gave in to the Red regime. In exchange for recognition and "support" by the church, the Hungarian state promised to support the church financially for the next 18 years, to guarantee "complete freedom of religion," and to return to the church eight parochial schools it had closed.

Why did the bishops surrender after two years of valiant resistance? Because the alternative would have been complete liquidation of the church in Hungary. Last June the Communists showed that they would stop at nothing when they raided Catholic monasteries and convents, imprisoned monks and nuns by the thousands. Soon afterwards the bishops started to negotiate. They had decided that a church with some liberties, however limited, was preferable to no church at all.

"NOTHING WAS LEFT": One week after the Hungarian Com- SEPT. 18 munist government had announced the signing of a church-state agreement, a government decree directed all but four Roman Catholic religious orders to suspend their activities. Ten thousand nuns and monks in 59 orders were given three months to get out of their monasteries and return to secular life. Said the bishops in a pastoral letter read in Budapest churches last Sunday: "We were deeply afflicted, and nothing was left to us but to protest."

HURRAH FOR STALIN!: Telephone operators at the Budapest OCT. 16 exchange were instructed last week to answer calls with: "*El-*

jen Sztalin, kivel ohajt beszelni? (Hurrah for Stalin, to whom do you wish to speak?)"

DEC. 18 **LOCKSTEP:** The Budapest monthly *Muvelt Nep* (Cultured People) laid out for its readers the Hungarian Communist line on dancing. The waltz and polka are "traditionally democratic." The tango, fox trot and English waltz, though "reflections of the capitalist decline . . . cannot be classed with American dances. They may now be danced with taste." But the samba, swing, boogie-woogie, rumba, conga and the like "are tools of aggression let loose by the bosses of America against human culture and progress."

However, warned *Muvelt Nep* Hungarian youth need not react by dancing "in overalls and with a hammer clenched in the hand." That would be "leftist deviationism."

India

FEB. 6 **REPUBLIC DAY:** A sovereign democratic republic, in the Hindi language, is *Sampoorna Prabhutva Sampanna Lokatantratmaka Ganarajya.* Last week, that is what India became. After weeks of work, laborers with chisels and paintbrushes had managed to remove hundreds of British crowns from furni-

President Prasad and Prime Minister Nehru. They order the British crown chiseled from buildings as India becomes a sovereign republic.

ture, doorways and walls of New Delhi's great sandstone Government House. The words "Royal" and "His Majesty's" had been taken off mailboxes, trucks and ships.

India was breaking her last symbolic bonds to Britain [which had granted India independence in 1947]. Declaring Jan. 26 Republic Day, the government gathered in New Delhi's Durbar Hall to inaugurate its new constitution and install its first President, 65-year-old Rajendra Prasad. Pandit Jawaharlal Nehru was sworn in as Prime Minister.

In the afternoon, President Prasad drove five miles through New Delhi's cheering streets. The magnificent viceregal coach (with crowns removed) was drawn by six horses, and escorted by the mounted viceregal bodyguard, in scarlet tunics and flowing rainbow turbans. Said an observer: "This show is more British than the British would ever dare be."

Not all of India, however, rejoiced on Republic Day. In Calcutta, three people were killed when police fired on a Communist demonstration. In Bombay, scores were injured during a Red-provoked riot. In Hyderabad, the Nizam barely escaped injury when a hand grenade thrown at his car failed to explode. And in Madras, a government spokesman announced that the specter of famine "is already sitting on a million thresholds."

TWILIGHT OF THE PRINCES: "Need we cavil at the small price MARCH we have paid for a bloodless revolution which has affected the destinies of millions of our peoples?" With this eloquent plea, Deputy Prime Minister Vallabhbhai Patel last year won over reluctant Congressmen to his plan for pensioning off India's princes. In return, the princes peacefully turned over their 587,888 square miles and 88 million subjects to republican administration. Last week in a white paper, Patel's Ministry of States disclosed the "small price": 56 million rupees (some $2,600,000) a year in "purses" paid out to 283 princes.

The price was low, at that. The princes have not only taken a 75% cut in income, they have also surrendered to the government at least 700 million rupees' worth of securities, palaces and lands.

BLOOD FOR BLOOD: A few weeks ago, Pakistan's Prime Minister Liaquat Ali Khan and India's Jawaharlal Nehru were APRIL hurling threats of war at each other. This week, the Pakistan-India crisis had grown so grave that it was no longer possible for responsible men to talk carelessly. Rioting between Hindus and Moslems had broken out again in Bengal. There was more burning and looting than killing, but the pattern was frighteningly like that of 1947, when over 200,000 Moslems and Hindus were killed.

In Calcutta, Hindu sidewalk orators, telling wild stories of atrocities against refugees, urged the people to "avenge" their Hindu brothers in Pakistan. Shouting "Blood for blood," Hindu mobs rushed through the city burning, looting and killing.

Even Europeans, usually not molested in communal troubles, were not safe. Alexander Leslie Cameron, 49, president of the Bengal Chamber of Commerce, and one of the leading British businessmen in India, tried to protect a friend's Moslem bearer from a mob, was himself beaten to death.

Calcutta's riots were one more triumph for the extremist Hindu Mahasabha Party, which opposes Nehru, accuses him of appeasing Pakistan. It would take all the skill that Nehru and (Pakistan Prime Minister) Liaquat Ali Khan could muster to bring peace out of the terror that stalked Bengal.

DEC. 4 **"HAVEN'T WE MET?":** Kalimpong, a zany Indian town straddling a ridge in the Himalayan foothills, is only 30 miles from Tibet. For that reason, Kalimpong has collected over the years a number of mystical characters—foreign cultists, scholars, artists, adventurers and missionaries—who plod Kalimpong's streets, panting to explore Tibet, but lacking permission to get in. Last week, as they have since the Chinese Reds invaded Tibet in October, Kalimpongians waited breathlessly to welcome the Dalai Lama should he flee from Lhasa into their midst, as his predecessor did in 1910. The town had one big worry. Would the Tibetan God-King bring enough sheets? In 1910 frenzied devotees of Buddhism kept ripping the exalted exile's linen to bits to preserve as sacred objects, along with dust from his room and his holy bath water.

Kalimpong's main social center is the Himalayan Hotel. In the dining room recently, a Buddhist Englishwoman thought she recognized another woman guest. "I beg your pardon," she said, "but haven't we met in a previous incarnation?"

"Yes," was the reply, "I believe we have. I was Joan of Arc and you were my brother." The Englishwoman drew herself up haughtily. "Certainly not," she snapped. "I have never been a male in any of my previous incarnations."

Indonesia

OVER THE FENCE: In Amsterdam's Royal Palace one morning JAN. 9 last week, 335 frock-coated Dutch and Indonesian officials gathered around a green baize table to hear Juliana, Queen of the Netherlands, end 340 years of Dutch rule in Indonesia. From her crimson-upholstered armchair, she spoke clearly and melodiously: "Immeasurable," said she, "is the satisfaction of a nation that finds its liberty realized. . . ."

Just before noon of the day after Queen Juliana's announcement, two C-47s bearing Indonesian President Soekarno and his official party swept over Jakarta from the mountains of central Java. Soekarno, whom most Indonesians regard as the personification of independence, had been driven from Jakarta by the Dutch almost exactly four years ago.

Almost as soon as Soekarno arrived at the palace, a torrent of Indonesians surged through the gates onto the lawn. Others enthusiastically kicked the slats from a wooden picket fence and poured in unchecked. In a matter of minutes, the sprawling, mile-wide Koningsplein in front of the palace was an unbroken expanse of brown faces.

"*Sudara, sudara*, brothers," said Soekarno. "Be quiet. Thanks to God Almighty, today after four years I have again set foot on the earth of Jakarta."

"*Merdeka*," the crowd thundered, "*Tetap merdeka* (Freedom, Freedom forever)!" One foreign diplomat waved in the direction of the crowds and said to a colleague: "Could the Dutch ever have held this, in the face of that?"

THE MAGIC SCISSORS: The black financial magic by which MARCH governments raise or lower the value of their currencies amid incantations of economic mumbo-jumbo is apt to baffle all but the most sophisticated spectators. But last week the government of "backward" Indonesia, whose guilder was badly inflated, devised an ingeniously simple new method, that anyone could grasp, for letting the air out of their currency. Indonesian Finance Minister Sjafruddin Prawiranegara ordered Indonesians to get out their scissors and cut in half their paper money above five guilders.

The left halves of the banknotes will be legal tender at half their face value until April 9. Then they are to be turned in for a new currency, worth half of the old. The right halves will, "in due time," be redeemable for 3% government bonds. All the Indonesians needed now was scissors and some money —and a great many of them had neither.

Mexico

APRIL 3 **PIES IN THE SKY:** In Mexico City's bustling Barrio Santa Maria, a huge crowd gathered, staring intently up into the sky. Darío Moctezuma joined the skygazers, but complained that he could see nothing. An obliging stranger threw an arm around his shoulder, pointed up—and sure enough, Darío thought he discerned a white globelike shape floating by. When his gaze returned earthward, he saw the stranger disappearing around the corner. Darío slapped the pocket where his wallet had been and began to yell: "*Polícia, polícia!*"

All over Mexico last week, pickpockets, adding a hypermodern wrinkle to their ancient profession, did a booming trade among crowds gathered to scan the skies for *plativolos* (flying saucers). For the saucer-hysteria that still flickers occasionally in the U.S. was sweeping Mexico.

Others besides pickpockets made hay while the *plativolos* shone. A chiropractor advertised: "Stiff neck from looking at the saucers? Come and see me for a massage."

NOV. 27 **SLOAN & BILL:** When American Airlines Flight 157 wheeled up to the customs shed at Mexico City's airport one day last week, a *mariachi* band struck up *Guadalajara*. Then smiling Sloan Simpson O'Dwyer, wife of the 41st U.S. envoy to Mexico, appeared in the plane's doorway. Ambassador William O'Dwyer followed her.

Bill O'Dwyer seemed a happy choice for a sunny job. Mexicans were complimented by his political prominence in the U.S., pleased that he is a Catholic, and tickled with his pretty

U.S. Ambassador William O'Dwyer and his wife, ex-model Sloan Simpson. Mexico likes him because he likes bullfights.

wife and his appreciation of bullfighting. Said a *torero*: "A good fan of the bulls cannot be an imperialist."

[O'Dwyer had served as Mayor of New York City from 1946 to 1950, when he resigned after a local grand jury began investigating gambling and police corruption. A widower, he had married ex-model Sloan Simpson, a divorcée, in Florida in 1949. She was granted a divorce in Mexico in 1953. O'Dwyer died in 1964.]

Nepal

SRI[3] WINS AGAIN: In 1846 the reigning monarch of Nepal was NOV. 20 Rajendra Bikram Sahi, a blue-blooded Rajput (Hindu warrior caste) and a descendant of Vishnu the Lifesaver. For all that, the King was nuttier than a pecan tree in October. He and the Queen persuaded one of their generals, Jung Bahadur Rana, to murder their Prime Minister, who happened to be the general's uncle. Then Jung Bahadur helped the King murder the Queen's lover and obligingly helped the Queen kill 55 nobles and 500 lesser folk whom she had assembled. The Queen was so pleased that she made Jung Bahadur Prime Minister. He knew what to do next. He exiled the King and Queen and put their minor son on the throne.

Since then, as anyone would expect, the Kings of Nepal have been Kings in name only, and the Ranas have been hereditary Prime Ministers. They have made a good thing of it. Half of Nepal's $10,000,000 state revenue finds its way to the Rana family.

Languishing in obscurity, the Kings retained the right to throw barley grains to the people on festival days, and they continued to bear the honorary title Sri Sri Sri Sri Sri (Sri means "Mr.") which is sometimes written Sri[5]. The Rana Prime Ministers bear the lesser title Sri Sri Sri, or Sri[3].

The present King, Sri Sri Sri Sri Sri Tribhubana Bir Bikram Jung Bahadur Shah Bahadur Shum Shere Jung Deva, came to the throne in 1911 when he was five. Little is known of him except that he is said to be able to ride two horses at the same time, one foot on each. Also, he married two sisters on the same day.

Of his public life, even less was known until December, 1948, when Loy W. Henderson went to Nepal as the first U.S. diplomatic representative to that kingdom. Prime Minister Rana was somewhat embarrassed to learn that Minister Henderson bore a letter from President Truman addressed to the King, in person. After due deliberation, Rana decided that the privilege of getting letters from Harry Truman be added to barley-throwing and being called Sri[5]. A TIME correspondent who accompanied the U.S. mission noticed that the King seemed very shy, as if he had not been allowed to associate with many people his own age (45).

Whatever his Rana-enforced limitations, the King is the hero of the anti-Rana Nepal Congress Party, which seeks to establish a constitutional monarchy. Recently, leaders of this party moved in from India, stepped up their agitation against the Ranas. When a plot to assassinate the Prime Minister was thwarted, the King asked Prime Minister Rana for permission to leave the country. Sri[3] refused to let Sri[5] go into exile. The King, with some of his jewels and both of his wives, sneaked into the Indian embassy, claimed the right to asylum.

At the request of India's Sri[1] Nehru, Sri[3] finally agreed to let the Indian government send in two planes to pick up Sri[5] and friends. When they landed at New Delhi, Nehru came out to meet the plane and a red carpet was rolled out. Watching their beaten King fly away, the good people of Kathmandu could shake their turbaned heads and murmur the Nepalese equivalent for: "They never come back."

Puerto Rico

Luis Muñoz Marín had been elected governor of the territory of Puerto Rico in 1948 in its first free popular gubernatorial election. He opposed the idea of Puerto Rican independence, and this stand resulted in an attempt by extremists to assassinate the governor in San Juan and President Truman in Washington. Muñoz Marín was re-elected governor in 1952 after Puerto Rico was granted Commonwealth status.

INSURRECTION: One morning last week, a green sedan rolled NOV. 13 into the palm-shaded cobblestone square before San Juan's Fortaleza, the 300-year-old residence of Governor Luis Muñoz Marín. Out of the car burst six members of Puerto Rico's desperate little Nationalist Party. Armed with pistols, rifles and a machine gun, they sprinted for the palace entrance. Yelling *"Viva Puerto Rico libre,"* one Nationalist got off a wild submachine-gun burst. From the arcade, from parapets, from rooftops, guards poured fire down on the attackers.

Dust and chips flew as bullets rattled off the old Spanish walls. One attacker got as far as the portico. There he fell, sieved by bullets. Another, hit a dozen times, moaned: "I'm already dead. Please don't shoot me any more." The answer was another blast of fire. Of the six Nationalist attackers, four died, another was badly wounded, the sixth taken prisoner.

That was the first sign of trouble stirring in the U.S.'s tiny (3,435 sq. mi.), poverty-stricken Caribbean territory—trouble which quickly spread to the steps of President Truman's residence in Washington.

Soon violence erupted in a blaze of gunfire all over the island. Seventy Nationalists seized the town of Jayuya, killing four policemen, firing the post office, police station, Selective Service headquarters and 20 homes. In Ponce, Mayaguez, Utuado, half a dozen other towns, Nationalists attacked police stations.

From San Juan, Governor Muñoz Marín called out the National Guard. In scores of sharp, bloody little battles, the guardsmen hunted down the terrorists with bazookas, tanks and planes. By the end of the second day, Governor Muñoz could report that Puerto Rico's worst uprising since the U.S. took over the island from Spain in 1898 seemed well under control. When police cornered diehard Nationalist Chief Pedro Albizu Campos, 59, in his San Juan headquarters, Governor Muñoz Marín ordered the besiegers to move cautiously. He wanted to cast no cloak of martyrdom over the Nationalists' hero.

Before the uprising, even Puerto Rican police had no real conception of the Nationalists' full, fanatic plans. They had begun to look on sickly, *yanqui*-hating Pedro Albizu Campos as no more than a noisy reminder of the days when "independence" was the rallying cry of all diehard Caribbean extremists.

Most Puerto Ricans had come to realize that independence, with the accompanying loss of tariff advantages and tax refunds, would be economic suicide. And in recent years, Puerto Rico had won more & more self-rule. Last weekend, just before the rebellious Nationalists struck, the islanders were to register for a plebiscite, preparing the way for a constitution they would write themselves.

By week's end the island's calm was restored and Puerto Ricans showed authoritatively what they thought of Albizu Campos' Nationalist terrorism. In even greater numbers than in the election year of 1948, they turned out to register for the vote on a constitution reaffirming self-rule, but keeping for themselves the rights and privileges of U.S. citizens.

Spain

JAN. 16 **LOVE IN THE AFTERNOON:** Take a haughty old duke, his love-sick daughter and her forbidden lover, a handsome bullfighter, and the cast is complete for one of Spain's beloved zarzuelas (romantic operettas). In this case, the duke was Carlos Pérez Soane de Pino Hermoso (beautiful pine), a grandee of Spain. One of his three daughters, Angelita, was a willowy, dark-eyed 19, a chip off the old pine. About a year ago she met Luis Miguel González, who is called Dominguín and is one of Spain's most highly regarded matadors. It was love at first sight.

When the duke caught on, he cut Dominguín from his guest list. The duke ordered that Angelita be watched closely during the day, locked in a third-floor room every night. At dawn one morning, Angelita tied bedsheets together and slid to freedom. A few minutes later, she was in Dominguín's arms.

Next morning, the enraged duke swore he would kill Dominguín. Instead, he called the police. They arrested Dominguín. Angelita was found in a hiding place. "Mind you," the duke explained, "I like Dominguín. He has the heart of a lion and the legs of a deer. What's more, he will probably end up much richer than I am. But there is one thing I simply cannot change—his family."

Bullfighter Dominguín. He must leave the duke's daughter alone.

The Duchess of Valencia. She keeps a kit packed for prison.

Last week, the duke prepared to send Angelita on a tour of the Middle East. Sorrowful, but determined to renew his suit when possible, Dominguín boarded a plane for Venezuela, where he will fight bulls. Most zarzuelas have happy endings. For Dominguín and Angelita no happy ending was in sight until Angelita reached the age of 21. [Dominguín eventually married another girl.]

MARCH 6 **ROUNDUP:** The bells of Madrid's venerable Town Hall pealed out a quarter to midnight. In front of the unpretentious apartment house at No. 10 Calle de la Vega the night watchman clanked a ring of keys, then unlocked the door for a party of four plainclothesmen. The visitors walked up the stairs to the apartment of Don Bernardo Bernardez, 63, respected executive and well-known elder of Spain's monarchist movement. "Don't worry about me. I will be back soon," the old man told his family. Then he was led off to jail.

Francisco Franco's government, after years of tight-lipped toleration of the anti-Franco monarchists, was cracking down. It looked as if Franco had finally decided that the monarchists had become more dangerous to his regime than the Communists. By week's end more than 30 members of the militant monarchist faction *Avanzadilla Monarquica* had been jailed incommunicado.

Banker Bernardez had been head of the *Avanzadilla* brain trust, and a shrewd political adviser to Leader Luisa Maria, 34, the handsome, impetuous Duchess of Valencia. When the duchess heard of his arrest, she still had time to flee. Instead, she chose to stay. When she was nine and a convent student, Luisa Maria had upset a plate of bean soup in protest against the quality of convent food. Reprimanded, she upset the inkwell on the mother superior's desk. Last week, still a rebel, the duchess made the rounds of Madrid's foreign embassies and newsmen, hoping that publicity would help her arrested friends.

Hatless, her curls flying, she motored to the Associated Press office. When her black Cadillac convertible (with ducal escutcheon enameled on its door) halted, a taxi pulled up just behind. From it hurried two men in the typical trench coats of the secret police. "Duchess," one of them said, "you must come along with us."

The rebel tossed her curls, then turned to her white-faced chauffeur. "There now, Felix," she said. "Don't look so worried. Go on home and send me my prison kit. Take good care of the dogs. Everything will be all right." Later she was taken to Las Ventas women's prison on Madrid's outskirts. Her butler stood waiting with her "prison kit," a large suitcase containing grey flannel slacks, leather jacket, woolen undies, sleeping bag, cologne water and salmon silk pajamas. The duchess has been jailed four times since 1947, always kept her kit ready.

REDHEAD'S EXIT: Last week, red-haired, two-fisted Luisa JULY 3 Maria, Duchess of Valencia, formally announced that she was giving up her political crusade. On doctors' orders she would undergo a long rest "to recover from ailments caused by imprisonment." From his Lisbon exile, the Spanish pretender, Don Juan, had himself urged his faithful follower to withdraw from the monarchist fight for the sake of her health. Spain's political scene would be a duller place without Luisa's fiery manifestoes, Spain's prison a duller place without her silk pajamas.

Yugoslavia

Yugoslavia came out of World War II a Communist state, ruled from 1945 on by Marshal Tito, hero of the anti-Nazi resistance. Complying at first with Soviet leadership of the Communist movement, Tito gradually developed an independent policy for his country and finally broke with Stalin in 1948. He accepted Western economic aid while remaining firmly Communist.

REPORT ON YUGOSLAVIA: The U.S., far from perfection it- JAN. 30 self, has many political allies who are incompetent, reactionary, corrupt. But the U.S. has one transcendent political and moral responsibility: to prevent war by stopping the extension of Soviet power. To discharge that duty, the U.S. needs allies —clean or dirty. One U.S. ally (in a way) is Tito. What kind of regime is he running?

Deep discontent and resentment smolder throughout Yugoslavia. Although some new factories, schools and offices have been built, what the average worker really sees ahead is a life of slavery for which he is not even beginning to receive compensation in the form of consumer goods.

Behind the façade of a puppet parliament and puppet courts stands the single real power of the Communist party, which has the police and the army firmly and totally in its hands. Atop this pyramid of power stands 57-year-old Josip Broz-Tito. There are a good many songs about him. Example:

Comrade Tito, our red rose,
Our famous country is with you;
Comrade Tito, you strawberry in the dew,
Our people are proud of you.

This 200-lb. strawberry has a personality which exudes strength and assurance. The former locksmith apprentice, soldier, agitator, machinist and army marshal is a fierce patriot and a convinced Communist. He talks fluent German and Russian, smokes a lot of cigarettes in a curved holder, wears a diamond ring on his left hand. It is a year and a half since Tito & Co. broke with the Kremlin. Must a Communist state outside Russia be a Soviet satellite? Tito said it need not, and he has proved it—so far. He has split the political atom—he has separated Communism and Soviet imperialism.

Marshal Tito, making friends on election day. His people call him "our red rose" and a "strawberry in the dew."

But having denounced and destroyed democracy, Tito could not re-embrace it even if he wanted to, because in so doing he would disown his Party, his secret police, his army. He is, in short, the willing prisoner of his own system. But he is taking no chances of a Russian invasion.

In this complex situation, the U.S. is pursuing in Yugoslavia perhaps the most difficult and most adult policy it has ever followed in Europe. It has been conducted with great skill, tact and coldbloodedness by U.S. diplomats, and it boils down to attacking Stalin in what he considers his own backyard by helping Tito and asking nothing in return. The aid of decadent capitalism is being accepted by Tito simply as a means of survival. "Tito is a son-of-a-bitch," ruefully remarked an American in Zagreb. "But he's our son-of-a-bitch now."

MILESTONES

DIED: Edna St. Vincent Millay, 58, fragile, elf-eyed poet laureate of the Golden Twenties; of a heart attack; in Austerlitz, N.Y. The respectable versifying of her last years never recaptured the fine girlish frenzy of the '20s:

> I cannot say what loves
> have come and gone,
> I only know that summer
> sang in me
> A little while, that in me
> sings no more.

MARRIED: Shirley Temple, 22, cine-moppet star of the '30s; and Charles Black, 31, California TV official, son of a public-utility mogul; she for the second time; in Del Monte, Calif.

DIVORCED: By Robert Anthony Eden, 53, Britain's No. 2 Tory, successor presumptive to No. 1 Winston Churchill: Beatrice Helen Eden, 44, baronet's daughter now living in Manhattan; after 27 years of marriage (three of separation), two sons; in London. Grounds: desertion.

DIED: Al Jolson, 64, black-faced mammy-shouting musicomedy star, whose brassy voice in *The Jazz Singer* for Warner Brothers in 1927 gave talking pictures their first real start; of coronary occlusion; in San Francisco. Jolson (real name Asa Yoelson) had only recently returned from singing for the soldiers in Korea.

MISCELLANY

A MAN'S HEART: In Metz, France, Jean Rozaire, hospitalized for three months after his wife carved him with a scythe, asked the court to free her before her year's sentence is up because he doesn't know how to cook.

CASE CLOSED: In Painesville, Ohio, Policeman Leon Debolt investigated a girl's tearful complaint against her father, wrote his report on the case: "Daughter, 15 years old, stayed out till 3 a.m. Got paddled. Needed it."

DUE CAUTION: In Dansville, N.Y., a classified advertisement appeared in the Dansville *Breeze*: WANTED —Farmer, age 38, wishes to meet woman around 30 who owns a tractor. Please enclose picture of tractor.

PRACTICAL POLITICS: In Cheyenne, Wyo., Dan Rees, elected county commissioner after a campaign in which he promised to be "reasonably honest," gave fair warning to the electorate in a newspaper ad: "All promises made in the heat of the campaign are hereby retracted; they are null and void and of no further value."

$$\text{PEOPLE}$$

"Names make news." In 1950 the following names made the following news.

A broad hint by the mother of lush, brunette Café Singer Gigi Durston that her daughter would marry ELLIOTT ROOSEVELT was called "premature" by Television Actress FAYE EMERSON, who pointed out that she and Elliott are still married. Said Faye: "I'm not put out, but I just like to announce my own divorces." [Two weeks later, Faye Emerson flew to Mexico City to get a divorce. Some four months after that Gigi called off her romance with Elliott.]

MAE WEST, announcing that she would shortly appear on television, said: "It will keep dad home at least once a week."

Near Callander, Ont., the DIONNE quintuplets turned 16. Said "Papa" (Oliva) Dionne: no dates for the girls for a couple of years yet.

Honored by the Williamsburg Settlement of Brooklyn with a gold medal for "her great efforts to transpose the ideals of social justice into realities": ELEANOR ROOSEVELT. The principal speaker, Playwright CLARE BOOTHE LUCE, said: "Mrs. Roosevelt has done more good deeds on a bigger scale for a longer time than any woman who ever appeared on the public scene. No woman has ever so comforted the distressed —or so distressed the comfortable."

Booked on charges of "giving an indecent performance" for the umpteenth time since she took up fandangling, SALLY RAND protested, "I'm sorry, I just don't tell my age. (Milwaukee Policewoman Geraldine Sampon, who had found Sally "nude as could be" in a lakefront carnival show, finally got her to admit to 46.)

Radio Moscow cried that the notorious spy, U.S. Supreme Court Justice WILLIAM O. DOUGLAS, was back nosing around the mountains of Iran. "In spite of his age, and he has already reached 50, Douglas has the effrontery to present himself as a mountain climber."

Ordered confiscated as "fascist literature" throughout the Soviet zone of Austria: *Crusade in Europe,* by DWIGHT D. EISENHOWER.

To Columnists Tex McCrary and Jinx Falkenburg, Fleet Admiral CHESTER NIMITZ confessed: "I always get seasick but I will not take any of those preventatives. I think a general cleaning out every once in a while is a good thing for the system."

Gloomy Author ARTHUR KOESTLER *(Darkness at Noon),* booked for punching a Paris policeman, candidly admitted that it was true. He said he celebrated finishing a new book by getting drunk, went to sleep at the curb in his car after deciding "the road seemed to be going uphill all the way." When he was taken to the station house, "conditioned by my past experiences with policemen, I lost my temper and struck this officer. . . . Later I was told I could go home. . . . The road had flattened out a lot."

Boxer-turned-Painter William Grant Sherry, 35, was in trouble again with his cinemactress wife BETTE DAVIS, 42. When he heard that highstrung Bette had resumed divorce proceedings, the ex-pug unburdened himself to the press: "I'm tired of being pushed around. She was the breadwinner, and I was the housewife and I've loved doing it. . . . I'd always have dinner ready for her when she got home. I'd take off her shoes and bring her her slippers. . . . I pressed her dresses when her maid wasn't there. I'd draw her bath and give her massages. . . . My wife is a troubled, mixed-up girl."

Crooner FRANK SINATRA, separated from his wife, flew to Spain and presented Cinemactress AVA GARDNER with a $10,000 emerald necklace.

JAN. 16 **BEN COMES BACK:** The crowd pressed close around the first tee at Los Angeles' Riviera Country Club. A bare-kneed em-cee in kilts and tam strode forward. "Ladies and gentlemen," he announced, "this is the greatest event in the history of the Los Angeles Open, but I have been requested by Mr. Ben Hogan to introduce him and say nothing else. On the tee— Ben Hogan."

To the gallery at the Riviera, once known as Hogan's Alley, there was little more that needed to be said. Everybody re-membered Ben's auto crash last February, how he lay for weeks after that in an El Paso hospital, his pelvis, collarbone, ankle and a rib broken. First it had been a question of whether Ben would live at all, then whether he would ever walk. But a couple of weeks ago, after a few practice rounds in Texas, 37-year-old Ben had made up his mind to come back. The gallery, schooled to remember that "they never come back," gave him a rolling cheer for heart.

Tight-lipped Ben Hogan touched his cap in acknowledge-ment. Then he sent the ball screaming down the fairway. Except for a slight stiffness about the hips and a shorter backswing, he looked like the old Hogan. When his strength began to ebb on the 13th, he leaned against a tree to pull himself together. His first-round score was 73, only five strokes off the pace.

That night he was almost beyond caring how well he had done. He fell into bed so tired he could hardly move a muscle. Next morning he developed a troublesome hook, but dug in-to his bag for brilliant recovery shots. One of his putts curled 60 feet over an undulating green before it dropped into the cup as though pulled by a magnet. On the long 17th he paused wearily and grinned: "You know, I've played this hole for ten years and I just realized it's uphill all the way." This week, after a brilliant 69 in the second round and another in the third, Blazin' Ben moved into the last day's play in second place, just two strokes behind Tournament Leader Jerry Barber of Pasadena. Coming back had been uphill too, but Ben was back. [Hogan tied Sam Snead for first place; Snead won the play-off.]

THE NONPAREILS: In the last half century in sport, which FEB. 13 names glittered brighter than all the rest? This week, after polling some 400 U.S. sportwriters and broadcasters, the Associated Press completed its line-up of the nonpareils and their runners-up:

BASEBALL: Babe Ruth (253 votes), Ty Cobb (116), Lou Gehrig (8).

BASKETBALL: George Mikan (139), Hank Luisetti (123), Nat Holman (31).

BOXING: Jack Dempsey (251), Joe Louis (104), Henry Armstrong (16).

FOOTBALL: Jim Thorpe (170), Red Grange (138), Bronko Nagurski (38).

GOLF: Bobby Jones (293), Ben Hogan (40), Walter Hagen (29).

HORSE RACING: Man o' War (305), Citation (36), Whirlaway (15).

SWIMMING: Johnny Weissmuller (132), Hironoshin Furuhashi (20), Adolph Kiefer (11).

TENNIS: Bill Tilden (310), Jack Kramer (32), Don Budge (31).

TRACK: Jesse Owens (201), Jim Thorpe (74), Paavo Nurmi (31).

The only one of the champs still in regular competition last week: towering (6 ft. 10 in.) George Mikan, who was busy rolling up about 30 points a game for the professional Minneapolis Lakers.

INFLATION: Slugging Ted Williams, baseball's best batter, FEB. 20 signed a 1950 contract for the most money ever paid a big-league player, an estimated $110,000.

NUTS: It is bad business to sell peanuts at ball games, rea- FEB. 2 soned practical President Paul Fagan of the San Francisco Seals: "It costs us $20,000 every season to sweep up peanut shells." One day last week, under-estimating the power of the peanut, Paul Fagan announced he was banning its sale in Seals Stadium this summer.

For the next 24 hours Fagan's ears burned. Newspaper editorials and radio commentators from Seattle to San Diego denounced his decision and he got telegrams of protest from peanut planters. Swelling by the minute came the anguished cries of fans. Next day, Fagan admitted defeat. Said he: "The public wants peanuts. Peanuts the public shall have—large, fresh-roasted ones."

Golfer Ben Hogan. Following a serious auto crash, he is making a comeback.   *Ted Williams, baseball's best batter, gets a new paycheck: $110,000.*

MARCH 6   **TEN & OUT:** For a while, Lavern Roach seemed to be a fighter who knew when to quit. A husky, young ex-marine and *Ring* magazine's Rookie-of-the-Year in 1947, he had learned a dreadful lesson when he climbed into the ring against the late ex-Middleweight Champion Marcel Cerdan. That night two years ago, he crawled around the ring on his hands & knees as Cerdan's sledgehammer blows smashed him to the floor seven times in eight rounds. After that beating, handsome Lavern Roach, a good fighter who had been brought along too fast, went back home to Plainview, Texas, with his wife and daughter, and took a job selling insurance.

But even in Plainview Lavern Roach still heard the roar of the crowd and the money-jingling song of the promoters. Last week, after three tune-up fights along the comeback trail, Middleweight (159½ lbs.) Roach shuffled his feet in the rosin box at Manhattan's St. Nicholas Arena and waited for the bell. He insisted that he felt as strong and fast as ever.

In the eighth round swarthy George Small of Brooklyn let go a desperation right and it crashed flush on Roach's jaw. It ripped the flesh inside his mouth and blood gushed from his lips. Roach's legs buckled; staggering, slack-jawed and glassy-eyed, he hung on. He lasted through the ninth, his wavy brown hair damp and matted, his body streaked with red from Small's blood-smeared gloves. When the bell sounded for the tenth round Roach doggedly came out into the ring again. Small jabbed a soggy left to his mouth. The blood trickled down from Roach's battered mouth, splattering down on his boxing trunks.

Then a vicious right put Roach down for a count of nine. Even Manhattan's bloodthirsty boxing fans seemed to sense what was about to happen and began yelling: "Stop it! Stop it!" Referee Frank Fullam did stop it—after another punch had sent Roach sprawling to the deck. By then it was too late.

Subconsciously, Lavern Roach seemed to know what was happening. "Damn it," he said, "my luck is running out." Then he lapsed into a coma. Fourteen hours later, in nearby St. Clare's Hospital, Lavern Roach, 24, died of a brain hemorrhage. He was the first boxing casualty of 1950. Last year there were nine U.S. ring deaths.

THE COMPETITIVE INSTINCT: Ted Williams of the Boston APRIL 10 Red Sox looked as fit as an Indian buck. After a winter out of doors, including a month of lazy fishing at the edge of the Florida Everglades, he was tanned to a light mahogany. His brownish green eyes were clear and sharp, his face lean, the big hands that wrapped around the handle of his 34-oz. Louisville Slugger were calloused and hard. He had 198 lbs., mostly well-trained muscle, tucked away on his 6 ft. 3¾ in. frame. He expected, he conceded, "to have a pretty good year."

What would satisfy any other man in baseball is not enough for Theodore Samuel Williams. As a boy in San Diego, Calif. he resolved, simply and forever, to become the best ballplayer of his generation. Big Ted has never forgotten his boyish decision, and, at 31, he has come within a bat-length of achieving it. There are plenty of fans who maintain that Ted has already achieved it. Last year, for the second time, Ted was voted the Most Valuable Player in the American League.

No one could deny that Ted was great, but some players, scores of sportwriters and not a few thousand fans thought that he was also a great pain in the neck. They rode him for blurting that his 1940 salary of $12,500 was chicken feed for a star of his magnitude, and for saying, in a rare moment of complete discouragement, that he would rather be a fireman than play baseball. The fans razzed him for seeming to loaf in the outfield, and for ignoring the tradition of tipping his cap to the applause after he had hit a home run.

Ted's reaction to the riding he took (and still takes) was typical. Boos burned him up. "They can all go to hell. I'll never tip my cap to them."

MAY 22 **"SORRY, FELLOWS"**: Hard-hitting, trigger-tempered Ted Williams came in for another round of raspberries after fumbling a tricky grounder and letting three runs score during a doubleheader with Detroit last week. Before he reached the dugout, he replied with a gesture from the international sign language of obscenity which Boston sportwriters primly described as a "vulgar motion." Then, while waiting his turn at bat, Ted added one more gesture that even the most proper Bostonians were sure to grasp: he turned and spat disgustedly in the direction of the grandstand.

Next day the Boston newspapers almost unanimously shellacked Ted. The Hearst tabloid *American* went so far as to suggest that he be suspended, concluded its editorial with the reproving observation: "This man is not the great baseball player he thinks he is. . . . Yesterday he was . . . a dirty little man."

But the Red Sox badly needed "little" Ted. The club front office hastily issued a press announcement: ". . . Ted is sorry for his impulsive actions on the field yesterday. . . ." That second-hand apology seemed to work. Two days after Ted's "impulsive actions," the applause actually drowned out the boos when Ted stepped up to bat.

JUNE 12 **GOLDEN MILE**: At California's Golden Gate Fields last week, Citation ran the mile in 1:33$\frac{3}{5}$, two-fifths of a second better than the world record set by his stablemate Coaltown at Washington Park last year. A moment later, the announcer verified what everybody at Golden Gate already knew: Big Cy had also beaten Stymie's alltime money-winning record. His earnings to date: $924,630 as against $918,485 for retired Stymie. [Citation's winnings finally totaled $1,085,760.]

AND STILL CHAMPION . . . : "The little man," said ex-Open JUNE 19 Champion Lloyd Mangrum, "is the only one in golf I've ever feared." The little man was Texan Ben Hogan. After the first round of the National Open last week, Ben Hogan was trailing eight strokes behind the leader. As the second round began, the 165-man field was as keyed up as invasion troops on D-day.

Hogan's real test came on the third day. The morning round left him two strokes back of Lloyd Mangrum's leading pace. In the afternoon, going into the final four holes, he needed par golf to win by two strokes. Tired and sagging, he could not quite make it. He missed an 18-inch putt on the dog-leg 15th. On the 17th he lost another stroke by trapping his tee shot, settled for a three-way tie with Mangrum and Washington, D.C. Pro George Fazio.

But with that hurdle past, there was no stopping little Ben Hogan in the play-off. Hogan curled in a clinching 50-foot putt for a birdie on the 17th, wound up with another 69, four strokes better than Mangrum, six ahead of Fazio. With his second Open championship in the bag, little Ben Hogan was once again the man to fear.

MOTOR MADNESS: In the sticky, midsummer night air of the AUG. 7 U.S. last week the fans were turning out in droves for a new national pastime: stock-car racing. Sheer speed was not the point; nobody was after records. The main idea was to pack 20 or 25 hopped-up cars on a tight, sharply-turned little quarter-mile track, and let them go for the bacon. The result was motor madness—a deafening combination of roaring engines and screeching tires, cars careening against each other or spinning into fences at 60 m.p.h.

In Chicago, where the racing is done mostly in postwar-model Fords, Chevvies and Plymouths, the twice-a-week grinds in Soldier Field have been outdrawing night baseball, and the Hurricane Auto Racing Association, a stable of professional drivers, pours it on five nights a week for a guarantee of $35 a night regardless of where they finish.

The biggest wind in the Hurricane circuit in the last four weeks has been 23-year-old Jim Rathman of Los Angeles. His 1947 Cadillac is owned by two friends who do all the repair work, get 60% of the car's winnings. At Soldier Field one night last week, before a crowd of 31,065 (a 1950 record), Rathman put on his standard performance. The 25-lap final was expected to be a duel between Rathman's Cadillac and Bob Leatherman's midget red Crosley (labeled "$1/_2$ Pint"). It was for a while. On the eighth lap, the little Crosley got banged from behind coming out of the south turn, cracked into the retaining wall. Leatherman was lifted out unconscious. With his main opposition out of action, Rathman won handily, pocketed $200 for the night. [Rathman went on to set three world records—including the Indianapolis 500 in 1960.]

OCT. 9 **THEY NEVER COME BACK:** In the fourth round, it looked for a moment or two as if Joe Louis might do it. He shuffled in, jolted Ezzard Charles with a series of stiff lefts, trying to set him up for the old layaway punch. The 22,357 fans, thinly scattered through Yankee Stadium, began to wonder: Was

Joe Louis takes a hard right from Ezzard Charles in round 14 and loses the chance to regain his heavyweight title. Page 158.

tired, fat, old (36) Joe Louis going to make a comeback, and heavyweight history?

Before another round had ended, the sentimentally pro-Louis crowd had the answer. The doomsday lefts & rights that won Joe the title from Braddock, and turned Max Schmeling and Max Baer to butter, were gone. Louis was a paunchy shadow of the Brown Bomber. Charles out-jabbed and outsmarted him almost all the way.

When it ended, after 15 bruising rounds, Louis stood silently in his corner and heard the judges' decision: unanimous for Ezzard Charles. Only one judge awarded Joe as many as five rounds.

Said Joe Louis: "I'll never fight again." His last fight had earned him $102,840, about $97,000 short of what he owes the U.S. Treasury in back income taxes.

THE OLD GENTLEMAN RETIRES: Philadelphia Athletics fans OCT. 30 have long lived on their memories of Connie Mack's last great teams, the American League pennant winners of '29, '30 and '31. But for 18 years Athletics fans have had little worth remembering. Despite his 87 years, Connie Mack, finishing his 50th year as Philadelphia manager, could read the red ink without spectacles. And though financial control of his club had been vested in his sons, Earle and Roy, "Mr. Mack" could still make a decision. Last week, he made the hardest one of his life: he stepped aside. Then he named Coach Jimmy Dykes as the new manager. Said Connie firmly: "I am not quitting because I'm too old. I am quitting because I think the people want me to quit." Still president of the A's, Connie added a wistful afterthought: "I'll travel with the team and watch the games from the stands."

THE THEATER

JAN. 2 OLD PLAY IN MANHATTAN: *Caesar and Cleopatra* remains after half a century one of George Bernard Shaw's, and hence the modern theater's, most vigorous plays. The tone is prevailingly wry and ironic. The air seems very chill at times for all the Mediterranean sunlight. A bald and aging conqueror withholds his heart from a violent young girl rather than have her torture it; then, with a rueful smile, promises to send her a dashing young Marc Antony.

Though 93 years old and 3,500 miles away, Playwright George Bernard Shaw kept a close, finicky eye on his latest Broadway revival. For nine months he badgered the producers with peppery cables, letters and postcards telling them just how to finance, cast and stage the play. He hand-picked Sir Cedric Hardwicke as Caesar (having coached him in the role in London in 1925), and gave Lilli Palmer his blessing as Cleopatra after Gertrude Lawrence brought her around for a visit last summer.

Still his own hard-bargaining agent, manager and lawyer, G.B.S. disposed brusquely of an early suggestion that the play be put on by Theatre Incorporated, a non-profit group. "I take no interest in non-profit enterprises," he wrote. "I am in business and prefer to deal with keen business managers who are out to make as much money as possible."

JAN. 9 THE WONDERFUL LEVELING OFF: In the center of the ballroom, somebody pressed a six-foot box jammed with 150 long-stemmed roses into the arms of a big, bewildered girl in a rented mink coat. As they watched, Noel Coward and his old friend Producer John C. Wilson suddenly and shamelessly burst into tears. "We just couldn't help it," explained Wilson later. "There on a platter before us was the whole essence of show business."

For the past few weeks the emotion of these hard-headed showmen has been echoing all up and down the glib middle aisle of show business, proclaiming the ascension of a star named Carol Channing. On Broadway, an authentic new star is almost as rare a phenomenon as it is in the heavens. Last week, the new star that glittered over Broadway was novel enough and brilliant enough to make all of show business seem once again like a glamourous, robust legend.

Carol Channing, displaying a variety of expressions, is the gold-digging Lorelei Lee in "Gentlemen Prefer Blondes."

As the gold-digging Lorelei Lee in the new musical version of Anita Loos's famed bestseller of the '20s, *Gentlemen Prefer Blondes*, strapping (5 ft. 9 in., 153 lbs.) Carol Channing is ludicrously miscast. Head topped by an unruly peroxide burlesque of a flapper's hair-do, sloping shoulders wrapped in the shapeless fashions of two decades ago, she gives the appearance of an amiable performing seal; and like a seal she seems naively anxious to please. For perhaps ten minutes an audience seeing her for the first time watches with something resembling embarrassed bewilderment. Then Carol Channing slides into her first solo; from that point on, the joke is obvious. Subtly and with never a false move, Carol's whole expressive body flows with the rhythm of the music. At the end of her first chorus, both Carol and Lorelei belong to the audience forever. "Everything," said Carol in her own peculiar idiom, "has leveled off just wonderfully."

JAN. 16 **"THE MEMBER OF THE WEDDING"** (adapted by Carson McCullers from her novel) has much the value of a bit of garden amid asphalt and city smoke. Laid in a Southern town, *Member* portrays the intimate relationship of three essentially lonely people: a motherless twelve-year-old girl, a middle-aged Negro servant and a small boy. Unfortunately, it suffers after a while from being so much less a play than a mere picture of people. As Berenice, Ethel Waters plays with sure and simple dignity; as John Henry, seven-year-old Brandon De Wilde is thoroughly captivating. In the much more difficult role of Frankie, Julie Harris is very effective up to a point. Yet she is never really moving, never conveys something inward that cannot be put into words.

FEB. 27 **"COME BACK, LITTLE SHEBA"** (by William Inge) tells of a couple, married for 20 years, who should never have married at all. Doc had gotten Lola into trouble; afterwards the baby died, and the sexy, good-natured, empty-headed girl turned into a shiftless housewife, her mind on men, her thoughts in the past. The play tries hard to be honest, manages in places to be effective, has a fierce moment or two, as when at the end Doc clings for help, like a drowning man, to the wife who has made him drown. As Lola and Doc, Shirley Booth and Sidney Blackmer prove a valiant acting team, bring a great deal that is human, perceptive, vivid to their roles.

ARCH 6 **MR. ELIOT:**   *How unpleasant to meet Mr. Eliot!*
With his features of clerical cut,
And his brow so grim
And his mouth so prim
And his conversation, so nicely
Restricted to What Precisely
And If and Perhaps and But . . .
How unpleasant to meet Mr. Eliot!
(Whether his mouth be open or shut.)

—T.S. Eliot

Few Americans have had the dubious pleasure of meeting Thomas Stearns Eliot. To most of them, he is an expatriate, obscurely highbrow poet who wrote an unreadable poem called *The Waste Land* and fathered a catch-phrase about the world ending not with a bang but a whimper.

Thanks to a Broadway hit called *The Cocktail Party*, his name at last was beginning to be more frequently encountered. Some of the higherbrowed reviewers had called the play "esoteric." But the people who crowded to see it night after night were not predominantly highbrows (there are not enough highbrows in New York to make a play a hit), and they did not, apparently, find the play esoteric—perhaps because they did not find Christianity esoteric.

Mr. Eliot himself was, as usual, far from Broadway, in his accustomed London haunts. Not long ago, on a bus, a large woman had sat down next to him, peered at him, and exclaimed: "Gracious me, aren't you Mr. T. S. Eliot?" Aghast, he had looked up, admitted his identity, and at the next stop he had fled down the narrow stairs and gone underground.

Thomas Stearns Eliot began his journey through the waste land in the heart of a land of plenty. He was born in Missouri. But after Harvard, Eliot went to study in Paris for a year ("on the old man's money"), and in a Left Bank flat wrote his first significant poem, *The Love Song of J. Alfred Prufrock*, the portrait of an aging man reviewing a life frittered away between timid hopes and lost opportunities:

> *For I have known them all already, known them all,*
> *Have known the evening, mornings, afternoons.*
> *I have measured out my life with coffee spoons. . . .*

By 1920, partly because of overwork in his dual career as banker and poet [he later shifted from banking to publishing], Eliot was on the verge of a breakdown. While resting, he finished *The Waste Land*. Some of the critics reviewing *The Waste Land* sniffed that it was indeed a piece that passed all understanding. (In its first issue, March 3, 1923, baffled, brash, bumptious TIME reported that *The Waste Land* was rumored to have been written as a hoax.) But it brought Eliot a literary notoriety that passed into fame.

One compelling reason why the audiences crowd his *Cocktail Party* is that they recognize it, in the sense that people always recognize a compelling restatement of the old and certain truths. They like Eliot for being clever, and at the same time clear; but what counts most is the common sense, the humility and the hope expressed in such lines as these:

> *The best of a bad job is all any of us make of it,—*
> *Except of course, the saints. . . .*

APRIL 10 **CHAMPION:** *South Pacific*, celebrating its first anniversary by taking an eight-day Lenten vacation, looked this week more than ever like the biggest hit in Broadway history. Except for a few seats in August, the Richard Rodgers-Oscar Hammerstein II-Joshua Logan musical was sold out through September, and the ticket demand was still big. The advance sale: $800,000. [It ran on Broadway for 1,694 performances—until May 16, 1953. The biggest Broadway musical hit at the time *South Pacific* closed was *Oklahoma!*,which had opened March 31, 1943 and ran for 2,212 performances.]

APRIL 17 **LAURELS:** After Novelist Carson McCullers turned her *The Member of the Wedding* into a play, the script languished in producers' offices for three years. One producer suggested to the 33-year-old Georgian that she tear it up and try something else. Last week, its 13th on Broadway, Mrs. McCullers' drama about a sensitive twelve-year-old girl's entry into adolescence won the New York Drama Critics' Circle Award as the best of the season. As the best foreign play, the Manhattan critics chose T. S. Eliot's verse comedy, *The Cocktail Party*. The award for the best musical play went to *The Consul*, written, composed and directed by Gian-Carlo Menotti.

The day after the critics presented their scrolls, the board of the American Theater Wing passed out its annual Antoinette Perry Awards, the stage's closest approach to Hollywood's Oscars. *South Pacific*, produced too late to qualify for last year's honors, was named the "outstanding" musical, and individual "Tonys" went to its producers, Director Joshua Logan and four of its players: Mary Martin, Ezio Pinza, Juanita Hall and Myron McCormick. The outstanding play: *The Cocktail Party*.

Among the other winners: Shirley Booth and Sidney Blackmer for "distinguished" performances in *Come Back, Little Sheba*, Actor-Manager Maurice Evans for producing the New York City Theater Company's winter season.

OCT. 23 **"CALL ME MADAM"** (music & lyrics by Irving Berlin; book by Howard Lindsay & Russel Crouse; produced by Leland Hayward) opened with an advance sale of over $1,000,000 and the sort of fabulous buildup that can all too easily backfire. But *Call Me Madam*, while far from stupendous, is perfectly satisfactory—and at least can boast of one stupendous performer, Ethel Merman.

Call her madam—or Madame Du Barry, or Panama Hattie, or Annie Oakley—she remains unsurpassed in putting over a song (and a show). No lungs can send forth more compelling sounds, no lips can enunciate words more clearly. She functions with the precision of a machine and the animation of a cheer leader, and is as American—and as lowdown—as chewing gum. Beyond that is her showmanship: even when her material lays an egg, she makes it seem a golden one.

Ethel Merman in "Call Me Madam": no lungs can send forth more compelling sounds, no lips can enunciate more clearly.

"THE LADY'S NOT FOR BURNING" (by Christopher Fry) is NOV. 2 laid in the Middle Ages, written in verse, and rife with imagery. It sounds like dust and cobwebs; what it turns out to be is a broom. With great impish strokes and elaborate flourishes —and winking and singing as he works—Christopher Fry sweeps the prosy and the plausible off the boards for an hour. It is the performance of a fellow who not only knows how to handle a broom, but at intervals can ride off on the broomstick.

The not-too-momentous story tells of a discharged soldier, who, in an effort to divert attention from a witch hunt to himself, bellows that he has committed murder and insists on being hanged. But once he sees the young and beguiling witch, he is willing to be cleared of murder and in a fair way to be cured of misanthropy. The play's forte is fireworks, not illumination. As the soldier, John Gielgud gives a dashing if slightly unmodulated performance. As the lady, Pamela Brown proves that Fry did not write the part for her in vain; no one ever made standoffishness more come-hitherable.

With a mixture of pleasure and outrage, the audience began to realize that this fellow Fry was breaking all the rules. He was writing verse which, like a drink on a hot day or a kiss on a cold night, gave pleasure and satisfaction. Fry's audiences prance out into the welcoming night, their eyes peeled for a pretty girl to hug or a fellow being to clap on the shoulder. It was time somebody like Fry came along. Poetry and the theater were beginning to regard themselves, and to be regarded, as hopelessly frigid old maids.

"THE COUNTRY GIRL" brings back Dramatist Clifford Odets to the land of the living. It by no means brings him back in triumph; even when his play throbs, it is not always with honest life. But it has passages of fierce feeling that only Odets could write, and characters that at moments are bitingly real.

The play tells of a once-famous actor who is a down-at-heel drunk, of his loyal, long-suffering wife, and of a bright young director who gives him a shot at a comeback. Odets creates for a time something like a new-angled triangle, and Paul Kelly as the husband, Uta Hagen as the wife and Steven Hill as the director give it tingle and intensity wherever possible.

Beset by the problem of having to make the play run till 11 o'clock and of wanting to make it run till June, Odets stages a double retreat from life into show business, filling out the play with colorful back-stage detail, phonying it up with facile on-stage emotions. His talent is flowing again, but from a faucet in dire need of a filter.

NOV. 27 **"BELL, BOOK AND CANDLE"** (by John van Druten) comes up with a bright comedy idea and, for perhaps better than half the evening, with a bright comedy. Playwright van Druten has assumed not only that there are modern-day witches but that they can be modish and highly efficient, and that one of them is attractive enough to ensnare a bright Manhattan publisher. When the publisher discovers she is a witch, he walks out on her—only for her to discover she is now a woman. Hoist on her own broomstick, she has fallen in love.

Lilli Palmer—whether murmuring endearments or, cat in hand, muttering incantations—is seductive and vivacious, and even in the fast company of demons, Rex Harrison provides a mere human being with dash.

"GUYS AND DOLLS" (music & lyrics by Frank Loesser; book DEC. 4 by Jo Swerling & Abe Burrows) whizzes through the whole first act hardly once having to stop for a light. If the second act slows things up a bit, *Guys and Dolls* emerges a thoroughly good, lively, lowdown musical. Using fleecelined tough material of Damon Runyon's, it takes a full-in-the-face but indulgent view of Broadway's cop-fleeing dice players and their dolls.

MILESTONES

DIED: Frank ("Bring 'Em Back Alive") Buck, 66, animal catcher extraordinary; of lung cancer; in Houston. Buck estimated that in 38 years of hunting he had brought back 100,000 birds, 65 tigers, more than 50 elephants, hundreds of other mammals and reptiles.

MARRIED: Looking scared, but still beautiful in a billowy white satin $1,200 wedding gown (a gift of M-G-M), Cinemactress Elizabeth Taylor, 18, became the bride of Conrad Nicholson Hilton Jr., 23, son of the hotelman.

DIED: Field Marshal Jan Christian Smuts, 80, world statesman, soldier, author, scientist, philosopher; after long illness; in his home near Pretoria, Union of South Africa. A commando general against the British in the Boer War, Smuts afterwards supported Britain, suggested the new name for the British Empire: "The British Commonwealth of Nations"; helped write the preamble of the United Nations Charter; for 40 years made the voice of his country heard in the world.

MISCELLANY

FRANKLY...: In Jamaica, N.Y., Judge Joseph M. Conroy listened patiently while Donald and Mary McClay each recited reasons why the other was unfit to have custody of their two-year-old daughter, then gave his decision: "Neither of you will get custody. In my opinion you both stink."

LOCAL TALENT: In San Diego, when officials at the county jail were unable to open a jail door, they called on an inmate who did the job in four minutes.

CONFORMIST: In Detroit, George Taylor, 56, petitioned to change his name to Pappados on grounds that his Greek friends could not pronounce Taylor.

ART

JAN. 23 **BATTLEGROUND:** What's wrong with the human face? Nothing, says Pablo Picasso, not a thing. Two eyes, a nose and a mouth are nice in themselves; furthermore it is great fun to add and subtract them, multiply and divide, maul, chop, smear, twist and shred them.

Last week seven garbled girls by Picasso were hanging on the wall of a Manhattan gallery by way of example. In the exhibition catalogue, William Carlos Williams, a poet-pediatrician, gave Bad Boy Picasso a clean bill of health.

"What is a face?" Williams wrote. "What has it always been, even to the remotest savagery? A battleground. Slash it with sharp instruments, rub ashes into the wound to make a keloid; daub it with clays, paint it with berry juices. This thing that terrifies us, this face upon which we lay so much stress is something they have always wanted to deform by every possible means. Why? To remove it from the possibility of death by making of it a work of art. . . .

Pablo Picasso, topped by a dove, approves the human face.

A Picasso face: the artist chops, shreds, twists and mauls it.

"We may humanly disagree with Picasso's tactics, but with his strategy we cannot disagree. His success has been phenomenal."

SUCCESS STORY: This week an amateur painter of pretty, neo-impressionist country scenes broke into professional ranks. For an undisclosed price, Kansas City's Hallmark greeting card company bought reproduction rights to 18 of Winston Churchill's canvases. [The proceeds were donated to Churchill College, Cambridge.] FEB. 27

GLOOMY PRODIGY: Paris, surfeited with aging masters, has taken a 22-year-old painter to its bosom. He is a shadowy figure, shy, ascetic and wire-thin, named Bernard Buffet. Two years ago, Buffet's first show won the coveted annual *Prix de la Critique*; his latest exhibition in Paris was a near sell-out (at prices which average one-third the going rate for a Braque or a Picasso). Last week Buffet's first show in Manhattan was doing fine, too. MARCH

In Paris, Buffet's work was described as "conscientious and cruel," but "thin and dingy" would do just as well. Buffet's "nudes" were bony yellow or grey creatures hovering, paralyzed, in huge, dirt-colored squares. In his "still lifes," cast-iron pears, shriveled, lozenge-shaped lemons, tortured cutlery and inedible fish writhed on wrinkled tablecloths.

Not even his ardent admirers could describe Buffet as a master of line or color. The most graceful lines in his work were those of his big, angular signature, which made an eye-catching spider track across the top of each picture. [Buffet had a great vogue in the 1950s, but in the 1960s his popularity declined.]

WITH A HAMMER: In London one morning last week, Sculptor Jacob Epstein got up early, donned a dirty cotton shirt and frayed, clay-soiled suit. After breakfast he stuffed a hammer and chisel into his sagging pockets, pulled a long-billed baseball cap down over his bald dome, and shambled hurriedly off to the Leicester Galleries. His first exhibition in three years was due to open there at 9 a.m. Epstein arrived at 8 to put some last-minute nicks in a major work, his $1\frac{1}{2}$-ton, $7\frac{1}{2}$-foot-tall *Lazarus*. MARC

Bernard Buffet. His spiny silhouettes strike the eye with mighty force.

Grandma Moses. Her farm pictures are a triumph in Europe. Page 172.

An hour later, when the critics came, Epstein stepped down from his ladder with a sigh of satisfaction. "I have tried," he said, "to express the idea of a man coming from death to life." He had succeeded. *Lazarus*, swathed in a cocoon of burial wrappings, was shown at the moment of Christ's command: "Come forth." Stone though it was, the loosely bound body almost semed to breathe.

"The man in the street," Epstein once remarked, "is a fool, and I care not a whit for his opinions. I should be a fool too if I were in the least influenced by him." The sculptor's damn-it-all individualism has led Epstein to create some monumental shockers. His new *Lazarus*, which seemed likely to offend no one, might go a long way toward persuading "the man in the street" that Epstein is among the most intense and skillful sculptors alive.

APRIL 3 **THE WANDERER:** Until recently only three painters rated special rooms in Paris' National Museum of Modern Art. They were Matisse, Braque and Picasso. Last week 60-year-old, Russian-born Marc Chagall had his own room too, filled with the strange gravity-defying pictures he has been painting for the past 40 years.

The room may be the closest thing to a permanent home that wispy-haired little Painter Chagall will ever know. Since

1910, when he left Russia and its harrowing threat of po-
groms for Paris, he had never really settled down. Haunted
by his memories and searching for escape, he found it only
in his unearthly, richly colored paintings, more like astral
visions than the real world, with ghostly men & women,
wandering violins, fish, cows and roosters floating across
them like derelict balloons. Like the figures in his paintings
he was hard to pin down. "My mother used to tell me, 'God,
sprich nicht.' It is the same with art."

ON THE COUCH: Modern art was on the couch last week. A APRIL 24
Viennese psychiatrist, Dr. Eva Henrich, had shown 30 pictures to a panel of 158 rank & file Viennese. Half the works
were by modernist painters—Picasso, Max Ernst, Yves Tan-
guy, Enrico Donati and Joán Miró. The other half were by
schizophrenic patients in mental hospitals. Asked to decide
which were the outpourings of patients and which the works
of artists, the panel scored a perfect zero. They were right
half the time, wrong the other half.

Picassophobes could take grim delight in Psychiatrist Henrich's findings. For them, the test proved that moderns are
mad. Picassophiles would be forced to conclude that the
average Viennese layman is no judge of art.

CAPTAIN PABLO'S VOYAGES: Once long ago, Pablo Picasso JUNE 26
warned an inquisitive American lady not to "ask questions
of the man at the wheel." At mid-century, Protean Pablo is
still grasping the wheel of modern art, and most people are
still wondering whether the boat is hopelessly lost or merely
off on an extended voyage of exploration. This week in Europe, hundreds of dauntless American ladies and their husbands were once again doggedly searching for a first-hand
answer. There the Venice biennial, the world's oldest, biggest
and best-known international art show, had assembled a record exhibition of 4,000 art works from a record 22 nations,
to celebrate its silver anniversary.

One impression stood out unmistakably: the same little
group of French painters who had dominated 20th Century
art right along were still the class of the show. No one had
ever tended the flames more assiduously or mistreated nature
with more zestful enthusiasm than the little barrel of a man

with the wonderful name: Pablo Diego José Francisco de Paula Juan Nepomuceno Crispín Crispiniano de la Santísima Trinidad Ruiz Picasso.

"Repeatedly I am asked," he once grumbled, "to explain how my painting evolved. . . . Variation does not mean evolution. If an artist varies his mode of expression, this only means that he has changed his manner of thinking. . . . It might be for the better or it might be for the worse."

That is certainly true of Picasso. To a somewhat lesser degree, it is also true of his contemporaries:

Henri Matisse is one whose brilliance equals Picasso's own. The ailing 80-year-old master lives in a huge hotel apartment in Nice, spends most of his time in a bedroom hung with dozens of his own cheerful works and some of the darkest, dourest Picassos in existence. At present he is completing designs for a Dominican chapel to be constructed in nearby Vence.

Maurice Utrillo, 66, no longer visits his old haunts; he sits at home in suburban stucco villa, staring at his buxom energetic wife and dreaming of the dear, drunken, amazingly productive old days.

Marc Chagall, a wanderer at 60, recently moved to the south of France and resolved to take up ceramics.

Fernand Léger looks hard as flint at 69, lives in a chaotically cluttered Montparnasse studio, and has 100 pupils—most of them ex-G.I.s.

Georges Rouault feels "very tired" at 70. Far more self-critical than most moderns, Rouault two years ago burned 315 old, unfinished works he had come to dislike.

Georges Braque, 68, collects and polishes old bones to embody in the ceramics he is making nowadays. In his spotless Paris studio, Craftsman Braque works at his complex, heavily textured canvases slowly and with obvious enjoyment.

Maurice de Vlaminck thinks the trouble with modern art is "too damned many artists and would-be artists." "French art is dead," roars Vlaminck, still volcanic at 74, "and Picasso is its gravedigger. He is not an artist, he is a virtuoso who changes his act ever week."

Raoul Dufy, a 73-year-old wisp of a man, is now in the U.S. undergoing treatment for arthritis in a Massachusetts hospital. One of the most charming masters of the atmospheric sketch who ever lived, Dufy maintains that "classicism is perfection. Unfortunately, I do not have perfection."

Picasso and his contemporaries are nearing the end of their journey. To some seasick critics it has seemed a trip aboard a Walloping Window Blind, but no one can deny that it has vastly broadened the horizons of art.

GRANDMA GOES TO EUROPE: Vienna's tiny Neue Galerie JULY 3 was bright last week with crude, cheery pictures of U.S. farm life, New York State style. The paintings were the work of 89-year-old "Primitive" Grandma Moses, making her first appearance before a European audience. Judging by her reception in Vienna, Grandma Moses' grand tour through The Hague, Berne and Paris will be something of a triumph.

"At last," exclaimed one young gallery-goer on opening day, "a happy world!"

MILESTONES

MARRIED: Marva Trotter, 34, former wife of retired Heavyweight Champ Joe Louis; and Dr. Albert Lee Spaulding, 30, internal medicine specialist; in Chicago.

DIED: Victoria, Dowager Marchioness of Milford Haven, 87, granddaughter of Queen Victoria, sister of the last Czarina of Russia, widow of Prince Louis of Battenberg (Mountbatten), first Marquess of Milford Haven, mother of Earl Mountbatten of Burma, grandmother of the Duke of Edinburgh, Princess Elizabeth's husband; in London.

MISCELLANY

A DOG'S LIFE: In Montgomery, Ala., Marion D. Perry, kept awake by his neighbor's dogs, was fined $10 for sitting on his porch at night, howling back.

CALL OF THE WILD: In Nashville, members of Vanderbilt University's Kappa Alpha Order (Southern) eagerly chased what they thought was their deodorized pet skunk, name of General Sherman, learned too late it was another skunk.

LIMITED CHOICE: In Oklahoma City, Federal Judge Stephen Chandler considered the case of two persistent moonshiners again found guilty of plying their craft in Oklahoma, delivered the sentence: spend three to five years in prison or move to "some place like West Texas."

GALLANTRY PLUS: In Glasgow, Scotland, Patrick McCusker kept raising his hat to women waiting for a streetcar, was finally arrested for disturbing the peace because perched on his head under the hat he carried two white mice.

LOVER'S CHOICE: In Detroit, Mrs. Patricia J. Stephens won a divorce after testifying that her husband thought "it was very funny to kiss the dog, give me a pat on the head and walk out the door."

$$\text{SCIENCE}$$

JAN. 23 **THE THINKING MACHINE:** On Oxford Street in Cambridge, Mass. lives a sibyl, a priestess of science. Her devotees take their problems to her as devout ancient Greeks took their insolubles to Delphi. Her name is Bessie (short for "Bessel Functions," a mathematical tool analogous to logarithms); she is a long, slim, glass-sided machine with 760,000 parts, and the riddles that are put to her and that she unfailingly answers concern such matters as rocket motors, nuclear physics and trigonometric functions.

During World War II, old Bessie, built by IBM, was given the job of evaluating mathematically an electrically powered cannon that the Nazis were known to be building. Bessie chewed into a snarl of equations and proved that the weapon was utterly impractical. The U.S. relaxed while the Germans, who had no Bessie, went on wasting enormous effort.

Such comparatively simple tasks are not impossible for human calculators, but they are impractical because of the time they would take. For instance, one calculator has recently completed in 103 hours a job relating to uranium fission for Princeton University. The same job would have taken a flesh and blood operator more than 100 years.

The great new computers, cried Professor Norbert Wiener of M.I.T., with mingled alarm and triumph, are not mere mathematical tools. They are, he said, harbingers of a whole new science of communication and control, which he promptly named "cybernetics" [from the Greek word meaning steersman]. The newest machines, Wiener pointed out, already have an extraordinary resemblance to the human brain, both in structure and function. So far, they have no senses or "effectors" (arms and legs), but why shouldn't they have? There are all sorts of artificial eyes, ears and fingertips (thermometers, strain gauges, pressure indicators, photo-electric tubes) that may be hooked up to the machines. Such a development, says Wiener, is certain.

Professor Wiener says that some computers are already "human" enough to suffer from typical psychiatric troubles. Unruly memories, he says, sometimes spread through a machine as fears and fixations spread through a psychotic human brain. Robert Seeber of IBM says that his big computer has a very human foible: it hates to wake up in the morning. The operators turn it on, the tubes light up, but the machine is not really awake. A problem sent through its sleepy wits does not get far. Red lights flash, indicating that the machine has made an error. The patient operators try the problem again. This time the machine thinks a little more clearly. At last, after several tries, it is fully awake and willing to think straight.

A computer, as portrayed on a TIME *cover that became famous. Some machines are "human" enough to suffer from psychiatric problems.*

HYDROGEN HYSTERIA: Not long ago many scientists feared MARCH that the public was forgetting the menace of the atom bomb. What many responsible scientists fear now is public hysteria caused by exaggeration of the destructiveness of the hydrogen bomb.

Last week, on a radio round table sponsored by the University of Chicago, Associate Professor Harrison Brown sprang a chiller to top all chillers. The blast effects of hydrogen bombing, Brown told his nationwide audience, will be only the beginning; the radioactive aftereffects will be far worse.

Hydrogen explosions, he said, will fill the air with fiercely radiating isotopes. They will drift with the wind, he believes, like a swarm of invisible locusts, killing people, animals, insects, plants.

Brown described how the U.S.S.R. might attack the U.S. Hydrogen bombs could be exploded in the Pacific, 1,000 miles west of California. Their radioactivity, drifting eastward, would lawnmower the whole U.S., reaching and sterilizing New York in about five days.

This week, on a similar broadcast, Physicist Leo Szilard of Chicago added that 50 tons of neutrons released by hydrogen fusion could ring the earth with a radioactive dust layer capable of killing the earth's entire population. To this sort of talk, other equally informed physicists react with astonishment or distaste. They point out that there is an enormous difference between a bomb that will disrupt a city and kill its people and one that will wipe all life off the face of a continent or the earth.

All scientists admit that a sufficient number of hydrogen bombs (or uranium bombs, for that matter) might raise the radioactivity of the entire atmosphere. But to kill the world's inhabitants, the amount of reactive material used would have to be improbably large.

RCH 13 **CULT OF DOOM:** The prophets of hydrogen Doomsday got no support from David E. Lilienthal, former chairman of the Atomic Energy Commission and a man well qualified to judge: "I want no part of the new Cult of Doom that I see rising all about us. . . . I would like, if I can, to help counteract the growing mood. . . . The chief consequence of this wave of headline after headline about Doom and Utter Destruction, of One-Night Wars and the horrors that lie in atomic destruction, is this: a growing sense of confusion and helplessness among our own people. And hopelessness and helplessness are the very opposite of what we need. These are emotions that play right into the hands of destructive Communist forces."

CH 27 **ELEMENT 98:** Creating new heavy elements is a faint bit like working a pinball machine; it takes a nice judgment of speed. Last week a group of University of California scientists led by Professor Glenn Seaborg told how they created Element 98, which stands six steps up the periodic table of chemical elements from uranium. They did it by shooting alpha particles (helium nuclei) at curium, another synthetic element, No. 96, created by a Seaborg group in 1945.

The Californians knew that the alpha particles would have to move at just the right speed. If they moved too slowly, they would bounce off the curium nuclei. If they moved too fast, they would smash the more fragile nuclei. So the scientists adjusted their old reliable 60-inch cyclotron until it emitted alpha particles with 35 million electron volts of energy. It did the trick.

The scientists named their creation "californium" after their state and university. They did not manufacture much of it. The new element proved so radioactive that half of it disintegrated in 45 minutes. It took fast action to identify it before it vanished.

WEATHER OR NOT: In their various fashions, the people of AUG. 28 New Mexico had long prayed for rain. They were used to seeing the Rio Grande shrunk to a brookwide trickle, too thick to drink, too thin to plough. Many a sun-scorched New Mexican had said resignedly: "The Lord made the state dry. I guess He wants it that way."

Nevertheless, on the slopes above Socorro, a group of scientists thought it no impiety to see what could be done about changing New Mexico's weather. And they were not the only ones. All over the Southwest, and here & there throughout the rest of the U.S., a rainmaking boom was on. Many of the rainmakers were amateurs. But some were serious and hopeful scientists or hardheaded businessmen.

All of them worked on the principle of spraying dry ice or silver iodide into fat, moisture-laden clouds, forcing them to disgorge their watery vapors which fall as rain. The man behind the principle was an energetic, 69-year-old scientist named Dr. Irving Langmuir. Until Irving Langmuir began poking into the subject, meteorology was a passive science. Meteorologists observed and tried to forecast the weather, but when asked why they didn't do something about it, they simply looked reproachful. Modern meteorological engineering—the technique of doing something about it—was born four years ago in Langmuir's General Electric laboratory at Schenectady.

Experimenting first with dry ice and then with silver iodide, Langmuir and his G.E. associates found that the merest smidge of the magic iodide seemed to be enough. Here apparently was a tool of almost miraculous potency.

With such a handy device available, the G.E. men foresaw a prospect of endless legal problems. In the winter of 1946, Langmuir's men gave the dry ice treatment to a mass of clouds near Schenectady. Snow started falling. It fell and fell. The storm had all the usual effects of a blizzard: snarled traffic, accidents, a drop in business for department stores. It would be hard to prove that the dry ice was responsible (if it was), but the incident gave G.E. a serious scare. The big, rich company would be a tempting target for damage-suit lawyers. The company was much relieved when the Army got into the game and took Langmuir and his associates to New Mexico.

So far, neither Langmuir nor his associates are overanxious to publish their latest results. They feel that too much silver iodide is being sprayed around the Southwest these days. It might be just as well to leave matters as they are for a while before western clouds are overseeded or the chemicals drift to the east and cause too much rain.

Dr. Irving Langmuir, the weathermaker. Can a man be sued for a storm?

Dr. Eugene Gardner. He dies from a whiff of beryllium dust. Page 178.

HEART OF GOLD: Gold is a heavy element with a big, clumsy DEC. 4 nucleus in the center of its atom. Last week University of Illinois scientists reported just how big a gold nucleus is. It would take 3.3 trillion (3,300,000,000,000) gold nuclei arranged in a line to cover one inch.

WAR HERO: Dr. Eugene Gardner, a brilliant young nuclear DEC. 11 physicist, was working in 1942 with the Manhattan (atom bomb) Project. His secret work required him to drill a hole in an electrode made of beryllium oxide. Out of the hole a fine dust rose, and 29-year-old Dr. Gardner inhaled it. He did not know, nor did anyone know at the time, that the beryllium in the dust was a slow, implacable poison.

All through the critical years of the bomb project, Gardner worked at Oak Ridge and Los Alamos. As one colleague put it, his brain was "one of the nation's great natural resources." When he returned to Berkeley in 1945 his disease was well advanced. He complained of fatigue and shortness of breath. X-rays of his chest showed fibrosis in both lungs. But no one could tell the cause; no treatment did any good.

He had hardly enough strength for desk work. But his scientist's brain was as good as ever. In 1948 he became nationally known as co-discoverer of the man-made meson, a basic atomic particle. About the same time his disease was correctly diagnosed as beryllium poisoning.

Fame does not cure berylliosis. Tuberculosis attacked Dr. Gardner's poisoned lungs. He spent much of his time in the hospital, often under an oxygen tent. He was even forbidden to lift his newborn daughter, Claire, now two years old. But he kept a microscope near his bed and worked on his meson research when he had enough strength. During his final hours under an oxygen tent, knowing that death would no longer be denied, he worked with pencil and notebook, painfully gleaning his brain while he still had time for last bits of knowledge to pass along to the living. Last week, his work all but done, Dr. Gardner laid down his notebook and died.

RADIO & TV

Television became a major industry and cultural force in 1950. At the beginning of that year there were only about 3,000,000 TV sets in the U.S.; at year's end nearly 10,000,000 families had sets. Although this was still 30,000,000 fewer than the number of families with radios, in some localities, for the first time, more Americans were watching TV than listening to radio.

JAN. 2 **YOU'VE GOT TO BELIEVE:** "The moment I saw TV," says Burr Tillstrom, "I knew it was the one medium made expressly for puppets." Every weekday evening, Tillstrom's *Kukla, Fran & Ollie* brilliantly proves the rightness of his conviction. But in finding success, Tillstrom has lost his own identity. Like Singer Fran Allison, he has been swallowed up by the puppet world he made. The world revolves around Kukla, a pinch-faced, sentimental puppet, and Ollie, a one-toothed dragon whose posturings might have been conceived by Molière.

The puppets, all powered by Tillstrom's nimble hands and agile, nine-voiced throat, make their way through rambling shows that somehow seem to crackle with spontaneity. Large and devoted as is *Kukla's* children's audience, that show's delicately balanced humor has just as strong an appeal for adults. Before going on the air, the studio crew members talk to the puppets almost as they do with each other. Fran Allison refuses to go backstage because she feels ill at ease whenever she sees Kukla or Ollie hanging lifelessly upsidedown from their hooks.

Says Tillstrom: "You must believe in the puppets before you can enjoy them. If you don't do that, the program is just silly."

JAN. 30 **GRUNTS ON TV:** Television was promising either to kill or cure the sports world. Wrestling had a sweaty, dying pallor until it was hurried onto TV as an inexpensive fill-in. So astounding was its success that when Promotor Ned Irish put a wrestling match into Madison Square Garden last month, he grossed over $50,000—$10,000 more than any boxing card had drawn all season. Said Irish: "At least 40% of the customers were women—there's nothing you can attribute it to but television."

Midget wrestlers, and bigger ones, too, are a hit on television.

Groucho Marx: "I'm like a dame hot out of Vassar." Page 182.

OCEANS OF EMPATHY: "And here's that man himself," cried FEB. 27 the announcer—"*Arthur,* the-man-with-the-natural-look, *Godfrey!*" Wearing his earphones, a swept-up shock of copper hair and a winning, country-boy grin that belied his 46 years, the big-shouldered man at the desk shifted a candy wafer in his mouth and asked plaintively: "Now what am I gonna do with the last half of this Life Saver?"

Before Godfrey, no one on the network air ever had the unbuttoned nerve to talk with his mouth full, use sloppy diction, or blithely ad-lib whatever popped into his mind. Yet today he is the top money-maker and the outstanding personality on the air. He earns $1,500 for every minute he broadcasts. He is seen and heard—and apparently loved—by 40 million people.

Because of Godfrey's use of such words as "doggone," "ain't" and "gotta," Comedian Fred Allen has called Godfrey "the man with the barefoot voice." Some cynical observers think that Godfrey's greatest audience bait is the faintly smutty double meaning. "He's sweeping the country," says Fred Allen, "and, Lord knows, it needs to be swept. But I think Arthur must be doing it with a short-handled broom—he's nearer the dirt than most people."

APRIL 3 **WHO, ME?:** The skit was certainly no broader in its assault on humor than many another on *Arthur Godfrey & His Friends*. Dressed as whitewings, Godfrey, Crooner Morton Downey and Hollywood Comic Jack Carson appeared on the screen pushing street cleaners' brooms. Said Godfrey: "Well, we've dished a lot of it out. Let's clean some of it up."

On this occasion, Godfrey's usually good timing was off-base as well as off-color. Just the day before, Wayne Coy, chairman of the Federal Communications Commission, had said: "When a comedian gets so big that his network can no longer handle him, then we have a case of the tail wagging the dog. The boy who used to express himself with chalk on a wall is now provided with a television screen. . . . This type of comedian is still peddling livery stable humor."

In New York, the protests began to mount. At week's end, Godfrey had flown off to the rural quiet of his Virginia farm, where he complained that "the audience often thinks something is dirty that I don't mean to be dirty."

MAY 1 **HOT OUT OF VASSAR:** A year ago, Groucho Marx's *You Bet Your Life* was fighting it out for 75th place in the Nielsen-Ratings with such tired old rivals as *Dr. I.Q.* Last week Groucho had piloted his show in a sky-rocketing climb to sixth place.

The propulsion was supplied by Groucho's trademarked wit, which tends to explode in star shells of mutual misunderstanding. Beginning with a casual question about the contestant's background, Groucho is soon off in a blaze of barbed and ribald *non sequiturs*. Introducing a dealer in war surplus, he inquired solicitously: "How many times have you been indicted?" Learning from a dress designer that women dress for themselves, he observed with a happy leer: "If they dressed for me, the stores wouldn't sell much—just an occasional sun visor."

He is often topped. He was almost speechless for once when a burlesque-show employee identified a stripteaser as "an anatomy award winner." Last week Groucho was being wined and dined by NBC executives who were trying to lure him away from CBS. Said Groucho: "I'm being wooed for the first time in my life. I'm like a dame hot out of Vassar." [He was successfully wooed, shifted to NBC later in the year.]

BEGINNING OF THE END: Baltimore last week became the MAY 15 first U.S. city in which more people watched evening television (50.2%) than listened to radio. Just a year ago, according to Researcher C. E. Hooper, the figures were 82% for radio, 18% for TV.

REAL THRILLER: Most radio whodunits rely on tough-talking private eyes, glossy gun molls and satanic scientists. By avoiding such standard characters, *Dragnet* has won a devoted following among policemen who welcome its non-nonsense approach. Says 30-year-old Jack Webb, creator of the show: "We try to make it as real as a guy pouring a cup of coffee." Last week, as it rounded out its first year on radio, *Dragnet's* realism reached a new high: the criminal got away.

HE WENT THAT-A-WAY: Washington's "I Am an American MAY 29 Day" celebration went off smoothly this week without its two top guests of honor—President Truman and Hopalong Cassidy. The celebration committee's chairman, Colonel Waldron Leonard, didn't blame the President. But Washington and Colonel Leonard will be a long time forgiving Hopalong.

"Everything was all set," says Leonard. "The next thing I knew there was a telegram from Cassidy saying he couldn't make it because of 'conflicting engagements.' You know what my kids did last night? They took an old safety razor and cut their Hopalong Cassidy clothes to bits."

EDITORS' CHOICE: After polling U.S. radio & TV editors, the NOV. 20 tradesheet *Radio Daily* last week announced their favorite shows and performers of 1950. In the TV documentary field, MARCH OF TIME's filmed *Crusade in Europe* (ABC-TV) scored a repeat win (first telecast in 1949, *Crusade* won a Peabody Award).

Other winners:

RADIO

Man of the Year: Jack Benny (CBS).
Woman of the Year: Eve Arden (CBS).
Drama Show: Lux Radio Theater (CBS).
Comedy Show: Jack Benny (CBS).

TELEVISION

Man of the Year: Sid Caesar (NBC-TV).
Woman of the Year: Faye Emerson (NBC-TV and CBS-TV).
Drama Show: *Studio One* (CBS-TV).
Comedy Show: Milton Berle (NBC-TV).

DEC. 11 **ONE-MAN SHOW:** Jimmy Durante proved last week that the success of his first TV show was no accident. Returning for the second of his monthly appearances on *Four Star Revue*, he again effortlessly balanced 60 minutes of solid fun on his expressive shoulders and never once bobbled the load.

Though long a popular draw in theater and nightclubs, Durante was never a top smash in either radio or movies. It now seems clear that TV was invented, in part at least, as a frame for his special talents. The dynamic Durante personality, a sort of mixture of W. C. Fields and Donald Duck, triumphs over old routines and standard jokes.

Almost every other comic has nervously surrounded himself with elaborate props for his entry into television. Jimmy Durante brought only his nose, his piano, his rasp-voiced songs and patter, and sat down like an old friend in the televiewer's living room. He hymned his nose's birthday ("It was the first time in history that a nose outweighed the child!"), displayed an entertaining low comedy that is as innocent as it is rare on TV—bending a tall girl backward in his arms, little Durante observes: "When my women are too tall, I fold 'em in half." Durante and TV were a long time getting together, but it was well worth the wait.

RELIGION

42 HOURS OF REPENTANCE: Just after dinner one evening FEB. 20 last week, balding, spectacled President Victor Raymond Edman of Illinois' Wheaton College rose to begin a regular session of the Evangelistic Week that traditionally begins each term. Stepping up to the microphones in the brightly lit, rectangular auditorium of Pierce Memorial Chapel, he asked if any student would "like to give a word of testimony or praise on the blessings of this week."

President Edman was not surprised when several students trooped up to the rostrum. Such impromptu declarations are not unusual at Wheaton, a little (1,500 students), non-denominational college which still bears the stamp of its strict fundamentalist heritage: no movies, smoking, card-playing, dancing or drinking, a 10 p.m. weekday curfew. But as the first students finished speaking, a surge of confessional fervor swept through the auditorium.

Singly and in little groups, sweatered and blue-jeaned undergraduates streamed onto the stage, filling up the choir chairs to await their turns. Hour after hour they kept coming. All night long, all the next day, all through the following night and half the following day, students poured out confessions of past sins and rededicated themselves to God.

The auditorium filled up and overflowed into a smaller chapel downstairs. Classes had to be canceled altogether. Some speakers came forward boldly and eagerly, others were so overcome with shyness that they had to abandon the attempt and come back later to try again. Some broke down completely.

Sniffled a determined brunette: "I want to say this publicly so that those who hear me will know I mean business. I know it's mostly fellows who say they have impure thoughts, but girls have them too. And I want to apologize if I've ever tempted any of the fellows I've had contact with. I know I've tried, and I'm sorry."

Declared a cheerful, ruddy baseball star, "Twenty-four hours ago, this is the last thing I thought I'd be doing. . . . Last night I looked in my yearbook, and after my name it said baseball is my main interest. I want to change it to say: Christ is my main interest."

There was little audible response to the confessions. But when other confession-hungry heart probers began flocking in to Wheaton—followed by the simply curious—President Edman discreetly ended the public testimonies. After a few hours more of confessions, it was all over—42 hours and 40 minutes after it began. "These kids are tired out," explained President Edman.

MARCH 6 **MORAL ABSENTEES:** *But I say unto you that ye resist not evil. . . .*—Matthew 5:39

On these and other words of Jesus some Christians have based a stand of absolute pacifism. Last week the Roman Catholic Church made it clear that Catholic conscientious objectors are theologically in error.

"When the fathers of the early Church advised the young against embracing military careers in Roman legions," says Rome's official Jesuit journal, "they based their advice on necessity of avoiding idolatrous service to the emperor—never on the individual right of avoiding combat against the state's aggressors. . . . Neither did Christ warn the good centurion against fighting."

APRIL 17 **A BAD SITUATION:** People have grown "so keyed up" about things, the Rev. Norman Vincent Peale of Manhattan's Marble Collegiate Church told a group of policemen last week, that "I haven't seen anyone sleeping in church in years—and, I tell you, that's a bad situation!"

MAY 15 **THE MYSTERY OF THE CLOTH:** How big was Jesus Christ? Was He a strongly built man 5 feet 10 inches tall, with long, delicate hands & feet, a right shoulder slightly lower than the left? Did He have a brain weighing approximately 1,492 grams? These questions were debated for three days last week by 200 learned scientists and black-robed scholars in the huge, frescoed Hall of the Papal Chancellery in Rome. It was the first International Congress of Studies of the Holy Shroud.

During the 7th Century two early churchmen referred to the existence of a cloth venerated as the shroud in which the body of Christ was wrapped when it was laid in the tomb. But in 1349 the Church of St. Stephen in Besançon, France, where it was kept at that time, caught fire, and the shroud seemed to have vanished. The following year, King Philippe de Valois of France presented to one of his lords a cloth purporting to be the same shroud. Two bishops forbade veneration of it, presumably because it was a fraud, and in 1390 Pope Clement VII issued a special bull ordering that it should be treated only as "a painted representation of the original, authentic Holy Shroud, whose whereabouts are unknown."

Since 1452, the cloth has been the property of the Italian House of Savoy. In 1898, King Umberto I agreed to have the relic photographed. Secondo Pia, a photographer of Turin, was given the job. While developing the plate, he reported: "Suddenly I was so filled with fear that I almost fainted. For there grew plainly visible on the plate the face and body of a man whose head was covered with blood, whose wrists carried stigmata, whose expression was one of untold majesty."

Ever since, the argument has raged: Does the 14 ft. 3 in.-long cloth really bear the front & back imprint of Christ's naked body, as though it had enveloped Him lengthwise, or is it the work of a clever forger?

Last week's conference closed without final proof either way, but with an official hope "that a way may be found to examine scientifically, religiously and historically those aspects of the holy linen which may lead to determination of its authenticity." Colored photographs, X-ray and chemical analyses seemed indicated, but much red tape needed unraveling before they would be forthcoming. The shroud, still the private property of ex-King Umberto II, has not been exhibited since the Holy Year 1933.

LITTLE MARTYR: In Rome last week, for the first time in history, a mother heard her daughter canonized a saint. In a place of special honor near the papal throne, 86-year-old Assunta Goretti sat with her two sons and two daughters and wept. "My daughter, my daughter," she cried. "My little Marietta!" JULY 3

In 1902, Maria Goretti, daughter of poor sharecroppers on the Pontine marshes south of Rome, was eleven years old. When 19-year-old Alessandro Serenelli tried to rape her, she resisted him, even though he stabbed her to death. As she lay dying, Maria forgave Serenelli and promised to pray for him in heaven. Serenelli served 27 penitent years in prison for his crime and is now a handyman and pig-tender at a Capuchin monastery. There last week he spent the day of Maria's canonization "in prayer more intense than ever."

Fitted with a mask of wax, Saint Maria's skeleton had been brought to Rome for public veneration. Calling upon the world to follow the example of "the little sweet Martyr of Purity," Pope Pius XII asked the young people in the crowd whether they would resist any attempt against their virtue. *"Si!"* they shouted in chorus.

Saint Maria. In 1902 she promised to pray in heaven for a rapist.

Actress Jane Russell: "a born-again believer in Jesus Christ." Page 188.

JULY 17 **HOLLYWOOD CHRISTIANS?:** The readers of the monthly *Christian Life* are no friends of show business. Drinking, smoking, dancing, card-playing and movies they consider the Devil's traps. Last week their aggressively fundamentalist magazine brought them up short with an article called "The Truth about Hollywood."

Editor Robert Walker told about a group of movie-folk who had become "born-again believers in the Lord Jesus

Christ." Among the galaxy of "sincere and effective soul-winners": Stars Jane Russell and Roy Rogers.

Christian Life's readers lost no time in letting Editor Walker know where the Devil had trapped him. Wrote one minister: ". . . Let's not have a story of the Bartenders' Christian Fellowship, or the revelation of a Prostitutes' Christian Association." Henry Pucek of St. Louis, Mo. pointed to a recent magazine picture of Jane Russell in an "un-Christian pose," and asked: "Is this the priesthood which Miss Russell feels that God has called her to?" Mrs. Derrall Bodenhamer of Macomb, Ill. was simply puzzled: "I didn't know there were Hollywood Christians."

MILESTONES

DIED: Kate Cross-Eyes, ninetyish, widow of Geronimo, famed Chiricahua Apache leader who terrorized white settlers in Arizona and New Mexico in the 1880s; in Mescalero, N.Mex. The last of Geronimo's wives to die, Kate was captured in 1886, the year he and his war band surrendered.

MARRIED: Cinemactor Cary (*I Was a Male War Bride*) Grant, 45, and Cinemactress Betsy (*Every Girl Should Be Married*) Drake, 26, who became his screen protégée two years ago; he for the third time (No. 2: five & dime Heiress Barbara Hutton), she for the first time; after an elopement from Hollywood in a plane piloted by Best Man Howard Hughes; near Phoenix, Ariz.

DIVORCED: John Huston, 43, writer-director of topnotch U.S. Army and Hollywood films (*Treasure of Sierra Madre*); by Cinemactress Evelyn Keyes, 28, his third wife (he was her third husband); after 3½ years of marriage, one adopted son; in Ciudad Juárez, Mexico.

DIED John Francis ("Honey Fitz") Fitzgerald, 87, oldtime "Young Napoleon" of Boston ward politics whose shrewd common touch and honeyed rendition of *Sweet Adeline* made him one of Boston's most influential Irish Democrats, got him elected U.S. Representative for three terms, mayor for two; in Boston. [He was John F. Kennedy's grandfather.]

MISCELLANY

IRON CURTAIN: In Manhattan, Associated Fur Manufacturers Inc. ruefully disclosed that twelve live Russian sables sent to the U.S. (in trade for twelve U.S. minks) to be used for breeding purposes had been sterilized before shipment.

TRIAL & ERROR: In Pittsburgh, Daniel A. Marra admitted in court that he used to beat his wife, but gave it up "when I found out it was not doing any good."

CLEAN SWEEP: In London, thieves broke into the Avenue Hotel, made off with 4,800 cigarettes, 140 bottles of liquor, a radio set, the watchdog.

JAN. 30 **THE EXILE OF PRADES:** Almost every morning at 8, a tubby little old man in baggy pants, a wool shirt and a brown pull-over sweater emerges from the concierge's cottage of the Châ-teau Valrac in the sleepy little Franco-Spanish border town of Prades to take a walk. He seldom heads toward the center of the town; the townspeople of Prades are inordinately proud of Pablo Casals, the great musician who lives among them in self-exile, and he would have to shake the hand of everyone he met.

For eleven years, world-famed Catalan Cellist Casals has lived his life of simple but defiant exile in Prades. When he came to Prades, it was with a vow that he would never play again in his native Spain so long as Dictator Francisco Fran-co was in power. Then, soon after World War II, he de-cided not to play any more in public at all.

At 73, his life is nonetheless full of music. After his morn-ing walks he goes to the new grand piano sent to him by an admirer from Buffalo, N.Y. "As I have done all my life long," he begins his musical day with preludes and fugues from the *Well-Tempered Clavier* of Johann Sebastian Bach. He is composing some, teaching a good deal; pupils come to him from all over the world. Above all, he has never neglect-ed his cello.

Last week, his blue eyes twinkling with enthusiasm and excitement, Pablo Casals was practicing with a new will and fervor. To honor the great Bach himself on the 200th anni-versary of the composer's death, he had agreed to play in public just once more. Said he last week: "I am not coming out of retirement. I decided to play here this once, in spite of my retirement."

In a world that has forgotten much and forgiven more, Pablo Casals has forgiven and forgotten nothing. He will not play in Britain or in the U.S., where he last toured in 1928, because "I consider that we owe to England and America the

situation in Spain. . . . They abandoned us. . . . It is the greatest sacrifice of my life I am making. But someone must remember. Someone." [Casals later moved to Puerto Rico; in
1961 he played in the White House for President Kennedy.]

THANKS AND FAREWELL: Onstage, red-haired Bulgarian So- MARCH 13
prano Ljuba (*Salome*) Welitch was singing her first *Tosca*
at the Metropolitan. Backstage, there was more excitement
still. Whispered one anxious artist in a thick Italian accent:
"Do you know the words to this *For He's a Jolly Good
Fellow*?" Replied another: "I don't even know the melody."
Nevertheless, when the curtain went down on *Tosca*, then up
again on a gala pageant of recent Met history, every singer
present seemed to roar it out like a native, and from the
heart. There was good reason for their fervor: the pageant
was the Met's farewell to pink-cheeked, white-haired General
Manager Edward Johnson, who will retire when Manager-
Designate Rudolf Bing takes over at the end of May.

Johnson had given Met audiences many a performance
they might not have seen but for him: the Met's first *Abduction from the Seraglio* of Mozart, the first *Alceste* of Gluck.
He had resurrected the dusty *Marriage of Figaro* (now one
of the Met's best performances and biggest hits), *Boris Go-
dunov, Otello, Falstaff.* He brought the best of Europe's
singers to the Met, but he made his era the era of the American singer too: in this year's roster of 108 singers, more than
half are U.S.-born.

SIR JOHN & THE MAESTRO: Giuseppe Verdi composed his APRIL 10
most fettlesome opera, *Falstaff*, when he was nearing 80.
Last week, white-fringed little Arturo Toscanini, who learned
how to play some of Verdi's operas from the famed composer himself some 60 years ago, proved he still had the pep at
83 to conduct a fettlesome performance of *Falstaff.*

He had given his opera of the year his usual patient and
pernickety preparation, drilling his singers until they were
ready to drop, illustrating passages by pushing his hoarse old
voice up into squeaky soprano register and down into roaring baritone range as well.

When he got around to putting the orchestra through
Falstaff early last week, he found the orchestral parts full of

wrong notes. Stopping the music, he would summon flutists and violists to the podium, hold the offending scores up to his nose so he could read them.

At week's end, when a jammed studio audience and NBC's millions of radio listeners heard the first half of *Falstaff*, they found the result, as usual, more than worth all the fussing and finishing. They heard a *Falstaff* that was robustiously humorous without being rambunctious—all of it performed with the kind of brilliance, clarity and pace that brought the audience bravoing to its feet with the crash of the final chord.

MAY 1 **COMPOSER ON BROADWAY:** A few days after his new opera, *The Consul*, opened on Broadway, Italian-born Composer Gian-Carlo Menotti phoned Producer Chandler Cowles and said in a subdued voice: "Well, I guess we have a success on our hands. Now is when we must be humble."

The Consul, Menotti's first three-acter, opened on Broadway with a $100,000 advance sale; by last week all seats were sold out through June. It had also won the New York Drama Critics Circle Award for the year's best "musical" (opera was still considered too strong a word for Broadway). Decca Records was recording it with the original cast, and Hollywood was shouting offers.

What pleased Menotti considerably more was that Milan's La Scala, which snooted his first five operas, had asked permission to produce *The Consul* in Italian late this year. Menotti felt hopeful that his acceptance by La Scala, at long last, might even persuade his family back in Italy that he amounted to something. Wails Menotti: "I keep telling them I am famous in America, famous! They just look at me sympathetically."

MAY 29 **WHAT COUNTS:** Tunesmith Richard Rodgers well remembers May 17, 1925. That was the day a group of Theatre Guild youngsters bounced onto the stage of Broadway's Garrick Theater and sang, danced and mugged their way through a little revue named *Garrick Gaieties*. In the pit, conducting his own catchy, melodious score, was Richard Rodgers himself. *Garrick Gaieties* was supposed to be a one-night stand, to raise money for new tapestries for the Theatre Guild. But when it was all over and the audience had gone home hum-

Composer Rodgers "moves more peo-
ple to tears than the Met."

Composer Copland sounds like the
best the U.S. has produced. Page 195.

ming Rodgers' tunes ("Manhattan," "Sentimental Me"), the Guild had more than its tapestries. It had a hit show. And 22-year-old Richard Rodgers had been launched on one of the most successful careers in U.S. show business.

Last week, 25 years after the opening at the Garrick, the Theatre Guild called together some of the old gang and threw a silver anniversary party for Songwriter and Pulitzer Prize-winner (*South Pacific*) Dick Rodgers.

For Rodgers, composing melodious, palatable music has always been "easier than bending over and tying my shoe-laces." In restaurants, Pullmans, theater lounges or his own living room, he has been known to whip out a song in 15 minutes, even with interruptions. In 25 years he has written 32 Broadway shows including *A Connecticut Yankee, Pal Joey, Carousel* and *Oklahoma!* Last week Rodgers was busy with a new assignment: a musical version of *Anna and the King of Siam* due on Broadway next winter. Said satisfied Dick Rodgers: "We move a lot more people to tears at the Majestic [where *South Pacific* is playing] than they do at the Met. And that's what really counts."

MISTER JELLY ROLL: At the Library of Congress the oldtime JUNE 19 pianist sat at the keyboard, facing an open microphone. "Mister Morton," said Alan Lomax, assistant curator of the

The late pianist Jelly Roll Morton.   *."LeadBelly"wrote"Goodnight, Irene,"*
He wore garters of solid gold.   *said goodbye to prison. Page 194.*

Library's American Folk Song Archive, "tell about where you were born and how you got started . . . and maybe keep playing piano while you talk."

Famed Creole Pianist-Composer Ferdinand ("Jelly Roll") Morton (*King Porter Stomp, Jelly Roll Blues, Alabama Bound*), "the father of hot piano," talked and played almost every day for a month. The result, a book entitled *Mister Jelly Roll*, is the full-flavored story of a raucous, diamond-studded era of U.S. history, as seen and told by a mulatto genius who lived it from top to bottom.

The beginning for Ferdinand La Menthe (he changed his name to Morton because "I didn't want to be called 'Frenchy'") was much like the end. He was born hard by the cribs of New Orleans' tough and fabled Storyville. When Author Lomax met him in 1938, he was pounding the piano in a dingy Washington nightspot. That same year, Jelly Roll was stabbed in a brawl there, and he died broke in Los Angeles in 1941. Bordello pianist, pool-playing shark and pimp, he was in & out of trouble all his life.

In his most glorious days, in the '20s, when such youngsters as Benny Goodman and Bix Beiderbecke gathered around to hear Jelly's style, he was "all in diamonds." As his wife recalls: "His watch was circled in diamonds. His belt buckle was in gold and studded with diamonds. He even had sock-supporters of solid gold set with diamonds. Then you could see that big half-carat diamond sparkling in his teeth. . . ."

His own flamboyant claim was that "I personally originated jazz in New Orleans in 1902." Old Jelly Roll did not originate it all. But his legacy—a barrelful of folk-flavored tunes and a riffling, hard-breaking piano style—has influenced long-hair and short-hair musicians alike for a generation.

GOOD NIGHT, IRENE: "This here song," the late Huddie AUG. 14 ("Lead Belly") Ledbetter used to explain, "was made about a man an' a girl was walkin' along one Sunday evenin'. Jus' befo' this girl an' man got to de house, she said, 'You ask my mother for me, when you get home.' The man tol' her, 'All right.' . . . An' he went back to de girl an' she say, 'What did mamma tell you?' He looked at Irene—her name was Irene —an' here what he said. . . ." Then, his coal-black face gleaming fiercely and his horny hands scratching his twelve-string guitar, the murderous old Minstrel Lead Belly would sing:

> *I ask your mother for you,*
> *She told me you was too young. . . .*
> *Good night, Irene, good night, Irene,*
> *I'll kiss you in my dreams.*

Old Lead Belly himself thought that he had learned *Irene* from his Uncle Terrell, just before he [Lead Belly] was sent to the penitentiary in Texas for murder in 1918. Adding verses as they came to him, Lead Belly made *Irene* a prison favorite. Five years after he got out of the Texas jail on a pardon, he bounced into Louisiana's state prison farm for assault with intent to kill, and sweet *Irene* went right along with him.

Music-loving Governor O.K. Allen is said to have pardoned the old reprobate as much for *Irene* as anything. Until Lead Belly died in Manhattan last year, he sang *Irene* as his theme song. Last week the old minstrel's old song, prettied up and cut in half, was on the hit parade.

TRAIL BLAZER FROM BROOKLYN: In Manhattan's Aeolian NOV. Hall one afternoon in 1925, Conductor Walter Damrosch put down his baton, turned to the audience that had just listened to the first performance of a new work by an unknown young composer. Roared Damrosch: "If a young man of 23 can write a symphony like that, in five years he will be ready to commit murder."

Time has proved audience and conductor wrong. Nobody has ever accused Aaron Copland of murder, even murder of harmony and counterpoint, and this week he reached his 50th birthday the most-played and most honored of living U.S.-born composers.

U.S. composers in particular have a lot to thank Copland for. In a way, homely, friendly Aaron Copland blazed the trail for them. Born in Brooklyn, he survived the iron classical discipline of his first teachers, then, at 20, took off for Paris. Other U.S. composers were soon following.

One night last week, Manhattan's musical advance guard gathered in the Museum of Modern Art auditorium to help pay Composer Copland a birthday tribute. Taken all in all, if Aaron Copland had not yet carved himself a niche among the immortals, he sounded like the best composer the U.S. had yet produced.

DEC. 25 **THE WINNERS:** The top popular singers of 1949 held their own in 1950. Last week, with returns in from their annual jazz-fan polls, both *Down Beat* and *Metronome* found that rubber-throated Billy Eckstine and sultry-voiced Sarah Vaughan again led all the rest.

The taste in jazz bands had changed a bit, if only slightly: up into first place, nosing out last year's favorite, Woody Herman, went Progressive Jazzman Stan Kenton. For the second time in *Down Beat* blind British Pianist George Shearing and his Quintet won the "best instrumental combo" title. For the ninth time, Spike Jones was elected "King of Corn." Runner-up: Guy Lombardo.

MEDICINE

CONTINUING MYSTERY: More cases of infantile paralysis JAN. 2
were reported in the U.S. during 1949 than in any previous
year. Last week the total passed 43,000. As the sad statistics piled up, officials of the U.S. Public Health Service
combed through mountains of reports, hoping that locating
the outbreaks would help to explain them. The results
were discouraging. No clear geographical pattern was
apparent.

A lot of old theories about polio came into question: there
was no close relation between temperature peaks and polio
peaks; crowd-begetting holidays and fairs did not seem to
give the disease any extra encouragement. Three famed buga-
boos—swimming, travel and over-exertion—seemed to pre-
cede the disease only in rare cases. The old questions of how,
when and where people catch polio remained a mystery.

MOTHER UNION: By the considered diagnosis of Chicago's JAN. 16
Dr. Robert N. McMurry, disputes between labor and management are not so much social or political as psychological
conflicts. Psychologist McMurry, a Freud disciple with a
Vienna Ph.D., gets $125 an hour for giving advice on labor
relations to companies manufacturing everything from auto-
mobiles to candy bars. Last week he summed up his findings:
"Management has failed to be the kindly protective father,
so the union has become the caressing mother who gets
things from that stinker of a father."

NEW ANTIBIOTIC: After testing scores of thousands of soil FEB. 6
samples from all over the world, researchers for Charles
Pfizer & Co. Inc. announced last week that they had isolated
a new and promising antibiotic from a piece of Indiana dirt.
The drug, named terramycin (earth mold) by its Brooklyn
discoverers, is secreted by a tiny organism, *Streptomyces ri-
mosus*, of the same group which has produced three other

major antibiotics—streptomycin, aureomycin and Chloromycetin.

In laboratory animals, terramycin kills heavy growths of bacteria which cause one of the commonest forms of pneumonia, streptococcal infections, typhoid fever, and many intestinal and urinary tract infections.

FEB. 13   **OLD SERGEANT SYNDROME:** In the ranks of World War II's foot soldiers, there were always the iron men—tough noncoms who stood out as the most efficient, best disciplined men in their outfits. But sometimes even the iron men cracked up and had to be carted to the rear muttering the confused soliloquies of soldiers suddenly smitten with combat fatigue.

Major Raymond Sobel analyzed the crack-ups of 50 seasoned men who had fought battle after battle without a misstep. The aggregation of symptoms was so similar in each case that Psychiatrist Sobel gave it a name—the "Old Sergeant Syndrome."

Sobel and his associates found that a five-layer cushion of psychological defenses had protected the old sergeants—and presumably all soldiers who survived long stretches of combat in good mental health—from caving in. As the layers were peeled away, normal combat anxiety eventually turned into psychoneurosis and the old sergeant became a casualty:

¶ "Distant ideals"—a reliance on such intangibles as "the four freedoms," democracy, and the desire for "keeping the enemy out of the United States"—were the first to dissolve.

¶ "Hatred of the enemy was the next defense to go. . . . It was not of sufficient force to counteract the effects of long-sustained combat."

¶ The soldier then lost faith in short-term objectives—his hope that once a given hill was taken or a town was entered he would be relieved.

¶ Next went pride in himself. Pride was a "mainstay" of the old sergeants' personalities, "but once a break in efficiency occurred, self-confidence weakened progressively."

¶ "Loyalty to the group was the last and most important line of defense. . . . Even this . . . weakens with the passage of time."

But once the patient was out of combat, Army psychiatrists found that the old sergeant syndrome was easy to treat.

By giving him a job out of shellfire range but close to the front, the Army found it could cure him and still get a lot of good service out of a rusty iron man.

DEATH IN THE CRIB: Every time a baby is found dead in his MARCH 6 crib, apparently smothered by bedclothing or a soft pillow, the mother is tortured by the feeling that she should have been more careful. Neighbors and kin often brand her as negligent. Almost all such blame and remorse are pointless, says Dr. Keith Bowden in the current *Australian Medical Journal*: cases of "baby smothering" are usually due to unsuspected disease. A baby may be overwhelmed in a few hours by a disease of such an "explosive" type that no symptoms are showing when the child is put to bed.

A healthy baby actually being suffocated would fight for life and yell to attract attention, says Dr. Bowden. "Why," he asks, "should a healthy baby die without much fuss just because he is face downward or his face is covered? But a baby dying of natural disease might well be expected to make a quiet exit."

ROUGH STUFF: The best way to get rid of acne scars, Plastic MARCH Surgeon William G. McEvitt of Detroit announced last week, is to rub them down with coarse sandpaper. He puts his patients into the hospital, gives them a general anesthetic, and sandpapers the whole face (using No. $1\frac{1}{2}$ or No. 2 grade of sandpaper). Then petrolatum gauze and a pressure dressing are applied. After ten days the wrappings come off, and the patient's face is usually healed. Self-conscious teen-agers are sternly warned against trying the treatment on themselves.

LEGAL RASH: Doctors are becoming more & more wary of MARCH laying themselves open to malpractice suits. And nowhere are they warier than in Los Angeles, where such suits are commoner than anywhere else in the U.S. The epidemic in Los Angeles is especially severe because Southern California is full of elderly hypochondriacs. Says Doctor-Lawyer Louis J. Regan: "We have so many people in the fringe group here —the lunatic fringe, that is." Examples: one woman, accusing her surgeon of having left needles in her arm, stuck 26 sewing needles into herself; another woman, claiming that she had been examined without her consent, sued under the Fourth Amendment guarantee against unlawful search & seizure. Both plaintiffs lost.

Because malpractice suits are costly to defend, even when the doctor wins, Dr. Regan and the County Medical Association are concentrating on trying to prevent them. For example, a doctor must not tell a patient that a broken limb will be "as good as new," for that can be regarded as a verbal contract. He must not promise a cure.

THE WEEPER SEX: After tests on 231 people, two ophthalmologists at the Mayo Clinic and Foundation proved what everybody knew (or thought he knew) all along: once they start to cry, young women can weep more tears than young men. The doctors squeezed out two more drops of information: from ages 30 to 60, men & women seem to have about the same capacity for tears; beyond 60, women seem to be slightly drier-eyed than men.

UNE 5 **SWEETEN TO TASTE:** Michael Sveda was working for his doctorate in chemistry at the University of Illinois and his laboratory bench was cluttered. One day Sveda lit a cigarette without bothering to wash his hands, was surprised to find that the cigarette tasted sweet. To track down the cause, Sveda tasted every compound on his bench. The sweetener proved to be sodium cyclohexylsulfamate. It was a lucky accident for people who want sweetness without sugar.

Last week, after 13 years of testing on animals and men, Chicago's Abbott Laboratories announced that it was putting Dr. Sveda's synthetic sweetener on the market under the trade name Sucaryl Sodium.

NE 19 **"DIETARY SUPPLEMENT":** In easygoing Lafayette, La. (pop: 19,210), 425 factory workers bustled each working day last week turning out more than 100,000 bottles of a murky brown liquid that tastes something like bilge water, and smells worse. The patent medicine called Hadacol has been such a resounding success in 14 Southern states that its backers expect this year to sell $20,000,000 worth.

The man responsible for the murky brown medicine is Louisiana's plump State Senator Dudley J. LeBlanc, 56, who had to rustle up a new business after he made the mistake of running against a Huey Long candidate. LeBlanc got a barrel and a batch of supplies, stirred his mixture up with a paddle, added 12% ethyl alcohol as a preservative, ladled out his first brew with a coffee cup.

Testimonials have poured in, extolling the work of Hadacol on ills such as headaches, gas pains, ulcers, loss of weight, drowsiness. Samples: From an 80-year-old Mississippian: "I was disable to get over a fence, disable to get up out of a chair without help, but after I took eight bottles of Hadacol I can tie up my own shoes and feel like I can jump over a six-foot fence and getting very sassy."

100,000 SYPHILITIC CHILDREN: There are more than 100,000 JULY 3 syphilitic children (under ten years) in the U.S. who have had the disease from birth. This shocking report came last week from two bureaus of the Federal Security Agency. Another fact from the report: 14,000 new cases of congenital syphilis are reported each year in the U.S.—about a third of them children of four or younger.

Last week's report concluded: "Any one of these children is a candidate for blindness, mental deficiency, physical deformity or premature death. Not one of them should have been born with syphilis. This is especially so now since penicillin . . . has been widely available in recent years." [Penicillin is still an effective cure, and the subsequent resurgence of syphilis is due to the fact that many victims do not submit to treatment.]

TRANSPLANTED KIDNEY: Openhanded nature gives people two kidneys, but only one is really needed to do the job (regulating the body's water balance and preventing the accumulation of waste products).

Last week in Chicago, trying a desperate experiment on a woman doomed to die because both kidneys were hopelessly diseased, doctors performed the first human kidney transplanting on record.

Both the mother and sister of Mrs. Ruth Tucker, 44, had died of the disease which sent her to Chicago's Little Company of Mary Hospital. While Mrs. Tucker stayed in the hospital for five weeks, staff doctors looked for a suitable donor.

Finally they found a dying woman of Mrs. Tucker's age, general size and blood type. Ten minutes after the donor died, Surgeon Richard Lawler, 54, and Dr. James West began operations in adjoining rooms.

Forty visiting surgeons and doctors watched Dr. Lawler transplant the dead woman's healthy kidney into Mrs. Tucker's body, skillfully fastening vein, artery and ureter. When the clamps were removed, 45 minutes after the donor had died, the kidney in Mrs. Tucker's body took on a healthy pink color.

Some doctors, doubting that the operation would work, pointed out that similar transplant operations on animals have not been entirely successful. At week's end Mrs. Tucker seemed to be fairly on the mend. What pleased the doctors most: she was calling for the bedpan at regular intervals. [Mrs. Tucker died in 1955 after a coronary attack, complicated by pneumonia.]

DEC. 11 **NO SECRET WEAPON:** Aureomycin attacks some viruslike organisms, and some common colds are caused by a virus. So, in a rigidly controlled test, the medical staff of the U.S. Military Academy at West Point tried the golden antibiotic on 154 cadets with colds. At the same time, they gave harmless yellow capsules to 155 other grey-uniformed snifflers. The medics had to admit defeat: aureomycin is just one more thing that doesn't cure a cold.

DEC. 18 **THE FARMER & THE DRUG:** Husky young T.C. Gaines, an Arizona farmer, had promised to lend his tractor to a neighbor. One day last May, as good as his word, he delivered the tractor and drove his truck over to the neighbor's farm to explain its workings. As he filled the tractor's tank with gas, a hired hand lit a cigarette. A split second later, panic-stricken Gaines was streaking across the field, his gasoline-soaked clothes a flaming torch. His friends managed to halt his flight, put out the flames and got him to the truck. No one else knew how, so Gaines himself had to drive 40 miles to the nearest hospital, a 42-bed affair maintained by the Bureau of Indian Affairs.

Once there, he collapsed. Receiving doctors, spotting the ugly third-degree burns which covered a full three-quarters of his body, had little hope that he would ever rise again. After giving him the standard treatment, they sent him to Phoenix. There he was put under the care of Dr. James Whitelaw. With little to lose, Dr. Whitelaw decided to play a hunch. He ordered all other medication stopped. Then he began injecting his patient at six-hour intervals with 20-milligram shots of ACTH, the new synthetic hormone. Within five days the patient's most dangerous symptoms had vanished. He was resting comfortably, "a normal man," in the words of one doctor, "only without much skin."

Last week, well on the road to complete recovery, Gaines appeared in person at Chicago before doctors from all over the country, as Exhibit A in a two-day conference on ACTH. By stimulating the adrenal glands during a crisis, the hormone injections serve to forestall most of the early complications (shock, pain, fever, infection, impairment of kidney function, loss of body fluids) which make burns most dangerous.

RUNNER-UP: Between Jan. 1 and Dec. 2 of this year, there DEC. 25 were 31,989 cases of polio in the U.S. This fearsome figure, announced last week by the National Foundation for Infantile Paralysis, made 1950 the second worse polio year on record. Worst year of all: 1949, with 41,442 cases.

MILESTONES

BORN: To William Samuel Paley, 48, board chairman and principal (19%) stockholder of Columbia Broadcasting System, and Barbara Cushing Mortimer Paley, 32, youngest of the late Dr. Harvey Cushing's three millions-marrying daughters: their second child, first daughter (each has two children by a previous marriage); in Manhattan. Name: Kate Cushing.

DIED: Countess Tatyana Tolstoy, 86, eldest daughter of Russian Novelist Leo Tolstoy; in Rome. Her sister Alexandra, a U.S. citizen and president of Manhattan's Tolstoy Foundation (which aids Russian refugees), is now the only survivor of Tolstoy's 13 children.

MISCELLANY

FAMILY RATE: In Edinburg, Tex., in Hidalgo County court, Reynaldo Gutiérrez was sentenced to six months in jail for beating his girl friend, José Guzmán de León was sentenced to only 30 days in jail for beating his wife.

THAT OLD FEELING: In Fond du Lac, Wis., Mrs. Jennie Schussman, 79, arrested with Charles Slater, 63, on a charge of drunk and disorderly conduct, explained: "It was our first date."

$$\boxed{\textbf{BUSINESS \& FINANCE}}$$

JAN. 16 **SQUARING THE CIRCLE:** As U.S. television-makers showed off their new 1950 models last week, Chicago's Hallicrafters Co., which is small in size but big in know-how, stole a march on the industry. It showed the first set with a rectangular picture tube.

Since the TV broadcast image is also rectangular, the new tube has two advantages over the old round tube. It permits the whole tube-face to be utilized, and it saves about one-half in cabinet space. Boasted Hallicrafters' President William J. Halligan: "This will be the only revolutionary thing in television this year."

FEB. 13 **CARD SHARK:**

> *There is only one who brightens all my everyday affairs,*
> *There is only one, My Darling, who understands and cares.*

In the greeting-card business the company that understands and cares the most is Kansas City's Hall Brothers, Inc., world's largest greeting-card makers.

Last week, in the midst of its biggest season next to Christmas, Hall Brothers was turning out more than 1,000,000 of its "Hallmark" cards every day. There were no fewer than 500 different designs for St. Valentine's Day alone. (The romantic holiday is believed to commemorate the death of two Roman priests in 269 A.D., each called Valentinus. One of the priests is supposed to have been executed for marrying lovers who came to him, despite a decree of Emperor Claudius II forbidding marriage because single men made better soldiers.)

Behind all the hearts and flowers is Joyce C. Hall, 58, a lean and solemn man who started out, at 18, to become a greeting-card shark by selling postcard greetings in Kansas City. Rollie B. Hall, a brother, joined him there, but they soon realized that postcard greetings were losing favor. They switched to cards enclosed in envelopes, were soon so successful that they took in another brother.

The Hall brothers claim to have fostered quite a few innovations. They developed the unfolding card that tells a continued story, and leveled out the seasonal peaks and valleys of the business by pushing the "everyday" card for birthdays, weddings, anniversaries, sympathy and the sick. Other tricks of the trade: white kittens on cards will always outsell brown ones; geraniums are never good, but pansies are surefire sellouts. One thing that doesn't worry Joyce Hall is a recession. In bad times, says he, people send greeting cards instead of presents.

Hallmark's Joyce Hall: geraniums don't sell, but pansies are surefire.

Mrs. Rosenberg's advice for girls: "Get along with the men." Page 209.

IRON BOTTOMS: When 20-year-old Levi Strauss sailed from FEB. 27 Manhattan around Cape Horn to San Francisco in 1850 to seek a fortune in the gold fields, he carried a roll of canvas in his baggage. He intended to sell it to a tentmaker to get enough cash for a grubstake. But when he got ashore, the complaint of a friendly miner gave him a better idea. "Pants don't wear worth a hoot up in the diggins," said the miner. "Can't get a pair strong enough to last no time."

Levi promptly went into the clothing business. He had a tailor cut a pair of trousers from his canvas roll, and soon the miner was strolling all over town, boasting how strong were these "pants of Levi's." Strauss soon found he had a steady stream of men who wanted "Levis." When Levi Strauss & Co. celebrated its 100th birthday last week in its San Francisco factory, it had turned out its 95,000,000th pair.

MARCH 20 **BUTTER FINGERS:** After years of debate, Congress last week repealed the 64-year-old federal tax on oleomargarine. But oleo will still not be easily mistaken for butter. Oleo sold at retail must be conspicuously identified on the wrapping, while yellow margarine served in restaurants must be either triangular in shape or clearly identified. Quipped one Congressman: "Maybe we should require Florida orange growers to sell all their artificially colored oranges in a square shape."

MARCH 20 **DON'T BE REPULSIVE:** As an Iowa farm boy, Stan Talbott had a slick way of convincing roadside customers that he sold only freshly laid eggs. Stan would duck into the henhouse where he keeps his ready-packaged eggs, push the hens about to make them cackle, and presently reappear with the eggs carefully sprinkled with pillow feathers.

In due course Salesman Talbott became advertising vice president of Joyce, Inc., one of the world's biggest makers of women's play shoes. To get a line on women's likes and dislikes, he packed a laundry bundle and started talking to women at self-service laundries. Besides talking, he read magazine ads to the women to see which words got a rise out of them.

Last week, 47-year-old Arthur Stanley Talbott told the Los Angeles Advertising Club the results of his survey on "How To Open Women's Purses." Certain words in ads and sales talks are "repulsive" to women, he said. Examples: *habit, bra, leathery, parched, matron, clingy, model.* Good sales words, which "appeal to women's hearts, emotions and vanities": *poise, charm, dainty, twinkle, blush, bloom, crisp, garden, bachelor.*

Talbott is now making a new test: showing women photographs of shoe clerks to see which sales faces they like and dislike. He expects to prove that "certain types of faces should be kept in the rear."

THE SUN NEVER SETS ON CACOOLA: In Brazil, some mis- MAY 15
guided people vow that it increases sexual prowess, others
are under the delusion that it makes a man impotent. Bright
red signs proclaim its worth in the shadow of the Matterhorn
and beneath the blank unastonished eyes of the great Sphinx
where it is locally known as "Cacoola." Its name, of course,
is Coca-Cola. Coke's peaceful near-conquest of the world is
one of the remarkable phenomena of the age.

Last week, as Cokemen surveyed their empire, on which
the sun never sets, their blood almost audibly fizzed with
pride. Coca-Cola is currently selling about 50 million Cokes
a day all over the world—enough to float a light cruiser.
Last year, the Coca-Cola Co. took in nearly $128 million,
a third of it from foreign business. This did not constitute
American exploitation, as the Reds bellow. For at the
same time, Coca-Cola's 270-odd foreign bottlers and 3,000-
odd foreign retail dealers grossed roughly $150 million.

GOOD NAME: Looking for an ear-catching name for his new,
low-priced car, Automaker Henry J. (for John) Kaiser set
up a $200,000 contest. The result was prodigious: some
450,000 people submitted names. Last week Kaiser-Frazer
picked the winner. It wasn't easy, since about 100 contestants
had submitted the same name. K-F awarded first prize of
$10,000 to Mrs. Charles Atkinson of Denver because she had
written the best 25-word reason for her choice. The winning
name: Henry J.

A NEW PEAK: On the crowded trading floor of the New York JUNE 5
Stock Exchange there was no gloom, only pent-up excitement. The huge cavern buzzed with talk of the General Motors' new five-year contract with the C.I.O.'s United Auto
Workers. Under the spell of the good news, the market
surged up: the Dow-Jones industrial average reached 222.57,
a new peak, the highest since September 1930.

UP FROM THE POTATO FIELDS: On 1,200 flat acres of potato JULY 3
farmland near Hicksville, Long Island, an army of
trucks sped over new-laid roads. Every 100 feet, the trucks
stopped and dumped identical bundles of lumber, pipes,
bricks, shingles and copper tubing—all as neatly packaged

as loaves from a bakery. Near the bundles, giant machines with an endless chain of buckets ate into the earth, taking just 13 minutes to dig a narrow, four-foot trench around a 25-by-32 ft. rectangle. Then came more trucks, loaded with cement, and laid a four-inch foundation for a house in the rectangle.

After the machines came the men. Under the skilled combination of men and machines, new houses rose faster than Jack ever built them; a new one was finished every 15 minutes. Three years ago, little potatoes had sprouted in these fields. Now there were 10,600 houses inhabited by more than 40,000 people, a community almost as big as 96-year-old Poughkeepsie, N.Y. Its name: Levittown.

Levittown is known largely for one reason: it epitomizes the revolution which has brought mass production to the housing industry. Its creator, Long Island's Levitt & Sons, Inc., has become the biggest builder of houses in the U.S. In his building year ending next March Builder William Levitt will have put up about 5,900 houses.

An ex-G.I. could buy a Levitt house with no down payment and installments of only $56 a month. The new projects made possible by this financial easy street are changing the way of life of millions of U.S. citizens, who are realizing for the first time the great American dream of owning their own home.

The Levitt houses, which sell for a uniform price of $7,990, cannot be mistaken for castles. The community has an almost antiseptic air. Like a hospital, Levittown has rules of its own. Fences are not allowed. The plot of grass must be cut at least once a week; if not, Bill Levitt's men mow the grass and send the bill. Wash cannot be hung out to dry on an ordinary clothesline; it must be arranged on rotary, removable drying racks and then not on weekends or holidays.

But there are perquisites as well as rules. For the young children there are parks and countless playgrounds. There are baseball diamonds, handball courts, swimming pools, shopping centers. Says one housewife: "Whenever I tell people where I live I get the same old freeze. Some of them think that everyone who lives in Levittown is on relief. But the only people who criticize the place are the ones who don't live here."

THE BEARS OF WAR: In the Communist credo, Wall Street JULY 10 provokes war because it is good for business. In the Wall Street credo, war is bad for business and for the stock market. Last week, the credo of Wall Street once more proved true. In the first day's trading after the Korean fighting began, the Dow-Jones industrial average tumbled 10 points. Then came the news that President Truman had ordered U.S. intervention in Korea, and a huge wave of selling swamped the market. Big and little traders, amateurs and professionals scrambled to unload. The market lost in one week all the progress it had made in five months. An estimated $8 billion in paper values had been wiped out. The market had cracked because investors knew that business, under wartime excess-profits taxes, could not maintain its current peacetime profits.

WIDER RIPPLES: Like ripples from a pebble dropped in water, JULY 24 the war's effects last week spread in ever widening circles through the U.S. economy, stirring a mild backwash of inflation. Consumers were doing little to help keep prices down; their growing rush to stock up on nylons, tires, sugar and anything else they felt like hoarding was creating shortages where none existed. In Kansas City, when department stores hiked the price of nylons from $1.35 to $2 a pair, the crush to buy grew even bigger.

PEACETIME AXIS: On Manhattan's Fifth Avenue recently, AUG. 7 an odd-looking, snub-nosed little car drew some mildly curious stares. Few of the onlookers realized that it was a postwar model of the *Volkswagen,* the car which Hitler once promised to put in every German garage. With an air-cooled rear engine, and a luggage compartment under the hood, it was the first of 600 which Germany is shipping to the U.S. to sell at $1,280 to $1,997.

The *Volkswagen's* appearance was the latest example of a new business phenomenon: the growing revival of export trade in both Germany and Japan.

THE PRICE OF GREATNESS: The world's biggest manufacturing SEPT. 25 company filed a tax return to fit its size last week. General Motors Corp.'s income tax for 1949: $444,377,889.44.

DEC. 11 **LITTLE–AND LATE:** How is U.S. rearmament going? From worried U.S. industrialists who have the big job of rearming the nation, came the shocking answer: not very well. In fact, big-scale arms production has not even started. With the threat of global war deepening by the hour, the bitter truth is that the U.S. right now—after five months of a shooting war—is producing fewer weapons than it was when the Japs struck Pearl Harbor. Most businessmen agree that the trouble lies with the inability of the armed services to make up their minds what arms they want and how many.

DEC. 18 **MISS R'S REWARD:** After getting along for 92 years with nothing but male veeps, R.H. Macy & Co. last week appointed its first woman vice president. She is Brooklyn-born Beatrice Rosenberg, 52, who joined Macy's as a hat clerk 32 years ago, is now in charge of the millinery and shoe sales staffs, some 400 people. In the excitement of her promotion, Miss Rosenberg burbled: "This is the greatest thing that's ever happened to Macy's!" Then she caught herself: "Not me, mind you. But picking a woman for such a high position. It's an inspiration to all the little girls who work here." Her advice to the little girls who want to be veeps: "Get along with the men."

MILESTONES

DIVORCED: Audie Murphy, 25, most decorated World War II hero turned cinemactor (*Bad Boy*) and author (*To Hell and Back*); by Wanda Hendrix, 21, cinemactress (*Ride the Pink Horse*); after one stormy year of marriage; in Los Angeles.

DIED: Mrs. Mabel Young Sanborn, 87, the last surviving of Mormon Leader Brigham Young's 56 children; in Salt Lake City.

MISCELLANY

PROGRESS: In Washington, D.C., the monthly *Postal Record* of the National Association of Letter Carriers noted that although it took the fastest pony express something more than nine hours to deliver a letter from St. Joseph, Mo. to Kansas City, "the modern, streamlined postal service does the job in two or three days."

POWER OF THE PEN: In Knoxville, Tenn., Mrs. Julia Gideon Whaley was granted a divorce after she showed the court a postcard addressed to her on which her husband had written a little verse:
Your eyes may shine,
Your teeth may grit,
But none of my money
Will you git.
Phooey on you.

YASMIN: The script had been carefully polished, as a major _{JAN. 9} production should be, and Director Aly Khan had rehearsed the Lausanne police and the Lausanne-Palace Hotel staff time and again. As soon as Leading Lady Rita Hayworth felt the first labor pains, husband Aly was to pick up a phone and simply breathe the secret password: *"Malbrough s'en va-t-en guerre"* (Marlborough is going to war). At the other end, a police functionary would flash the word to the cops who were standing eagerly by to escort the couple to the clinic. Then, after Aly and Rita slipped out, the concierge would lock every exit of the hotel, thus trap the impatient representatives of the world press.

Shortly before 3 o'clock one morning last week, just seven months and a day after their wedding near Cannes, Rita gave Aly his cue, and Aly, in his own words, "blew up completely." Throwing away the script, he hustled her through one of the hotel's side exits and into a black Buick. Aly took the wheel himself and roared off to the clinic.

Catching word that something was up, two carloads of police screeched up to the clinic, a poor third behind Aly and the press. Around 11 a.m., rumpled and unshaven, Aly told the world: it was a $5^1/_2$ lb. girl. The baby would be called Yasmin, the Arabic word for jasmine. "I told you," he reminded a newsman, "that premature babies run in my family."

"TWELVE O'CLOCK HIGH" is the freshest and most convincing _{JAN. 30} movie of the current cycle about World War II. It avoids such cinemilitary booby traps as self-conscious heroics, overwrought battle scenes and the women left behind or picked up along the way.

Twelve O'clock High is the story of a stubborn flying general's mission: rebuilding a bomber group's shattered morale. Gregory Peck goes at the job with the cold passion of a martinet and the inner torment of a man of good will, with a strong, beautifully modulated performance that never lets the role down.

FEB. 6 **"THE THIRD MAN"** is already a smash hit in Britain, where most critics hailed it as the best movie of 1949. U.S. moviegoers are likely to find it one of the best of 1950.

The story employs the classic melodramatic gambit of the innocent who walks straight into somebody else's intrigue and can't get out. A well-meaning bungler in the tradition of Scripter Graham Greene heroes, Joseph Cotten decides to clear up his friend's death and reputation. Along the way he becomes involved with a sardonic major of the British military police (Trevor Howard), a melancholy actress (Valli), and, finally, the villain (Orson Welles).

In Director Carol Reed's hands, a shot of a cat licking a man's shoe becomes a chilling premonition of shock. And Reed gets a grotesquely comic sequence out of an eerie four-year-old boy leading a street crowd in pursuit of Cotten while the accompanying zither jangles like a nickelodeon piano.

FEB. 13 **A BASKET OF RICOTTA:** One afternoon last week, while the world's headlines featured nothing more exciting than the hydrogen bomb, Cinemactress Ingrid Bergman gave birth to a plump, blue-eyed, 7-lb. 14-oz. boy. Only a week had passed since she had filed for a quick Mexican divorce from Hollywood physician Dr. Peter Lindstrom, her husband of twelve years. It was just a year since the Swedish-born star, 34, had met the balding, 43-year-old Italian director, Roberto Rossellini and first talked of going to Italy to make *Stromboli* with him. It was just nine months since Dr. Lindstrom had spent two grim days in Sicily with Ingrid and Rossellini, trying to talk her out of her world-publicized romance and her demands for a divorce.

If Ingrid Bergman had found any of the privacy that her situation clearly called for, it was not the fault of newsmen, photographers and talkative clinic personnel. Reporters got hold of her nursing schedule. Obstetrician Dr. Giuseppe Sannicandro gave Rome's radio audience a play-by-play account of the delivery ("We used the same sort of sedative that

Rita Hayworth and daughter Yasmin.
The father: Aly Khan. Page 210.

Ingrid Bergman and son Renato. The
father: Roberto Rossellini.

was administered to Rita Hayworth"). Three jeeploads of the Rome riot squad were summoned to pull clambering reporters off the clinic wall and to guard Ingrid's room.

Meanwhile, on location outside Rome for a new film, Rossellini received from friendly local peasants their traditional gift to the father of a new-born son: a basket of *ricotta*, a cheese made from ewe's milk and eaten on coarse black bread in the open air.

"STROMBOLI": Any film by Director Roberto Rossellini and FEB. 27 Actress Ingrid Bergman would seem anticlimactic after their own stormy, thoroughly publicized private lives. As an anticlimax in moviemaking, this one can stand on its own feet. A bleak, draggy little picture, it fulfills neither RKO's prurient advertising claims, nor Rossellini's obvious intentions. Would-be moralists who are trying to punish Actress Bergman and Director Rossellini for their private transgressions by banning *Stromboli* might serve their own ends better by having the picture shown as widely as possible.

THIS SIDE OF HAPPINESS: It was not an auspicious debut. APRIL 24 Mom strummed the ukulele in the blind pig that she operated in Lansing, Mich., and onto the dance floor came a skinny, freckled five-year-old named Betty June Thornburg, with her sister Marion, seven. While the speakeasy patrons sipped needled beer, the blonde moppets sang and wriggled.

"Mom didn't do anything real bad," recalls Betty Hutton, as larger audiences have since come to know her. "Mom just ran a joint on a small scale. We'd operate until the cops got wise. How is a woman supposed to make her living with two kids when her husband deserted her?"

Last week 29-year-old Betty Hutton was a $260,000-a-year movie star on the verge of her splashiest success. She was still going strong on the momentum she had picked up on the wrong side of the tracks. Within the fortnight, U.S. moviegoers will see her in M-G-M's *Annie Get Your Gun*, 1950's biggest, costliest ($3,200,000) musical.

Betty had prayed, pleaded and plotted for the role of Annie from the time she saw Ethel Merman do it in the 1946 Broadway hit. With Judy Garland cast in the lead and shooting already begun, Betty still insisted on betting that she would play the part. Then Garland had a nervous breakdown, and the studio had to start again from scratch. M-G-M decided that it needed Betty just as badly as she needed the part.

Betty carries the show with such riotous energy that she threatens to carry it too far. She plunges into her first two numbers like a bronco out of a rodeo pen. And she lacks Ethel Merman's craftiness with comedy. But along with her unbridled vitality, she gives the role something that brassy Ethel Merman never attempted: she kindles the love story with poignancy, makes it seem something more sincere than a musicomedy plot.

MAY 29 **"FATHER OF THE BRIDE":** The picture opens with the camera poking among the abused remnants of a wedding reception—empty bottles, broken glasses, cigarette butts—and finally settles on the most pathetic: the father (Spencer Tracy) of the bride (Elizabeth Taylor). The fun rarely lets up. Actress Taylor, perfectly cast, gives a winning performance. But in a production that makes a happy blend of many talents, Veteran Spencer Tracy is by far the most conspicuous. The role of the harassed, neglected father is his best in years, and from start to finish his flawless playing is a joy to watch.

"KIND HEARTS AND CORONETS" is a blue-ribbon British JULY 3 comedy filled with wit, irony and impudent fun. In detailing the memoirs of an Edwardian gentleman who systematically murders his way into the peerage, it combines the overcivilized urbanity and understatement of the English comic style with the saucy irreverence of the French comic spirit.

Alec Guinness' eight-role performance (of all the victims) is a brilliantly successful tour de force, with each character so sharply defined and acted that it is hard to see how eight different players could have done as well.

"TREASURE ISLAND" is Walt Disney's first movie made with JULY 24 live actors only. It offers the fun of watching an eye-rolling, lip-twitching Robert Newton as he wallows outrageously through the role of Long John Silver, one of fiction's most ingratiating scoundrels. Disney apparently liked him well enough to let him steal the whole treasure (as well as the picture), instead of the single sack of coins that Stevenson let him get away with.

"THE MEN" ranks with the handful of extraordinary movies that do credit not only to their makers but to Hollywood. In an industry that lives by the box office, the film is remarkable for tackling a touchy subject: the salvage of war-wounded paraplegics. More remarkable, the subject has been handled with frankness, taste and dramatic skill. The result is realistic, unsentimental and emotionally powerful.

Marlon Brando, in his first movie appearance, does a magnificent job as the embittered patient. His halting, mumbled delivery, glowering silences and expert simulation of paraplegia do not suggest acting at all; they look chillingly like the real thing.

Broadway's 26-year-old Marlon Brando spent his first four weeks in Hollywood learning to live in a wheelchair with 31 paraplegics in a veterans' hospital ward. By the time shooting started on *The Men*, intense, moody Actor Brando knew, as well as any whole man could, how it feels to be paralyzed from the waist down. Such wholehearted concentration on his craft may partly explain Nebraska-born Brando's rapid rise to stardom. Without much formal education, he left home at 19 to make a name for himself. After a year's study at Manhattan's Dramatic Workshop and in summer stock, he got fat parts in quick succession. In 1947, he found himself an overnight Broadway sensation as the brutish lout in *A Streetcar Named Desire*.

In Hollywood, Brando appeared to be the first genuine "character" since Garbo. Dressed in his usual cotton T-shirt and greasy jeans, Brando shunned the big stars and their glittering parties, spent most of his time roaming the back alleys and bars, sometimes without shoes.

AUG. 14   **"SUNSET BOULEVARD"** is a story of Hollywood, mostly at its worst, brilliantly told by Hollywood at its best. It brings Actress Gloria Swanson back to the screen after a nine-year absence. The role of Norma Desmond, a great star of the silent movies, is as juicy a part as any actress could hope for, and Actress Swanson squeezes the last drop from it. As a young hack scripter who blunders into her eerie world, William Holden plays the picture's most difficult role to perfection.

A 51-year-old grandmother, Gloria Swanson has made 63 movies, five marriages (all ended in divorce) and even two or three comebacks. She looks younger than her years, is still energetic enough to have taken on a three-month tour of 30 cities as advance agent for *Sunset Boulevard*. She insists: "It is *not* the story of my life."

Gloria Swanson and William Holden in "Sunset Boulevard": a story of Hollywood at its worst told by Hollywood at its best.

"THE BREAKING POINT" is the latest turn in the cinematic SEPT. 25 fortunes of Ernest Hemingway's 1937 novel, *To Have and Have Not*. The result is an expert piece of hard-boiled cinema. Harry Morgan (John Garfield), a rough and ready veteran of PT boats, scrounges a living for his wife (Phyllis Thaxter) and two daughters by chartering his cruiser for fishing trips.

Besides stinging melodrama, the film offers some unusual dividends. Its love story involves the hero with—of all people —his wife, and it is played with a passion that U.S. movies never seem to find in married couples who have school-age children. In the other woman (Patricia Neal), who gets nowhere with Morgan, the script fashions an acid, quip-studded portrait of a smart tart on the make.

"ALL ABOUT EVE," a needle-sharp study of bitchery in the OCT. 16 Broadway theater, crackles with smart, smarting dialogue, matches some penetrating characterizations with top-drawer acting. The movie shows the swift rise of young Broadway Actress Eve Harrington (Anne Baxter) from a stagestruck unknown to an adulated star. Subtly at first, then with fine crescendo effect, Director Joseph L. Mankiewicz reveals her as an ambitious fanatic who stops at nothing—deceit, betrayal, assignation, blackmail—to knife her way to the top.

The two main victims of Eve's rise (Bette Davis, George Sanders) are just as keenly drawn. Actress Davis, who submits to deliberately harsh lighting, unflattering camera angles and messy make-up, gives the picture's showiest role what may well be the best performance of her career.

"BORN YESTERDAY," Garson Kanin's 1946 stage hit, ran DEC. 25 for almost four years on Broadway. After paying $1,000,000 for the movie rights, Cinemogul Harry Cohn spent two years trying to cast it, wound up with the perfect choice for its dumb blonde heroine: Judy Holliday, who created the role on the stage. Thanks largely to Actress Holliday's hilarious performance, the movie deserves to repeat the play's success.

EDUCATION

FEB. 20 **THE THINGS THEY TEACH:** Southern Methodist University in Dallas reported that 13 undergraduates were enrolled in its new one-credit course: bait-casting. S.M.U. heard rumors last week that the rival University of Texas was offering a course in lariat-throwing.

FEB. 27 **PEOPLE ARE EITHER:** Ever since 1943, when big, broad-beamed Lynn White Jr. became president of lively little (enrollment: 800) Mills College (for women) in Oakland, Calif., he has been something of a maverick in the world of higher education. So far as women are concerned, says he, higher education is a flop. Last week, in a new book called *Educating Our Daughters*, he told why.

Woman's lot these days is not a happy one, White says, and her education is to blame. Her colleges were modeled after men's, and the belief has persisted that "higher education is something like spinach which can profitably be absorbed without reference to the gender of the absorbent." As a result, women have clung to the "biologically fantastic notion that to be different from men is to be inferior to men." Since they no longer churn the butter, make the candles, plow the fields, or even bring their husbands a dowry, they are deeply plagued by a "sense of parasitism."

Raising a family is apparently not enough: that is being "just a housewife." White argues that the college must give women "a vision of the family and the rewards it offers." "We must agree with the feminists that 'women are people,'" says White, "yet hold to the supplementary truth that 'people are either women or men.'" One of the first tasks of the woman's college, says he, is to educate women to be proud that they are what they are.

MARCH 6 **SIGN HERE:** When the Board of Regents of the University of California drew up a loyalty oath last summer for its 11,000 teachers and staffmen, the faculty's Academic Senate flatly refused to accept it. Later, the oath was toned down a little; instead of having to swear that they had never joined, supported or even believed in a subversive organization, faculty members would simply have to swear that they were not members of the Communist Party. But after eight months, 13.5% of the faculty had still not signed. Last week the regents issued an ultimatum: any C.P. member, they said, automatically "has violated the terms on which he is employed . . . and shall be dismissed." For the 13.5% still holding out, it had become a question of signing or resigning.

STOP, LOOK & LISTEN: In Stamford, Conn. (pop. 50,000), MARCH 20 more and more names were turning up on the Burdick Junior High School's biweekly failure lists. Principal Joseph J. Franchina started to nose out the trouble—and he thought he knew what it was. Principal Franchina smelled television.

By last week, after a survey of 447 pupils, it looked as if he were right. At the end of each week, at least half of Burdick's pupils had spent as much time sitting before TV as before teacher. Whatever educational programs TV boasted the kids seemed to give low rating. Their preferences: Milton Berle, Ed Sullivan and *Six-Gun Playhouse*.

"DEEPER . . . DEEPER . . . DEE. . . .": Midday shoppers, clustered about a window on Washington's Connecticut Avenue, could hardly tear themselves away. Behind the glass, in strapless bathing suit, black-eyed Mary Jane Hayes, Miss Washington of 1949, climbed into a bed. On her pillow was a small black earphone and the words that she heard as she pretended to sleep floated outside through amplifiers. "*Bon soir . . .*" cooed the speaker. "Good night . . . *Bon* . . . good . . . *le soir* . . . the night. . . ." As onlookers soon found out, Miss Washington was modeling the newest type of French lesson.

Washington's Educational Services had arranged the show to promote the latest wrinkle in learning-while-sleeping devices. Each kit will contain a "Prelude" for lesson-takers about to retire ("You are going to sleep now. It is getting deeper and deeper and deeper and dee. . . .").

The theory is that when a person sleeps, his subconscious

is still open to suggestion and can therefore learn. Rudy Vallee is using a sleep machine to learn lines and lyrics. And one housewife solemnly reported that, by placing a machine under her husband's pillow, she had taught him to like salad.

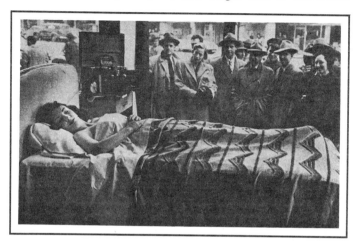

Miss Washington of 1949, pretending to be asleep in a store window, demonstrates a machine that teaches while you snooze.

MAY 1 **DISAPPEARING SCHOOLHOUSE:** The little red schoolhouse may be on the way out, but it is still far from extinct. Last week the U.S. Office of Education gave out the facts & figures. Though one-room schools have been folding up at the rate of twelve a day for 30 years, there are still 75,000 left. They account for nearly one-half of all public-school buildings, have an enrollment of 1,500,000 U.S. schoolchildren.

ARMISTICE IN CALIFORNIA: Peace finally came last week to end the winter-long war between the regents and the faculty of the University of California over anti-Communist loyalty oaths. From the beginning, both sides had agreed on one thing: they wanted no Communist teachers. But there agreement stopped. When the regents ordered faculty holdouts to the loyalty oath to sign or resign, most of the faculty rose in arms. Governor Earl Warren and President Robert Gordon Sproul sided with the faculty.

Last week, nine days before their own deadline, the regents met and reconsidered. Was the difference between the two points of view worth all the shooting? The regents decided not. By a vote of 21 to 1, they accepted the idea of a contract clause (stipulating that the signers were not Communists) instead of the oath.

BUSY MONDAY: This week the Supreme Court ordered the JUNE 12 University of Texas to admit Heman Sweatt, Negro, to its all-white law school, on the ground that the Negro law school that Texas had set up was not the equivalent of Texas' law school for whites. [This decision was the first of a series of legal steps leading to a landmark decision in 1954 in which the Supreme Court ruled that "separate but equal" schools for Negroes were inherently unequal.]

HO HUM: The editor of a Columbia University Press trade JULY 17 letter thought it might be fun to make a list of the ten most boring books. He polled several hundred U.S. librarians, editors, authors, reviewers and schoolteachers, asking them to send him a list of the ten classics that have bored most people most. The ten that led all the rest: Bunyan's *Pilgrim's Progress*, Melville's *Moby Dick*, Milton's *Paradise Lost*, Spenser's *Faerie Queene*, Boswell's *Life of Samuel Johnson*, Richardson's *Pamela*, Eliot's *Silas Marner*, Scott's *Ivanhoe*, Cervantes' *Don Quixote*, Goethe's *Faust*.

UH-HUH: Officials of Wellesley College this week announced NOV. 20 with evident satisfaction the results of a survey of 457 freshmen on what made them pick the school in the first place. By far the greatest number (42%) specified Wellesley's academic standards. Other chief reasons: Wellesley's prestige, a Wellesley tradition among family or friends. Only two girls said it was because Wellesley is just twelve miles from Harvard, 14 miles from M.I.T.

THE PRESS

FEB. 13 **RHAPSODY IN BLUE:** Must a fan dancer don bra and panties in a newspaper advertisement even though she doffs them in her act? Could Macy's guarantee to undersell Gimbels on Page 23, while Gimbels guaranteed to beat Macy's on Page 24? Probably the most influential voice in determining what is acceptable advertising is the New York *Times*. As "chief censor" of the *Times* for the past 18 years, Joseph W. Gannon sets the standards for the *Times*—which he calls "the strictest in the field." Last year, red-faced, blue-nosed Censor Gannon and staff reworded, revised or rejected 1,456 ads.

An ad describing underwear as "Naughty—but so nice. . . ." read in the Gannonized version: "Paris-inspired—but so nice. . . ." When a Manhattan nightclub boasted that it possessed "Fifty of the hottest girls this side of hell," Censor Gannon deftly made it "Fifty of the most alluring maidens this side of paradise."

The *Times* painted more clothing on Sally Rand, and airbrushed out the bare essentials of a model in a girdle ad. There are no "matchless, magnificent minks" in the *Times*; they may be "beautiful," but not "matchless." Only one unqualified superlative regularly passes the blue pencils of Gannon & Co. In full-page ads in the *Times*, the Chicago *Tribune* is permitted to call itself the "World's Greatest Newspaper." Explains Censor Gannon: "The *Times* can afford to be magnanimous."

APRIL 10 **ATOMIC INTERVENTION:** With the coming of the atom bomb, the U.S. press found itself confronted with one of the gravest and most difficult jobs in its history. It had the prime duty of giving readers the best possible understanding of the atomic age and of the technical processes that had brought it about. On the other hand, it had the responsibility of not giving away any information that might be of value to the enemy.

Last week AEC decided that one press enterprise had overstepped the danger line. It ordered the monthly *Scientific American* (circ. 78,878) to delete four technical paragraphs in a 5,000-word article on the hydrogen bomb by Dr. Hans A. Bethe, Cornell physicist and wartime chief of theoretical physics at the Los Alamos laboratory. Although the April issue containing the article had already gone to press, AEC summarily "requested" the presses stopped—the first time it had taken such a drastic step. It burned 3,000 copies already run off, melted down the type and impounded every galley proof and the manuscript of the original story. In AEC's view, technical expositions coming from such a person as Dr. Bethe, even if it was material previously published by lesser-known physicists, would give the Russians "verification" of the data.

WORLD'S END: The *Nation* (circ. 35,889), which usually takes itself and the world with knitbrowed gravity, took a lighter view last week of the current "apocalyptic writing." If the bomb destroys the world, wrote Associate Editor Robert Bendiner, "everyone will be prepared with the proper ironic comment." But if the end comes from a "brush with a . . . comet, we'll all be caught flatfooted. . . . Habits being what they are, the press will handle the calamity as follows:

New York *Times*—
END OF WORLD FORESEEN IN 24 HOURS
Stock Prices Tumble to Record Lows

New York *Daily News*—
BIG BANG TOMORROW
SERIES OFF—NO WORLD

Daily Worker—
CAPITALIST WORLD DOOMED
U.S.S.R. to Trim Five-Year Plan

Variety—
NO PIX BEYOND STYX

Chicago *Tribune*—
WORLD TO BLOW UP!
Voters Hail End of Democratic Misrule;
McCormick Bomb Shelter Faces Test

TIME—

As it must to all, death comes tomorrow to tired, harried, war-haunted Mother Earth. Sixth in size of the solar system's nine whirling satellites, fourth in distance from the sun, Earth alone has Man, was from the start hailed as planet most likely to fail. . . ." [Writer Bendiner's TIME erred. Earth is actually third in distance from the sun.]

JUNE 19 **OUT WITH SCHMIDT:** Fortnight ago, Czechoslovakia indicted able New York *Times* Correspondent Dana Adams Schmidt for espionage and subversion. After dutifully filing a straight story to the *Times* on the charges (which he denied), Schmidt fled to the U.S. zone of Germany. That left only three regular Western correspondents in Prague.

While Czechoslovakia seems to be working with clumsy stealth toward a purge of non-Communist correspondents, Bulgaria openly bars all Western newsmen. Rumania is still tighter; it does not even admit Communist reporters from Hungary. No Western correspondents are welcome in Soviet-occupied Eastern Germany except on special occasions. The propaganda-wise Russians sometimes plant phony stories, wait until Western newsmen swallow the Soviet bait, then denounce their "mendacity."

The latest country to vanish behind the censorship curtain is Communist China. On the Chinese mainland last week, there was one Western newsman left—a French correspondent at Shanghai who could not file a word.

JULY 31 **ANTICLIMAX:** In the New York *Post*, Columnist Leonard Lyons told a revealing anecdote about his self-trumpeting friend, New York *Mirror* Columnist Walter Winchell. Wrote Lyons: "Walter Winchell arrived at the Stork Club Wednesday night, and asked about the President's broadcast. 'Mr. Truman called for mobilization,' he was told. Winchell shrugged: 'I called for it last Sunday night.'"

AUG. 21 **COVERING KOREA:** In Korea last week, a harassed Public Information officer looked over half a dozen correspondents who had just flown in from Tokyo and muttered wearily: "By the time we start getting back some of the ground we've lost, there'll be a reporter in every rifle squad."

It wasn't quite that crowded. But by last week there were 271 correspondents from 19 countries reporting the Korean war. And they were still coming in.

In Korea, the going was almost as rough for correspondents as it was for soldiers. Most of them took their chances with the troops, ate and slept where they could, were soon covered with mosquito and flea bites, came down with dysentery.

Marguerite Higgins of the New York Herald Tribune, with South Korean troops. General MacArthur finally let her in.

One night in Taejon, Jack Percival, a peppery, tough Australian reporter, bedded down among his fellow reporters on the floor of an old house. Shortly after, he dashed out into the living room. "There's a woman in there," he gasped. "There was one fellow kept rolling over in his sleep. I gave him a good push and I found out it wasn't a he." Percival had unwittingly gone to bed between the only women correspondents then in Korea, the New York *Herald Tribune*'s Marguerite Higgins (who had fought a ban on women reporters in Korea, finally persuaded MacArthur to lift it) and *Collier*'s Charlotte Knight, who were getting the same treatment as the men. [Miss Higgins died in 1966 of a tropical disease she contracted during a trip to the Far East, including Vietnam. Miss Knight later became a free-lance writer.]

The following story was written after the Communist Chinese attack against U.N. forces in Korea—perhaps the low point of General MacArthur's career so far as his popularity was concerned.

DEC. 18 **STOP THE PRESS:** At printing plants in Concord, N.H. and Dayton, Ohio, the presses had run off a third of the 11-million-copy run of the January issue of the *Reader's Digest* last week before they were abruptly stopped. *Digest* Editor DeWitt Wallace and his staff had decided, after reading late war news, to replace the lead article on MacArthur's Korean triumph titled "The Right Man in the Right Place."

MILESTONES

BORN: To Major General Claire Chennault (ret.), 59, granite-faced onetime boss of the Flying Tigers and the Fourteenth Air Force, and second wife Anna Chan, 26, former news reporter: their second daughter (his tenth child); in Hong Kong. Name: Cynthia Louise.

DIVORCED: Milton Berle, 41, TV's No. 1 funnyman by Joyce Mathews, 29, actress; after seven intermittent years (married in 1941, divorced in 1947, remarried last June), one adopted daughter.

MARRIED: Eugene Ormandy, 50, conductor of the Philadelphia Orchestra since 1936; and longtime friend Margaret Francis Hitsch, 41; he for the second time; in Philadelphia.

DIED: Eugene O'Neill Jr., 40, teacher of literature at Manhattan's New School for Social Research, Greek scholar, critic, son of the playwright; by his own hand (slashing his wrist with a razor); in Woodstock, N.Y.

MISCELLANY

THE CRIMINAL MIND: In San José, Costa Rica, thieves broke into a chicken coop, carried off all the hens, left a note tied to the rooster's neck: "I was made a widower at 2 o'clock this morning."

YES, BUT HURRY: In Longview, Wash., Marine Reservist Thomas B. Meyers, ordered to report for active duty by 8 a.m., Aug. 5, wired for an extension so he could train a replacement for his job, was granted until 9 a.m., Aug. 5.

STRIKE THREE: In Tulsa, Okla., Coney Lee Coffey tried for the third time to rob the Lucky Seven Grill, for the third time got caught.

SEE HERE, PRIVATE. . . . In Danville, Va., a young man named Major General Robertson was directed to report for his Selective Service physical.

YES, MY DARLING DAUGHTER: In Newark, Internal Revenue Collector John E. Manning denied a tax deduction to a young woman after he found that for the third year running she had reported losing $20 bathing suits while swimming in the ocean.

BOOKS

"THE GOD THAT FAILED"—Many western comrades had JAN. 9 joined the Communist Party in the '20s and '30s with the notion that they were making a better, more decent world, only to find that the party was committed to indecent, inhuman calculation. At that point, the more courageous broke with the party. In *The God That Failed*, six of them tell the stories of their Communist pilgrimage, and the return trip. It is as goodly a company of such pilgrims as has yet been collected in one volume: Novelists Arthur Koestler, Ignazio Silone, Richard Wright, André Gide, Journalist Louis Fischer, Poet Stephen Spender. The stories the six contributors tell may be read as strange and dreadful *Canterbury Tales* of the 20th Century.

"DOWN AND OUT IN PARIS AND LONDON"; "BURMESE DAYS"; FEB. 6 **"COMING UP FOR AIR"**—India-born Eric Blair, who died last fortnight, was a frail, intense Englishman with an Eton education, a fine nose for humbug and a genius for exposing it. He was only 46 when he died, but in his lifetime he had seen too much of the super-humbug of totalitarianism to be complacent about it. No writer had done more to shatter the complacency of others.

As George Orwell, the name he long intended to legalize, he had written a dozen books, fiction and non-fiction. Only six have been published in the U.S., but all of them are distinguished by a forthrightness of mind and a limber, cutting style that are singularly Orwellian, unmistakably original.

To U.S. readers, Orwell is known chiefly through last year's *Nineteen Eighty-Four*, the grimmest, most credible preview of the totalitarian state in print. Two days before his death his U.S. publishers put out simultaneously *Down and Out in Paris and London, Burmese Days* and *Coming Up for Air. Down and Out* is the largely autobiographical account of Orwell's own depression battle with starvation.

Burmese Days, in some ways his best novel, is a colorful story of a few Englishmen loaded down with the white man's burden in a small Burmese settlement. By 1939, when *Coming Up for Air* first appeared, Orwell was deep in his personal war with everything political and technological that threatened individual freedom. Orwell's hero is Britain's average little man who the author was afraid would be a pushover for the superstate boys. He wasn't.

There are no replacements for a George Orwell, just as there are no replacements for a Bernard Shaw or a Mark Twain. Without being a great novelist, he engaged his readers more directly than his literary betters. He will be missed, if only because he kept begging modern man not to become an ultra-modern slave.

"THE HORSE'S MOUTH"—The world may be a grim place but British Novelist Joyce Cary is not the man to learn it from. Author Cary's distinction is that, almost alone among contemporary authors, he works in the tradition of the old English novel. His theme is simple. He sees his hero, Artist Gulley Jimson, as the epitome of the will to live and to create at all costs. Starvation, jail and beatings-up mean only one thing to dedicated Artist-Genius Gulley—they tend to interrupt his work.

FEB. 13 **"PATERSON, BOOKS I & II"; "PATERSON, BOOK III"**—Just off the main street of Rutherford, N.J. (pop. 16,000) stands the clapboard home and office of Dr. William Carlos Williams, M.D., 66, the best-known pediatrician in town. Doctoring is a busy life, but it is not enough for Williams: for over 40 years, on prescription blanks, old envelopes and other odd scraps of paper, he has been jotting down his impressions. A lot of the jottings turned out to be poetry. He admits that his patients often have trouble when they try to read Poet Williams. Says a patient in one scrap of Williams' poems: "Geeze, Doc, I guess it's all right but what the hell does it mean?"

For a good many years, Poet Williams has been working on a long four-part poem about nearby Paterson (pop. 150,000), of which the first three parts are finished. Despite a humorlessness and awkwardness that make Williams the

Dreiser of U.S. poets, the Williams eye sees with clinical honesty. His notion:

> *The province of the poem is the world.*
> *When the sun rises, it rises in the poem*
> *and when it sets darkness comes down*
> *and the poem is dark.*

George Orwell: a style that was limber, cutting, original. Page 226.

Dr. William Carlos Williams, poet and pediatrician.

"THE CARDINAL" by Henry Morton Robinson is one of those novels that may have the undesired result of cheapening a fair cause. In this instance the cause is the right of the Catholic Church to teach and sustain Christianity in its own way. The author has included so many banal fictional tricks that both tract and story quickly reach a sustained level of stupendous boredom. APRIL 3

"THE TOWN"—Once in a while a really good writer retells the story of the pioneer, his hardships, his courage, his eccentricities, and the story seems as fresh as the land he settled. Such a writer is Conrad Richter, and *The Town* is the third volume in his trilogy of Ohio from post-Revolutionary War times to the Civil War. It is written in pioneer idiom, and sometimes it gets to be a strain watching Richter strain for colorful expressions. But when he succeeds, they're good, *e.g.*, "You wouldn't reckon to look at her she could read a MAY 1 lick, but she'd turn the old page and suck out the meaning of the new like a bird pulling out a worm."

"THE GRAND ALLIANCE"—Historians of World War II may yet recognize their great debt to British Prime Minister Attlee. By enforcing a measure of leisure on Winston Churchill [whom Attlee replaced as Prime Minister in 1945], Mr. Attlee has probably hastened the progress of the finest single contribution so far to the history of the war. *The Grand Alliance* is the third and longest volume of Churchill's war memoirs and covers the year 1941. It seems to be more hurriedly written, as if against time, but it brings that critical year stirringly alive, conveys with enormous authority and engaging candor its crushing despair and growing hopes.

MAY 29 **"D.H. LAWRENCE: PORTRAIT OF A GENIUS BUT. . . ."**—Biographer Richard Aldington chose the subtitle for this book because, when he began to collect material, almost everyone who had known Poet-Novelist Lawrence used the phrase "Of course, Lawrence was a genius, but. . . ." Whatever Lawrence might have been as a literary man, they sniffed, he was no great shakes as a gentleman.

Biographer Aldington cannot restrain a few well-bred sniffs of his own. Even though he manages to explain and forgive much that struck others as deplorable, even in a genius, he cannot quite condone the fact that Lawrence was capable of the "atrocity" of drinking red wine with bouillabaisse.

JUNE 19 **"THE MAVERICK QUEEN"**—Novel No. 51 on Author Zane Grey's production line follows slim, grey-eyed Nebraska Cowboy Linc Bradway on an errand of justice to South Pass, Wyo., tangles him up with the lady leader of a gang of cattle rustlers, ultimately thrusts him into the arms of the queen's innocent niece. Before Linc and bride can turn "to face the dark patch against the distant hills which marked the valley that one day would be their home," straight-shootin' Linc calls the bluff of just about every shifty-eyed little skunk in South Pass.

With the appearance of Author Zane Grey's eighth novel since his death in 1939, the mystery of where all the new books are coming from will puzzle many readers more than the maverick queen's bloody secret. Mrs. Zane Grey's answer: her indefatigable husband, who sometimes polished off a novel in two or three months of fast scribbling, was 15 to 20 manuscripts ahead of Harper's schedule. That could well mean another decade of easy readin' and hard ridin' before Zane Grey's zealous fans reach the end of the trail. [Zane Grey's 67th novel, *Boulder Dam* was published in 1963. Some of his manuscripts remain unpublished.]

"COLLECTED STORIES OF WILLIAM FAULKNER"—A fat collection of 42 Faulkner tales written over the past quarter-century, *Collected Stories* will let a brand-new layer of U.S. readers judge for themselves what all the critical whooping is about. AUG. 28

This view of the South as an area trapped between Sartoris impotence and Snopes viciousness explains Faulkner's fury. He is a man possessed and tortured by his vision. The horrors of his books—the rapes and castrations, the incestuous romances and idiot flirtations with cows—fall into place, not as exhibits of sensationalism, but instead as images of the social and moral disease that he is constantly probing.

The final impression left by Faulkner's work is that he is a writer of incomparable talents who has used and misused those talents superbly and recklessly. But this book has the excitement that comes from never knowing when, amidst pages of failure, there will come a masterpiece.

"ACROSS THE RIVER AND INTO THE TREES"—Hemingway was the champ all right. He had said so himself, to a *New Yorker* writer: "It is sort of fun to be 50 and feel you are going to defend the title again. . . ." SEPT. 11

After reading Ernest Hemingway's new novel, *Across the River and into the Trees*, only the most sentimental referee could raise Hemingway's arm with the old chant: "The winner and still champion!" Hemingway likes to discuss his writing in prize-ring talk but the fact is that a writer can be licked only by himself. In *Across the River*, Hemingway never wins a round. The famed Hemingway style, once a poetic blend of tension and despair, is hardly more than a parody of itself.

DEC. 4 **"COMPLETE POEMS"**—Carl Sandburg did pretty well at West Point—for a poet. He lasted two weeks. (Among those in his class who finished the course: Douglas MacArthur.) Sandburg failed in arithmetic and grammar and now, 50 years later, in the preface to his fat *Complete Poems* he admits that he is "still studying verbs and the mystery of how they connect nouns," and adds, "I am more suspicious of adjectives than at any other time in all my born days."

Zane Grey. Eleven years after his death, new books keep coming out.

Frances Parkinson Keyes learned to type on a cash register. Page 232.

Of all major U.S. literary figures, Sandburg, during a long productive life, has developed least as a writer, changed least as a man. His poetry, dredged raw from the look and experience of "the people," is from start to finish a shrewd, tender, cantankerous and lovingly slangy impressionist folkportrait.

If Sandburg, as Critic H.L. Mencken guessed 20 years ago, has the best chance for immortality of any contemporary U.S. writer, it is not because he has written with the moving beauty or the condensed, quietly explosive intuition of Fellow Poet Robert Frost. His *Complete Poems* is one great song-story about the look of the U.S. It is a song with good swinging rhythms, but the tune is hard to remember and after hearing it all night only the mood remains in the morning.

"JOY STREET"—"When the final chapter of *Joy Street* was DEC. 11 dispatched," writes Frances Parkinson Keyes, "I was too completely exhausted to feel the slightest elation. . . . It had become one of those nightmares which apparently had no end, but goes on and on." Rare is the author who makes an accurate appraisal of personal work, even by accident. The happy quip in the publishing world is that Novelist Keyes learned to type on a cash register. With her last ten novels (including *Came a Cavalier*, *Dinner at Antoine's*) Novelist Keyes has rung up sales of more than 5,000,000 copies. Even the sourbellies will have to admit that such an author is a fact of U.S. life as unalterable as the soda-fountain whipped-cream gun.

MILESTONES

MARRIAGE REVEALED: Lena Horne, 32, sultry-voiced *café au lait* nightclub and cinema songstress (*Words and Music*); and Lennie Hayton, 42, onetime M-G-M music director; both for the second time; in Paris, in December 1947.

DIVORCED: By Betty Hutton, 29, bouncy blonde cinemusicomedienne (*Red, Hot and Blue*): Theodore ("Ted") Briskin, 32, Chicago camera manufacturer; after 4½ years, two daughters; in Santa Monica, Calif.

MISCELLANY

BIRDMAN: In Terre Haute, Ind., one Donald Duck enlisted in the U.S. Air Force.

HORTICULTURIST: In Pittsburgh, the *Post-Gazette* ran a gloating letter from a cat hater who boasted of shooting cats and burying them in his garden for fertilizer: "Last year I had tomatoes as large as cantaloupes."

HANDYMAN: In Cheektowaga, N.Y., the *Times* printed a classified ad: "WANTED—Man to wash dishes and two waitresses."

GREATLY EXAGGERATED: In Chicago, Mrs. Genevieve Lumley complained to the judge that, among other things, her husband told friends she was dead.

CLOSED CITY: In Washington, city officials held up the ceremony of welcome to visiting Japanese dignitaries because they could not find the keys to the cabinet containing the keys to the city.

Numerals in italics indicate a picture of subject mentioned.

PICTURE CREDITS

T

PRODUCTION STAFF FOR TIME INCORPORATED
John L. Hallenbeck (Vice President and Director of Production),
Robert E. Foy, Caroline Ferri and Robert E. Fraser
Text photocomposed under the direction of Albert J. Dunn and Arthur J. Dunn

QUOTES OF THE YEAR

President Truman *(in a letter to a music critic who had panned his daughter Margaret's singing—p. 23):* "Someday I hope to meet you. When that happens you'll need a new nose, a lot of beefsteak for black eyes, and perhaps a supporter below."

Secretary of State Dean Acheson *(after the conviction of former State Department employee Alger Hiss for perjury—p. 42):* "I do not intend to turn my back on Alger Hiss."

General Douglas MacArthur *(to one of his division commanders in Korea—p. 78):* "I have already promised wives and mothers that the boys will be back by Christmas. Don't make me a liar."

Marine General O. P. Smith *(as U.S. troops retreated in Korea in the face of heavy Chinese attack—p. 82):* "Retreat, hell! We're just advancing in a different direction."

Sir Winston Churchill *(commenting on the British Labor Government's economic programs—p. 97):* "Queuetopia."

Admiral Chester Nimitz *(p. 150):* "I always get seasick, but I think a general cleaning out is a good thing for the system."

Comedian Fred Allen *(commenting on Arthur Godfrey's racy radio style—p. 181):* "He's sweeping the country. But I think Arthur must be doing it with a short-handled broom—he's nearer the dirt than most people."

10393